Haynes

Car Builder's

manual

Designing and constructing your own car from scratch

Haynes

Car Builder's manual

Designing and constructing your own car from scratch

Lionel Baxter

First published in July 2001
Reprinted January 2003

A catalogue record for this book is available from the British Library.

ISBN 1 85960 646 6

Library of Congress catalog card no. 00-135963

Published by Haynes Publishing,
Sparkford, Yeovil, Somerset BA22 7JJ, UK
Tel: 01963 442030 Fax: 01963 440001
Int. tel: +44 1963 442030 Fax: +44 1963 440001
E-mail: sales@haynes-manuals.co.uk
Web site: www.haynes.co.uk

Haynes North America Inc., 861 Lawrence Drive,
Newbury Park, California 91320, USA

Printed and bound in Great Britain by J. H. Haynes & Co. Ltd, Sparkford

Illustrations courtesy the author except where credited.

WARNING
While every attempt has been made throughout this book to emphasize the safety aspects of building your own car, the publishers, the author and the distributors accept no liability whatsoever for any damage, injury or loss resulting from the use of this book. If you have any doubts about your ability to safely build your own car then it is recommended that you seek advice from a professional engineer.

Jurisdictions which have strict emission control laws may consider any modifications to a vehicle to be an infringement of those laws. You are advised to check with the appropriate body or authority whether your proposed modification complies fully with the law. The publishers accept no liability in this regard.

Contents

Foreword

by Ron Champion

This book is the result of the many years of experience that the author has had in the restoration and building of a wide variety of cars and motorcycles of all ages and types. Every aspect of car building is covered, from the stripping of the donor to final painting and finishing, and the legal requirements for putting the car on the road, including a synopsis of the SVA (Single Vehicle Approval) regulations.

The need for such a book became apparent when the author worked with me in the motor vehicle workshops at our local public school, where pupils, often with no previous knowledge or experience of motor vehicles but with great enthusiasm, spent some of their spare time building their own 'Locosts', buggies, or restoring their own vehicles. Activity in the workshops was often frenetic, with 30 to 40 projects being worked on at the same time, and a constant barrage of questions to the staff.

'What's this for?'; 'How do I do that?'; 'Can you help me?'; 'Will you show me what to do?', were the demands, and the author realised that while the pupils were privileged because they could get immediate answers and help from the staff, there were many builders and would-be builders of cars who had no immediate access to this information and advice.

Although this book is aimed primarily at the beginner, there is also help and advice for the experienced builder, and I expect that this book will be found in the workshops of many enthusiasts undertaking the restoration or building of cars, and on the book shelves of many 'armchair' builders.

Anyone who is contemplating building their own car will find this book very readable and an invaluable source of reference.

Ron Champion
Peterborough
July 2001

Acknowledgements

I am grateful to all who have helped with this book, and especially to those who have provided photographs or given facilities for photography. Included are:

Ken and Dan Freeman at AK Sportscars
Avenue Panels
Jan Baxter
Beauford Cars Ltd
BRA Motor Works
Mick Davidson at Car Spares
Chesil Motor Company
Chestnut Classics
Demon Tweeks
Driver and Vehicle Licensing Agency
Sue and Tom Duncan
Tim Earnshaw
Grant Educational Technologies
John Hardaker
Healey Brothers
Revolution Wheels
Royale Motor Company
Doug Sutton
Sykes-Pickavant

I am especially grateful to Ron Champion for his help and enthusiasm and for kindly agreeing to write the Foreword.

Introduction

This book is about the building of cars – specials and kit-cars – and, since for parts amateur builders rely heavily on production cars that are often old, it also deals with restoration. Although essentially a practical guide aimed mainly at the beginner, the experienced builder will also find this book useful. It should, as well, appeal to armchair enthusiasts, even if their dreams of building their own car never actually get translated into reality.

SPECIALS

I suppose that a 'special' is any car that is not standard. From almost the day motoring began, enthusiasts have been making their own cars, either because they could not afford to buy the one they wanted, or because they preferred a car that would express their own individuality and suit their needs more precisely than the standard production article. There are those, and I would count myself as one of them, who just like mechanical engineering, and see building a car as one of the highest Do-It-Yourself achievements.

In the early days, the 'specials' movement was mainly concerned with the building of racing cars to compete at Brooklands or other tracks, and there was a particular fascination, both before and after the First World War, with the fitting of huge ex-aircraft engines into the rather flimsy car chassis of the time. Monsters were created, like the 23-litre-engined 'Chitty-Bang-Bang I', and the gargantuan White 'Triplex' Special which had three aero-engines with a total of 36 cylinders and a capacity of 81 litres! Some of those cars have survived and are still active, like the Fiat 'Mephistopheles', a 22-litre Land Speed Record breaker, which not only still races but is also used on the roads. I have a happy memory of seeing it some years ago heading north on the M1, going very well indeed.

At the other end of the scale there were the motorcycle-engined specials built for hill-climbs and circuit racing, and the 750 Motor Club's Austin Seven specials, popular before and after the Second World War, some of which can still be seen performing impressively today. The heyday of the special was in the late-'20s and '30s, when there was an astonishing variety of machinery of different sizes and types, from the small Mercedes-looking single-seater designed and built by Alec Issigonis, later of Mini fame, to the most famous of them all, 'Bloody Mary'. 'Mary' was built by John Bolster in 1927 and had a wooden chassis with three parallel rails, steering that is best described as 'direct' since it had only one turn of the steering wheel from lock-to-lock, two 1000cc JAP motorcycle engines (most of the time), and a remarkable lack of sophisticated engineering. Bolster wrote: 'I had no machine tools of any description available. I hadn't even a bench drill and had to make all the holes with a breast drill, known throughout the engineering world as a "gut buster"...' So you do not *have* to have a fully-equipped workshop to build an outstanding special, but I have to say that it

A streamlined Austin Seven-based special with an early commercially produced GRP bodyshell, the Hamblin Cadet, which cost £37. (Ron Champion)

John Bolster's 1927 special, 'Bloody Mary'. (National Motor Museum)

helps! 'Bloody Mary', in its final form, now resides in the National Motor Museum at Beaulieu. Bolster also built, and raced for a short time, a car similar to 'Bloody Mary' but with independent front suspension and no less than four JAP twin-cylinder motorcycle engines.

About the same time that this was happening, the peculiarly British sport of 'trials' (or 'mud plugging') started. This consists of off-road competitions inevitably including steep hills with loose or muddy surfaces, with competitors competing against the clock, points being awarded for successful completion of the various 'sections'. In the days before 4x4 and off-road vehicles were available, there was usually a tractor or a horse or two available to clear the 'sections' for the next competitor when one had become stuck irretrievably in the mud, burnt out their clutch, or snapped a half-shaft. This rather specialised form of motor sport, which was very popular, had an effect on the design of some of the small production sports cars of the period, such as MGs, Singers and Morgans, leading to low gear ratios in the gearbox and differential (making them less competitive for road racing than their Continental counterparts), and twin spare wheels with special tyres that were fitted before the event in place of the rear road wheels. It also gave rise to a large number of home-made cars with light bodies, and usually with Austin or Ford chassis and engines. These cars were invariably driven to events and so had to be roadworthy. A small number of specialist manufacturers produced and offered for sale complete cars specifically for 'mud plugging' – Dellow, with its space-frame chassis designed to accept Ford parts, being the best known.

Frederick Henry Royce, a maker of superb electric cranes, bought his first car, a Deauville, in 1902 and, not thinking much of the noisy contraption, set about building his own special, which led on to other things. Others who had successfully built their own cars were asked by friends to build them one too, or they saw commercial opportunities and put their designs into production, like the Coopers (father and son). The Coopers started by racing motorcycle-engined 500cc specials, and went on not only to win Grand Prix races with cars of their own creation, but also to originate a completely new design

A Dellow trials special in action at Simms Hill. (National Motor Museum)

of racing car – the rear-engined racer, which remains the layout of choice today.

Perhaps the most famous specials builder of all was Colin Chapman. He had a leftover 1930 Austin Seven from a small commercial operation that he and a friend ran as a sideline when students, and decided to rebuild it as a trials car. Not wanting it known that it was an Austin Seven, he called it a 'Lotus MkI'. The subsequent MkIII was a one-off built for 750cc racing, and later came the Mk VI, which was the first Lotus production car, inspiring the famous 'Seven' and many look-alikes, as well as becoming the foundation of a famous company with many superb cars to its credit and a reputation for innovative engineering.

The 'specials' movement gained fresh impetus in 1996 with the first publication of Ron Champion's best-selling book, *Build Your Own Sports Car For As Little As £250* (Haynes Publishing). The car featured in the book has become universally known as the 'Locost' because of the author's claim that it can be built for as little as £250, and a cottage industry has grown up supplying chassis and other parts for the amateur to use in the construction of Locosts. As is right and proper in a special, no two cars are ever alike, each example bearing the imprint of the constructor's individualism and ideas. A thriving club has also sprung into being in the UK, and the Locost chassis design has been accepted for a racing class by the 750 Motor Club. Many Locosts have been, and are being, constructed in countries as far apart as the USA and South Africa.

A Lotus Mk VI. (National Motor Museum)

KIT-CARS

In the last 15 to 20 years kit-cars have come a long way, and there is now a wide choice of models, from high-powered sports cars, to saloons, recreational and utility vehicles. The bodies of the majority of these designs are moulded from glass-reinforced plastic (GRP), popularly known as glassfibre (or fibreglass), which we shall deal with later. When this material first became available to the amateur, some horrific creations, in both style and engineering integrity, were offered for sale, and new ones appeared almost monthly.

However, some designs were good from the beginning and have been refined over the years, and new ones have appeared to the same high standard. There are now over a hundred kits from which to choose, and when deciding which

An AK Cobra kit-car.

A retro-styled Beauford kit-car.

car to build it is worth reading the dedicated magazines which build, test and comment on the various cars in addition to advertising kits and specialist parts. Some of the well-established models have their own clubs, which are generally pleased to help with advice and information.

Kit-cars fall into three main categories; the small sports car, many of them based on or inspired by the immortal 'Seven' created by Colin Chapman; replicas (acknowledged or not) of famous makes; and completely original models, some of which are very advanced and exciting.

Kits vary widely in cost depending upon size and complexity, but in many cases you can spread the cost by buying components in stages so that, for instance, you may be able to complete the chassis before buying the body, and then the upholstery and trim.

Often a 'donor' car is required for the engine, transmission and running gear, but in some cases kit car manufacturers can supply reconditioned items, cleaned and ready for use – or even new ones – so that the dirty work of stripping and cleaning is avoided. In a few cases the car is designed to accept every component of the donor vehicle, providing in effect a new and differently-styled bodyshell. The choice of designs is very wide in style, power and price, and most of us can find at least one model that we would like to own.

By their nature, kit-cars are usually fairly quick to assemble, and often much of the time required is spent on stripping the donor and restoring the component parts. As the majority of kit-car bodies come with a coloured 'gel-coat', you do not even have to paint them.

A Chesil kit-car, styled after a Porsche Speedster.

RESTORATION

If you are a classic or vintage car enthusiast, you will probably prefer to restore a car rather than build a new one. If you already own a car, your choice is made, but if you do not, then you have a pleasurable time ahead of you deciding what to buy and scanning advertisements in the various specialist magazines.

Inevitably, your choice will be governed largely by your budget, but there are other factors that need to be taken into account, such as the car's suitability for the purpose it is to serve. If you are set on owning an exotic sports car, it may prove impractical for daily commuting or shopping use, and there is the question of garage space for a car that will only be used occasionally.

When you have narrowed down your choice, you need to talk to people who run the particular type of car that interests you. Gather as much information as possible, and try to get a drive in an example to see whether it lives up to your expectations and is really the car that you want. Find out if different models were made and, if so, which of them is the most desirable (and, if there is a price premium on it, is it worth it?).

It would be wrong to assume without question that a later Mark or model is better than its predecessors. It should be the case, of course, since manufacturers strive progressively to improve their cars, but it could be that the cost accountants influenced the building of later models and caused cheaper materials to be used or, like the E-type Jaguar, a design may put on weight and may have to be modified to conform with new legislation. Do you in any case know the difference between the various models, and can you identify them?

For nearly all classic and vintage vehicles there is at least one one-make club (a lot of which have international membership), and by joining you will gain access not only to many knowledgeable people who are generally prepared to give freely of their advice and time, but also to technical expertise, spare parts and social events. Moreover, most clubs have their own magazines, usually with advertisements of cars for sale, and although many of the cars advertised are good, usable vehicles, you may pick up a restoration project. Used spares and specially manufactured items are also often available. A full list of these clubs and the addresses of their membership secretaries can be obtained from the DVLA.

You also need to consider how skilled you are and what facilities you have at your disposal. You can buy a runner and gradually improve it as time and money permit (a 'rolling restoration'), or you can go to the other extreme and buy a rough, cheap car – the better option if you have the required skills and facilities.

If the model you want is a rare one, make sure that the example you buy is complete, since you are unlikely to pick up missing parts from a breaker's yard, and searching for them can take up much valuable time and can prove expensive. In particular, you should try to ensure that the car has those things that establish its identity and perhaps are exclusive to it, such as mascot, badges, wheel hub centres (properly known as 'nave plates') and instruments. These are easily lost or plundered, but are essential to complete an authentic restoration.

Finally, do not be too ambitious, and remember that every restorer finds that the final cost is always at least double the original estimate!

Barn find. This 1936 Standard Flying 12 is complete and restorable.

Chapter 1

Tools and equipment

TOOLS

I think that over the years I have wasted more money on tools than on anything else, as I have tended to buy and collect them on the off-chance that they will come in useful one day (and possibly just because they seemed a bargain at the time), rather than having any real need for some of them. Certainly I have some tools that I never use, and others that I lend out more than I use myself. I have now made a rule that I never buy tools until I am certain that I am about to need them, and I never buy the cheapest.

There was a time when, apart from a few open-ended spanners, sockets, screwdrivers and pliers, hand tools seemed to be the preserve of the professional mechanic and not easily available to the general public, while electrical equipment was limited to the electric drill and a few attachments. Now it is possible for the DIY enthusiast to buy the same range of tools as the professional uses, from trade outlets, high street shops and mail order catalogues.

Beware, though, since the quality of some of the tools and equipment on offer is doubtful. Over the last 20 or so years we have been swamped with cheap tools from all over the world. Some are of abysmally poor quality in fit, finish and construction – almost guaranteed to fail on first use – while others are surprisingly good. At the other extreme there are available, at a price, tools of superb quality and finish that are a joy to

Fig. 1.1. A good quality 5in or 6in mechanic's bench vice is a vital piece of equipment. (Draper)

Fig. 1.2. Over a period of time you are likely to need some or all of these hand-tools. (Sykes-Pickavant)

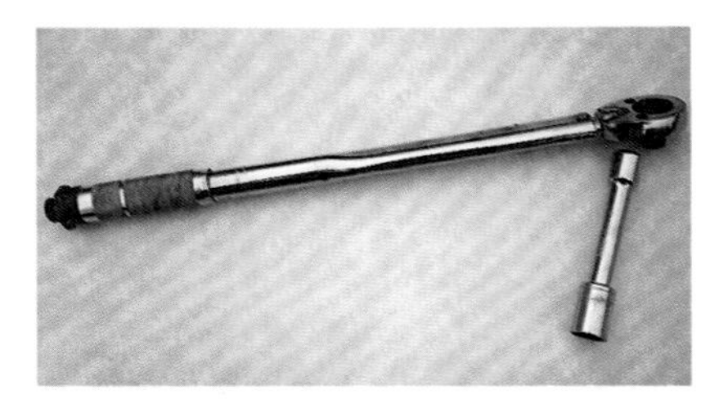

Fig. 1.3. A torque wrench is essential.

use. These are doubtless intended for the professional mechanic to whom they will give a lifetime of service in daily use. While I would dearly love a full set of such tools, they are, to some extent, a waste of money for the amateur, as they are unlikely to see the frequent use that would justify the high capital outlay for their purchase.

So, those of us who use tools for hobby purposes should look to buy satisfactory tools somewhere between the two extremes. There are many makes and qualities available but one of the widest ranges of tools and equipment comes from Sykes-Pickavant Ltd, whose tools are available, in the UK, from Halfords stores and from motor factors and automotive distributors nationwide, including Partco, Brown Brothers and Finelist branches.

Many hand tools, particularly sockets, are sold as sets in a fitted case. These are often convenient and certainly keep the various items in their places, making it easy to check at a glance whether any items are missing. However, I find that almost inevitably I later need one or more extras that will not fit into the case, which then requires additional storage space and makes the case less useful than was intended. You can, of course, get over this difficulty by storing your tools in tool boxes (where you can never find what you are looking for), or in the type of cabinet used by the professionals which has drawers and is mounted on castors so that it is moveable (if you don't overload it), but you still need to be disciplined, otherwise tools will get mixed up in the wrong drawers.

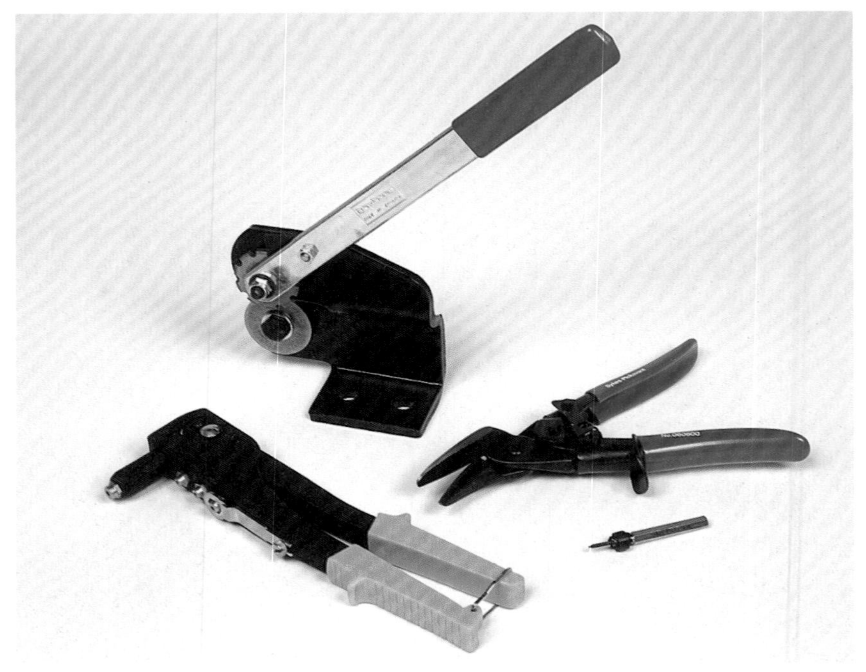

Fig. 1.4. Pop riveter, sheet metal cutter, snips and Zipcut. (Sykes-Pickavant)

Fig. 1.5. Electrical tools: wire stripper and crimper kit, soldering iron, multimeter and current tester. (Sykes-Pickavant)

Wall-boards with dedicated clips for each tool are useful but immobile, and one seems to spend a lot of time walking to and from them. I recently overcame the problem (for myself) by mounting peg-boards on a trolley which I made specially for them. This ensures that the tools are always returned to their proper places and that they can be brought close to the job, while shelves provide storage space for awkward objects.

EQUIPMENT

As far as equipment is concerned, much depends on what you are able, or want, to undertake, and how much work you will farm out.

Fig. 1.6. Author's home-made tool trolley – everything to hand and in its right place.

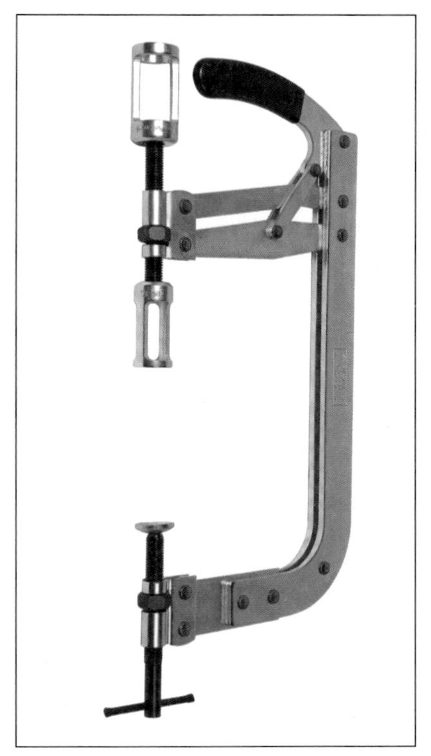

Fig. 1.7. A valve spring compressor. (Sykes-Pickavant)

Fig. 1.8. A pillar drill. (Draper)

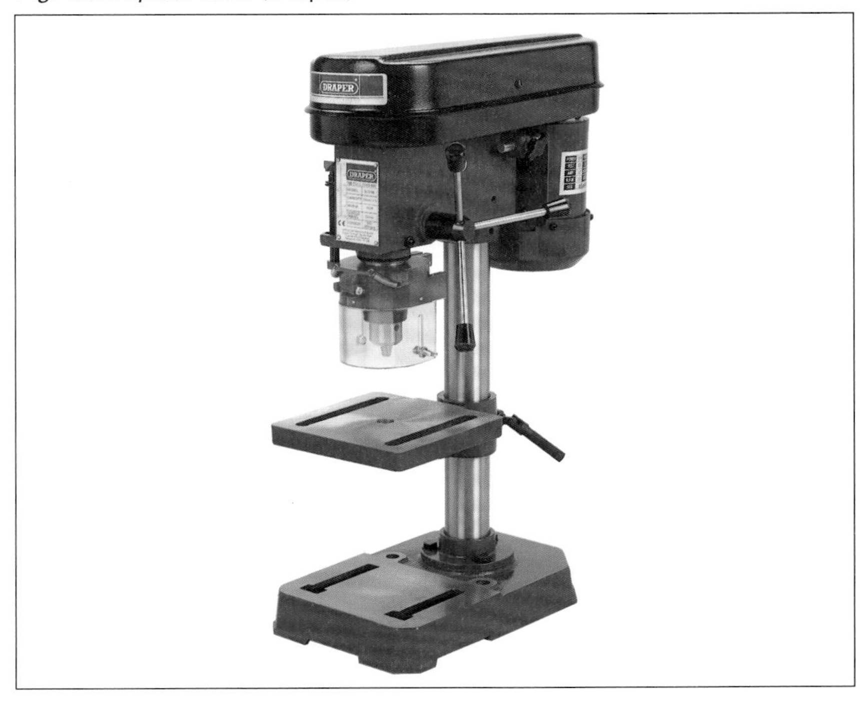

The choice of equipment also depends on how frequently you are likely to use it and whether you have space to store it. Some items, like compressors, can be hired when you get to the painting stage. As most compressor equipment is electrically operated, you will need to ensure that your workplace has an adequate electrical supply – 13amp is the minimum worth bothering with, and if you are going to install a supply, make it 30amp which will give you a safe margin and will allow you a wider choice of compressors, whether you hire or buy.

You may also wish to consider obtaining the following equipment.

Electric hand drill

Ideally, the minimum chuck capacity needs to be ½in (13mm), but you may get by with a ⅜in (10mm) chuck. Do ensure that you obtain a two-speed drill, or one with electronic speed control, as single-speed drills are much too

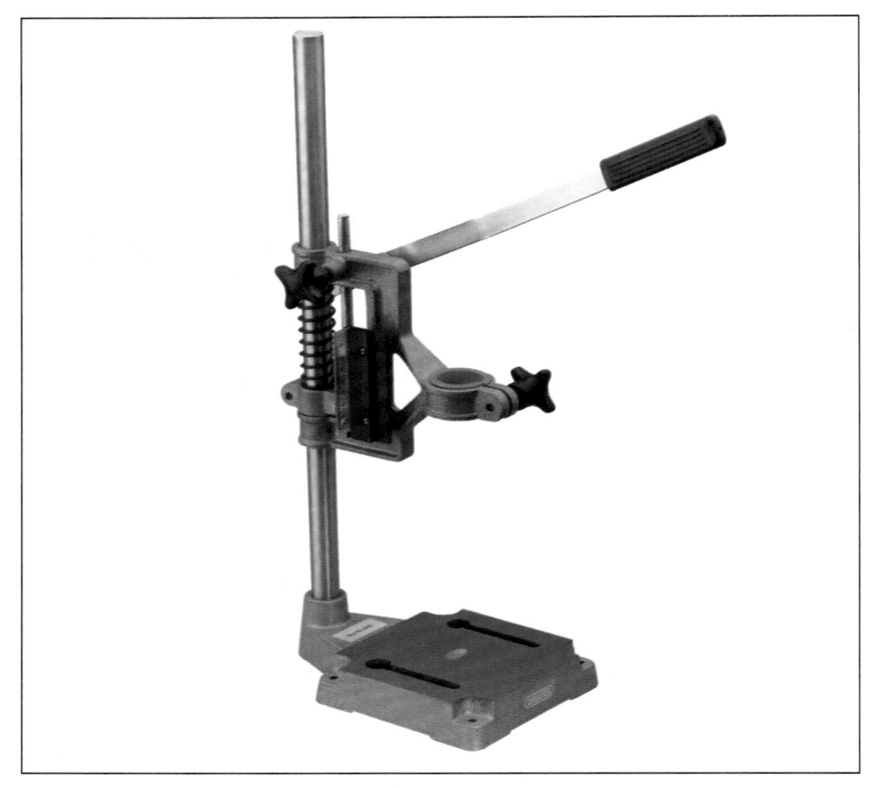

Fig. 1.9. A stand to convert a hand drill into a pillar drill. (Draper)

fast for drilling large holes in mild steel. If you cannot afford a pillar drill, a stand to convert a hand drill into a pillar drill is very useful.

Bench grinder

A bench-mounted grinder, with 6in (152mm) wheels for preference, is essential for sharpening tools, and a polishing mop or wire brush at one end is useful.

MIG welder

If you are restoring bodywork or building a chassis, you will need to weld. MIG welders are now very common, as they are easy to use. MIG welders operate like an electric arc-welder, but shield the arc with CO_2 gas. Small gas canisters of the throw-away variety are available and are useful for small jobs, but if you are likely to be tackling a larger job, or welding often, then you will need to hire a gas cylinder from the commercial suppliers. Although there is a hire charge and the initial charge for the contents is much greater, it is in fact very much the cheaper option in the long term. A welding mask is absolutely essential, and every sensible person will also wear welding gauntlets and appropriate overalls.

Angle grinder

An angle grinder will be required for cleaning up ('fettling') welds.

Air compressor

Compressors have been mentioned already. They have many uses apart from providing the air supply required to spray paint. An air supply can be used to operate a wide range of air tools, as well as providing a high-pressure air supply for cleaning and drying components (such as carburettor jets) and pumping up tyres, but a compressor is perhaps not as essential as the other equipment mentioned. If you do buy one, get the biggest you can afford which will run on your mains supply, with say a 50-litre air receiver. Most compressors will give a pressure of about 100–120psi (7–8.5kg per sq cm), but what is important both for operating tools and spraying paint is the quantity of 'free' air that a compressor can supply. This is expressed as a number of cubic feet per minute (cfm) or cubic metres. A 13amp supply will power a compressor that gives about 7cfm (0.20 cubic metres), a 20amp supply will give around 9cfm (0.25 cubic metres), and a 30amp supply is required for 14cfm (0.40 cubic metres). For the amateur, 7cfm (0.20 cubic metres) is adequate, as it will operate a number of commonly used air tools and will spray paint effectively, but I would have a larger compressor if I had a bigger mains supply.

Fig. 1.10. A spray gun complete with small compressor unit. (Draper)

Chapter 2

Designing a special

BASIC PRINCIPLES

You may already have decided what type of car you want to build and, doubtless, will at least have 'doodled' some sketches when in all probability you should have been doing something else. The time has now come to find out what is practicable both in terms of what will work, what is legal and what you are capable of.

The size and type of body will need to be decided upon first, and only you can do that, although you will be guided by the use you intend for the car.

Of course, if you are building a hill-climb or trials special there may not be much bodywork, but if your car is to be used on the road, then it must comply with certain requirements. A road car must have mudguards, lights, indicators, stop lights and, if it is to have a fixed windscreen, it must have windscreen wipers and a windscreen washer system. Inside the car, any seats must be fixed (or lockable on runners) and, of course, seat belts must be fitted.

You will have realised that if the car is to have a space-frame it cannot also have doors, and that a luxury saloon or tourer needs softer suspension than a sports car, whilst an off-road vehicle needs longer suspension travel than either. You also need to take into account the seating capacity and whether the car is to be an open car, a saloon or a utility vehicle.

Whether you have decided to build a replica of a car that you like, or something completely individual, in either case it is worthwhile looking at 'real' cars and taking some measurements from them if you can. If this is not possible, try to study scale models, as they will help you with relative dimensions and proportions.

In general, the low, sleek machines that many of us are fond of drawing tend to be impracticable, both to build and use, and are best avoided. One of the best ways of getting things right is to do what the professionals do and make a model of your envisaged car. Professional designers use clay, but you can make a model out of balsa wood and, when you are happy with it, scale it up to the actual dimensions you will use.

You should view everything from the safety angle – your own and other people's. For instance, if you plan to have an exposed exhaust system, will it be likely to burn anyone – including inquisitive children – or emit fumes into the cockpit? Will there be any internal or external projections with sharp edges that can cause damage? Will

Fig. 2.1. Use models to help to get measurements and proportions right.

Fig. 2.2. It is a good idea to make a balsa-wood model of your envisaged car.

there be enough clearance under the mudguards to allow for the full travel of the suspension and steering – or will you mount them so that they move up and down with the suspension and turn with the wheels? (This is in order for a light sports car like a 'Seven', but almost anything else will require fixed mudguards.) These and many other factors need to be taken into account.

In the UK, the *Single Vehicle Approval Inspection Manual* is helpful at the design stage, as it lays down certain parameters that must be observed for 'one-off' road cars. However, these are primarily to do with safety and do not take into account ergonomics or other aspects of the overall design.

CHASSIS DESIGN

If you are going to build a 'Seven'-type car, then you will presumably build (or buy) a space-frame type chassis – so much a feature of this type of car. You can do no better than buy a copy of the Haynes book *Build Your Own Sports Car for as Little as £250* by Ron Champion, which gives full details, not only of how to build a chassis from scratch, but also how to build the suspension units and, in fact a whole car, popularly known as a 'Locost'.

The 'Locost' design can be modified in both breadth and length. Some have been built as four-seaters and others widened from behind the scuttle to make room for those of more ample than average form. With about 15in (400mm) available per person in width, another 2in (50mm) or so each side works wonders and gives a wider(!) choice of seat type, but there is nothing wrong with sticking to the original design.

If you are not going to build a 'Seven', then you need to follow the time-honoured way of setting out the parameters for your car, and in particular the chassis. For this you need a clear garage floor, an assistant, a piece of chalk and a long straight-edge.

Sit on the floor of the garage, or on a low box, decide where you would like the pedals to be, and mark this position on the floor in chalk, together with the position of your bottom or the seat. It is going to be your car so you might as well be comfortable when driving it.

If you already have the engine and gearbox, place these in position with the gear lever knob at a convenient position for your hand if it has remote control, or slightly forward of the ideal position if you intend to make a remote-change mechanism. Chalk round the outline of the complete assembly. Depending on the position of the engine, there are a number of factors to be borne in mind. If the engine is transversely mounted, as is the case in many smaller cars, the assembly is likely to be fairly wide and it may be quite tall if the engine is above the gearbox/final drive assembly, both of which will affect the shape of the body. If the car is to be mid-engined, the same may be true, though the engine's dimensions in this position may be less important than the fact that if it is very close to the driver you will need some good sound insulation and you will need to make sure that there is sufficient space to service the engine. (The Fiat X1/9's engine was so close to the driver that it had to have a removable panel behind the driver's seat to allow access to the distributor.) You will also need to make decisions about the position of the radiator and any associated piping, as well as the heater.

A rear-engined car may be at a disadvantage in terms of handling, because the heaviest single item, the engine, may be outside the wheelbase. In this case, you will need to try to compensate for this by arranging the driving position as far forward as possible and putting anything heavy within the wheelbase and preferably at the front – the battery, radiator (if water cooled), and fuel tank will all help.

Once you have decided on the location of the engine, draw the

Fig. 2.3. The author's Locost.

centreline of the car, through the centre of the engine if rear-wheel-drive/front-engined or, if you have the complete suspension unit(s), by taking the distance between the left and right wheel hubs and halving it. Now draw a line on the driver's side, parallel to the centreline already drawn, to represent the outside of the car, using your body to establish its position. A similar line can be drawn to represent the outside of the car on the passenger's side by measuring the distance from the centreline to the line you have already marked on the driver's side, and drawing another corresponding line equidistant from the centreline on the passenger's side.

To give a comfortable width, you will need a minimum internal dimension of about 32in (810mm). On a rear-wheel-drive car you will need to add around 8in (21mm) for the transmission tunnel, giving a total of about 40in (1020mm) for the inside width of the car. This is a bit chummy, and is all right for a small open car, but you will need rather more for a closed car or a tourer.

If the car is going to be a four-seater, will it have four doors or only two? Access to the rear seats must be allowed for, and there must be enough room for the passengers to sit with comfort, unless it is to be of the 'close-coupled' variety of '2+2', which traditionally provides room for two small children, or for one adult squeezed in sideways.

Having established these dimensions and drawn them on the garage floor, you can now decide on the dimensions for the wheelbase and track. These are the distances between the centres of the wheels when viewed from the side, and from the front and rear respectively.

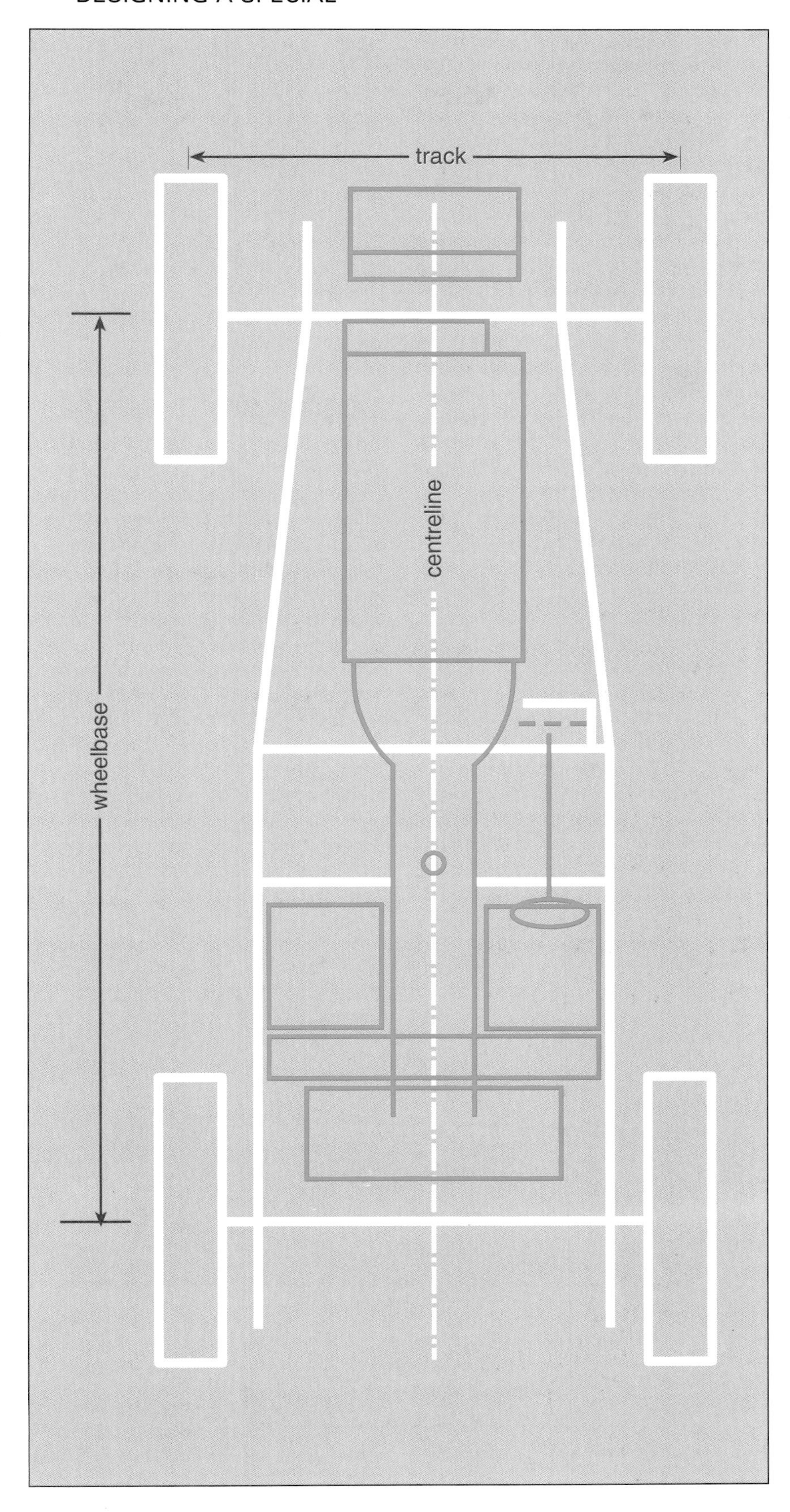

Fig. 2.4. Chalk out the dimensions on the garage floor, prior to drawing a detailed plan view on paper.

Whereas it is normal to have the same wheelbase on each side of the car (there have been a few production cars where one side has been slightly shorter than the other because of the type of suspension used), front and rear tracks are often different. Again, these will obviously depend on the size of the car you wish to build and how many people it is to carry.

If you are going to build a four-seater, do try to ensure that the rear passengers are sitting within the wheelbase, and not directly over the rear axle line as happened for so long on production saloons, including large chauffeur-driven limousines where the unfortunate owner sat in the most uncomfortable place possible.

Out of interest, and to give you some guidance, above is a list of the wheelbase and track dimensions of some popular cars (all dimensions in cm).

Car	**Wheelbase**	**Track (front)**	**Track (rear)**
Austin Seven	195	102	102
Mini	204	120	120
Escort	240	131	132
Jaguar XK	259	129	127
Lotus 7	224	124	131
Morgan +4	244	119	119
VW Beetle	240	130	127

It will be seen that, with the exception of the very small car – the Austin Seven – and the much larger Jaguar, the dimensions for all the other makes are quite similar, but before coming to any firm conclusions about track width, you need to decide whether to make your own suspension or whether to use suspension assemblies or parts from a donor car, as discussed in Chapter 5.

BODYWORK DESIGN

Some aspects of bodywork have already been mentioned, particularly the need for adequate clearances for the wheels, but you should also ensure that the car will be convenient to use, and that access to the various maintenance points will not be restricted.

In the past, some manufacturers, who should have known better, hid batteries away – for example stuffed into the back of a Mini or under the rear seat of an MGB – with the result that the once necessary routine job of topping-up was very difficult. The battery on my Triumph Stag cannot be taken out without first removing the power-steering pump, and you have to be very conscientious to find and uncover the brake master cylinder of a Morris 1000 in order to check the fluid level. When cars were maintained and serviced by garages or chauffeurs, the location of service items and maintenance points perhaps did not much matter, but anyone building their own car will probably be doing their own servicing, and will therefore need to make it as easy as possible.

Another factor to consider is body overhang. It has long been recognised that a car with 'a wheel at each corner' will hold the road well. This is because all the weight is carried within the wheelbase, where it should be. A car with an enormous overhang beyond its rear wheels can be a problem, particularly if loaded at the rear. If you need overhang for the sake of the styling of the car, ensure that the space it encloses will not be

Fig. 2.5. Shaping the bodywork. Use a line drawn through the wheel centres as a datum, and aim for ground clearance of about 6in (152mm), with 50:50 weight distribution over front and rear wheels.

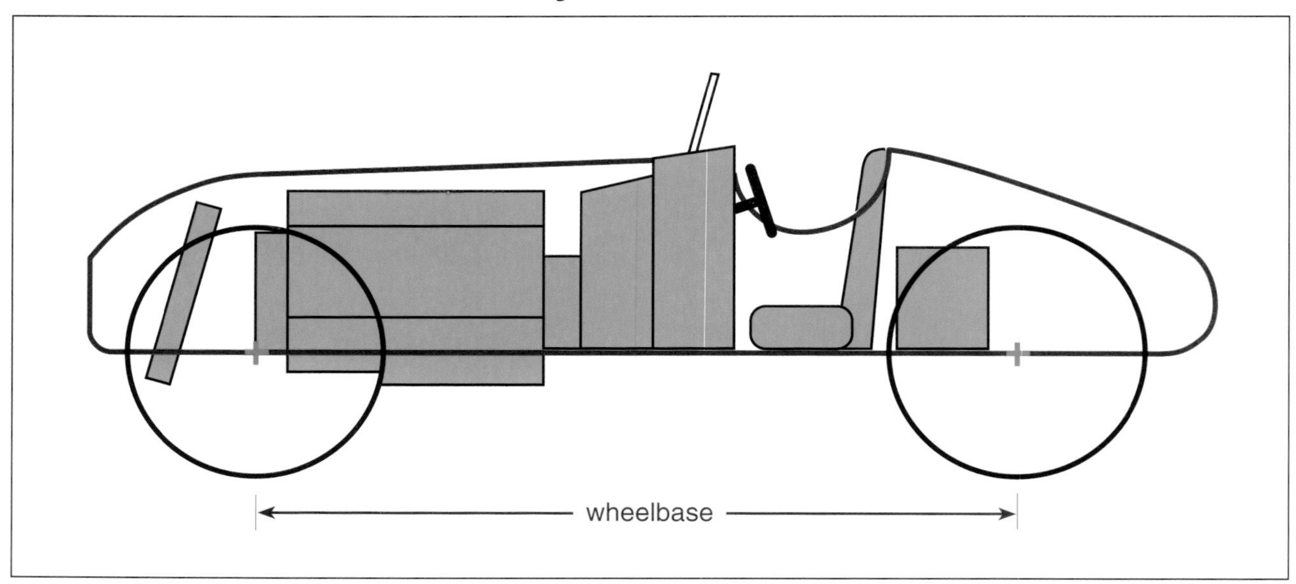

used for heavy weight carrying (no more than the spare wheel, say), and ensure that the overhang is well-supported from the rear of the chassis.

When you have established the basic body dimensions in plan view (looking down from the top) you can draw the side elevation and ascertain whether the shape that you want is feasible.

Draw a line through the wheel centres and use this as a datum. Unless you are going racing, for which you will want minimum ground clearance and suspension travel, you should aim for about 6in (150mm) ground clearance, so nothing should be lower than this.

Starting at the front, the position of the radiator needs to be determined. This does not have to be upright, and you can slope it either way, but make sure that it will clear the engine.

Engine heights vary considerably depending on their stroke and method of valve actuation – some cam covers add considerably to the height, especially if these also have components mounted on them.

The scuttle needs to be high enough to accommodate your legs comfortably, and to offer weather protection, but not so high that you cannot easily see over it (the windscreen will be mounted on the scuttle). This also needs to be taken into consideration when deciding on the height of the seats.

Try to achieve a 50:50 weight distribution, or as near as possible, between front and rear wheels. A front-engined, rear-wheel-drive car has the weight of the rear axle, petrol tank, spare wheel and driver (if a two-seater) to help to balance the weight of the engine. A rear-engined car is less easy to balance, as all the weight of engine and transaxle is in one place which can cause the car to handle like a pendulum and be 'tail happy'. Front-wheel-drive cars tend to enjoy greater directional stability, as they have more weight at the front, though excessive weight can cause 'understeer', making a car want to carry on in a straight line rather than corner easily when steering lock is applied. A mid-engined car is the easiest design to balance, as it has a 'low polar moment of inertia', which means that the weight is concentrated in the middle and does not, therefore, affect the behaviour of either the front or rear end.

At the rear you need to consider the comfort of back seat passengers (if there is to be a back seat), and the positions of the petrol tank and the spare wheel.

Once you have considered all these factors, you can begin to 'clothe' your car with the shape of bodywork that you want.

Chapter 3

The donor car

OBTAINING A DONOR

If you are building a special or a kit car, you are going to need mechanical and electrical parts to add to the chassis that you are building or have bought. To buy everything new may be prohibitively expensive, so as an alternative, it is possible to use second-hand parts and assemblies. As you will need a lot of components, often from the same model, it is a good idea to buy a complete car (the 'donor') and remove the components that you want. This is generally cheaper and more convenient than buying individual components, especially if you buy from a 'vehicle dismantler' (or 'breaker', to you and me), as he will often deliver and, perhaps more importantly, take away the remains, as part of the deal.

You can, of course, buy privately – the small ads in the local newspapers are usually full of potential donor cars. They have the advantage over cars bought from breakers, in that most of them are runners, so you should be able to test them before purchase and thereby assess the state of the mechanical parts, brakes, steering, etc. This is useful, as you will then have a good idea of what work needs doing, and you can negotiate the price accordingly. Many of the cheap cars on offer are already, or are about to become, MoT failures. As such, they are often an embarrassment to owners who need the space – and cash – for their next purchase. More often than not, rotten bodywork is the problem, and the mechanical components are in satisfactory running condition. Mechanical repair is usually easy and, for most modern cars, cheap when compared with the cost of body repair and repainting. So, do not be put off if the brakes or steering are a bit dodgy – you will be renewing the worn parts of these systems, anyway, as you build up your new car.

Even if it is a 'banger' you are looking for as a donor, it is still worthwhile taking along a 'knowledgeable friend' as a check on impulsive buying, and because a more detailed inspection is possible when there are two of you. It also gives you someone to blame when undetected shortcomings are found later!

Breakers often have complete cars for sale (or, if you are not in a hurry, they may be able to source one for you from their network), but more often than not they will supply parts and assemblies. These may have been removed from different vehicles. It is important that you know and specify that they all originate from the same model, in case modifications were made to later 'marks' which might make it impossible to mate them with parts you have already obtained. In any case, it is usually better to buy a complete system rather than just odd component parts.

If you are buying from a breaker, you are unlikely to get any documentation unless the car is being sold as a roadworthy vehicle, as V5s (vehicle registration documents) are normally handed in to the DVLA when a car becomes 'scrap'.

There is a well-known legal maxim – *caveat emptor* – which means 'let the buyer beware'.

When buying a complete vehicle, make sure, before parting

Fig. 3.1. Full of treasure – a breaker's yard.

with your money, that the seller actually *is* the legal owner of the car. However hard it may seem, if you buy a car that has been stolen, even if the seller is unaware of it, when the legal owner traces it you lose both the car and the cash.

Before buying privately, insist on seeing the V5 and establishing that the identity of the seller is the same as that shown on the form – the address should help if you are at a private house. Avoid the deal that takes place in a deserted car park late at night when the seller promises to send you the paperwork later!

Getting the car home is the next thing. If it is MoT'd, taxed and insured, you can drive it home, or have it delivered by the seller (but do not pay the seller until the car has been delivered). If the car cannot legally be driven on the road, you can hire a trailer or, perhaps better, an 'A' frame, provided you have towing gear. Also bear in mind the distance for which you will have to tow the car, as towing over a long distance can be very tiring.

Before you buy the donor car, you should make plans for what you are going to do with it when you get it home. Storage can be a difficulty, and neighbours often object to having to live next door to a mini breaker's yard! If you have no option but to leave it in the front garden, the best course of action is to summon a few friends (we all enjoy tearing a car apart) and dismantle the car in as short a time as possible. You can then get the carcase removed immediately.

If you have covered storage space, and can hide the wreck in decent privacy, you can leave it as a whole and remove parts as required. Restorers and kit-car builders will need to bear in mind that a dismantled car, especially if it has a separate chassis, can easily take up the equivalent of three or four cars' space.

When you do dismantle, keep the assemblies in the largest units possible – for instance, engine and gearbox, front suspension and steering – and on no account take everything apart at this stage. Drain coolant from the system, oil from the engine and petrol from the tank, but keep oil in the gearbox and differential if these are separate from the engine. Batteries are always a nuisance when not fitted to a car. Unless you can make use of the battery

Fig. 3.2. Keep the assemblies in the largest units possible.

Fig. 3.3. A Ford Sierra rear suspension assembly.

immediately, you might as well dispose of it, as you are bound to forget to recharge it and, quite likely, it will be useless by the time you do need it.

In preparation for the great event, you will doubtless have collected a variety of boxes or containers in which to store the various parts when you do come to dismantle them. Try not to mix the parts and do label them – masking tape and a marker pen are very good for this purpose. Resist the temptation to clean anything at this stage, the oily mess will protect against rust and may help to show the source of any leaks that need attention.

It is as well to recognise at this point that building, and especially restoration, usually takes much longer than anticipated. With a kit car you can strip the donor vehicle and rebuild the various units while awaiting delivery of the kit. The anticipation keeps the adrenalin going and you get two bites of the cherry, but obviously you cannot start on a restoration until you have the car. When you have stripped the car and assessed the amount of work to be done, and experienced the drudgery of de-rusting and cleaning, motivation can flag and trips to the pub may become more frequent than those to your garage.

Progress on your project may be threatened by outside influences. A house move is perhaps the most disastrous, but job changes, new partners and other major changes in circumstances for good or ill can mean that a build or rebuild takes years rather than months. The moral is to label everything, make copious notes and drawings, and take plenty of photographs of every part of the car before and during stripping, as you will certainly not remember everything when you come to put it together again months later. Photographs such as the ones shown can be invaluable.

With the exception of the body shell, keep as much of the donor car as you can, whether or not you are likely to need the parts, and whether or not they are serviceable. Small things, like fittings, clips, spacers, relays and so on, are often hard to replace and can be difficult to make. Even if unserviceable, they can be useful as patterns.

Cut the wires near the components they serve if you are not intending to reuse the wiring loom, and do the same with pipes and their fittings to help subsequent identification and in case any of the fittings are special. Recognise, also, that there is only one satisfactory way of storing nuts and bolts, and that is not in a jam jar which you will at some time kick over or drop to the detriment of your fingers as you try to sort it all out. The proper place for nuts, bolts and studs is back where they came from in their original positions, with nuts screwed loosely back on their bolts or studs, or in labelled plastic bags. A few fasteners may be special and hard to come by, and some bolts will be longer than others. If, when rebuilding, you fit them correctly the first time, you will not cause damage or have to dismantle components to try again. Even if you need new fasteners, it is less embarrassing and more helpful to say to the supplier, 'I want three like this please', than to say, 'I'm not sure what they are, but I need three that are a bit thinner than these and with a different thread.'

DISMANTLING

A car is made up of hundreds of separate pieces. These are held together by various means depending on whether or not they are intended to be taken apart, and whether they revolve or need to be prevented from revolving. Welding and spot-welding is used on body panels and chassis members because they are intended to be joined permanently (except for repair), but doors, boot and bonnet lids are bolted in place, as adjustment may be necessary to make them fit properly.

Mechanical units contain parts that may be secured by rivets, if not intended to be serviced, or by threaded fasteners – nuts, bolts, screws or studs – if they are. In addition, rotating or moveable parts may be 'mated' to others by means of keys, tapers, pins or splines, some of which are not always obvious. Before you can take things apart you need to know how they are joined together, especially if you want to reuse them. *Figs. 3.4 to 3.19* show how various parts may be joined together and how to take them apart. Remember that the parts may have been fixed for many years and may be reluctant to be parted. Thumping them with a big hammer is unlikely to do more than damage the mating parts, so it is wise to use the appropriate proper method.

Nuts and bolts are often a nuisance as, especially on brakes and chassis, they are exposed to all weathers and dirt thrown up by the car from the road. Good quality, close-fitting spanners are essential, especially as nuts and bolts are sometimes difficult to reach. There are several ways in which you can tackle rusted nuts and bolts, depending on whether or not you need to keep them. If they are in any way special you may need to use them again, if not, it is satisfying to build or rebuild your car using new fasteners throughout. Scrub the exposed thread with a wire brush, then try soaking the nut and bolt assembly in penetrating oil (make your own using old engine oil and paraffin in equal quantities) or something like WD40. If this does not work, try heating the assembly with a gas blowlamp, if it is safe to do so. Heat will slightly expand the nut and bolt and break the rust seal between them, but be careful when doing this. Do not use a naked flame or heat near the petrol lines or tank, near anything that can be destroyed by heat, such as wiring, or close to anything which is flammable like plastic, and always have a suitable fire extinguisher or fire blanket ready to put out a fire if one should occur.

If you cannot use heat to separate the components, try sawing through the bolt, chiselling the nut off, or using a nut splitter, depending on how easy the problem is to get at. The majority of bolts used have a 'right-hand thread', that is they tighten up by being turned to the right (in a clockwise direction) but in some special cases, usually on rotating parts where the movement would tend to loosen them, left-hand threads are used. It is always worthwhile checking the thread to make sure that you are in fact trying to undo the assembly rather than tightening it further.

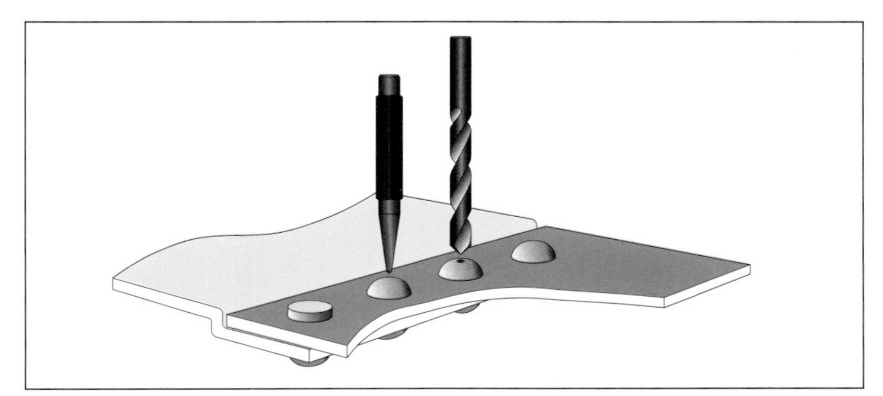

Fig. 3.4. Rivets. Centre punch and drill down to base of head. Drill diameter should be about half diameter of rivet head.

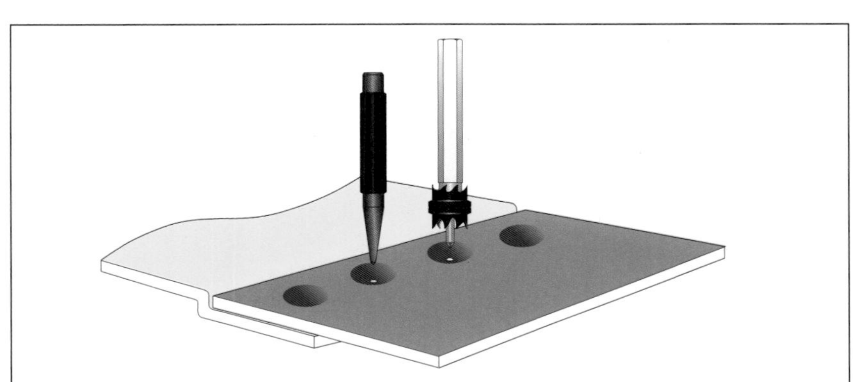

Fig. 3.5. Spot welds. If you need to reuse one of the panels, centre punch and cut through the weld on one panel with a Zipcut.

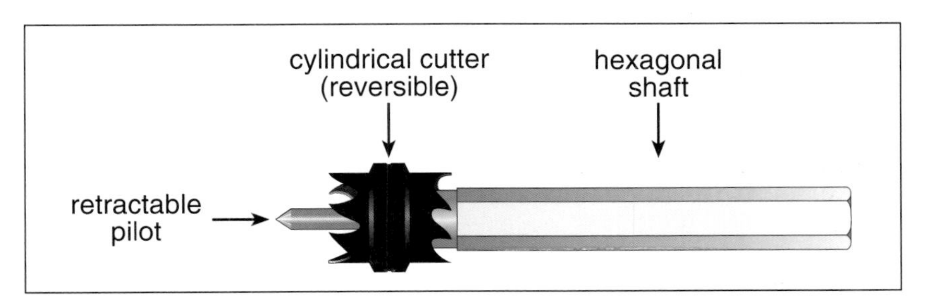

Fig. 3.6. A Zipcut in detail.

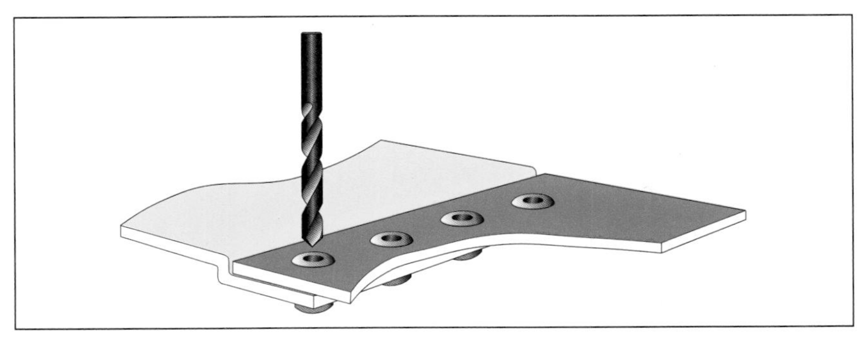

Fig. 3.7. Pop rivets. Drill to base of lip and knock out.

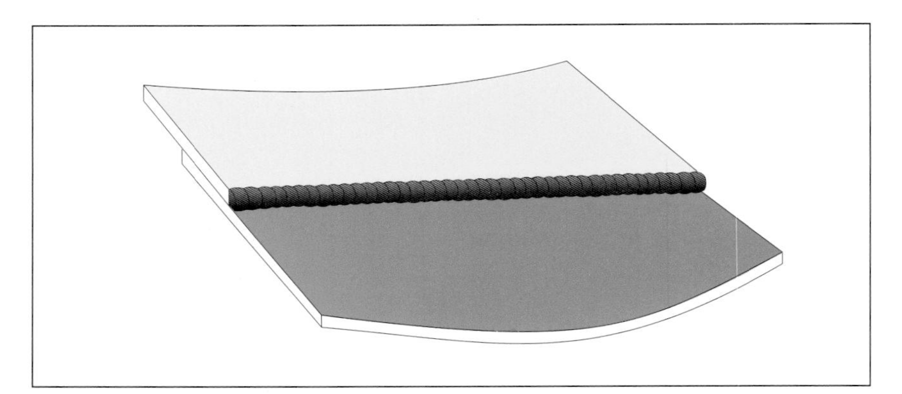

Fig. 3.8. Weld. Remove weld bead with angle grinder.

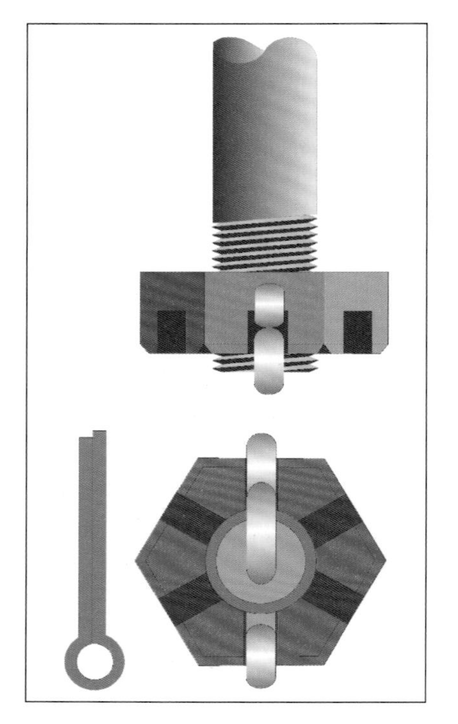

Fig. 3.9 (left). Castellated nut and split-pin (note correct way to fit pin). Straighten pin and pull out, or clip off legs with side-cutting pliers. If necessary, tap remains of pin out of hole with pin punch. Never reuse split-pins; always fit new ones of the correct diameter.

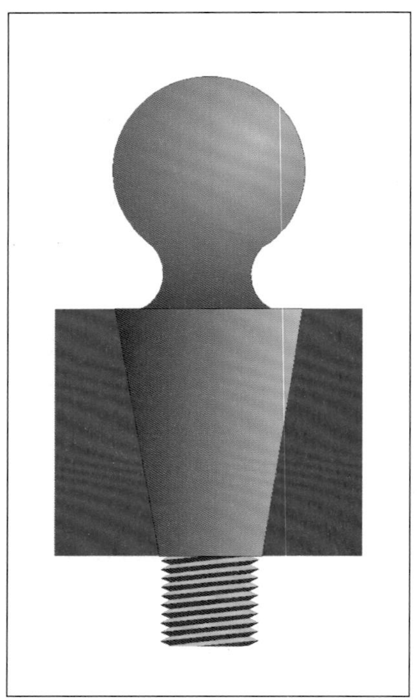

Fig. 3.10 (right). Taper. Remove retaining nut. Support one side with solid object and give a heavy blow to the opposite side with a hammer, or use special splitter.

Fig. 3.11 (left). Lock nuts. Hold lower nut with spanner and undo upper nut.

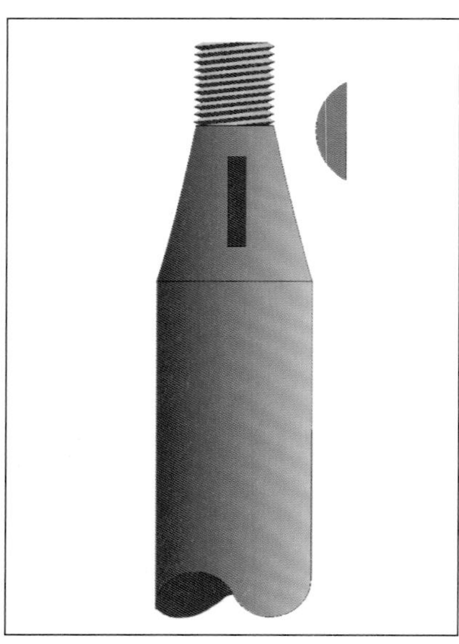

Fig. 3.12 (right). Taper and key. Used on rotating parts such as pulleys or gearwheels.

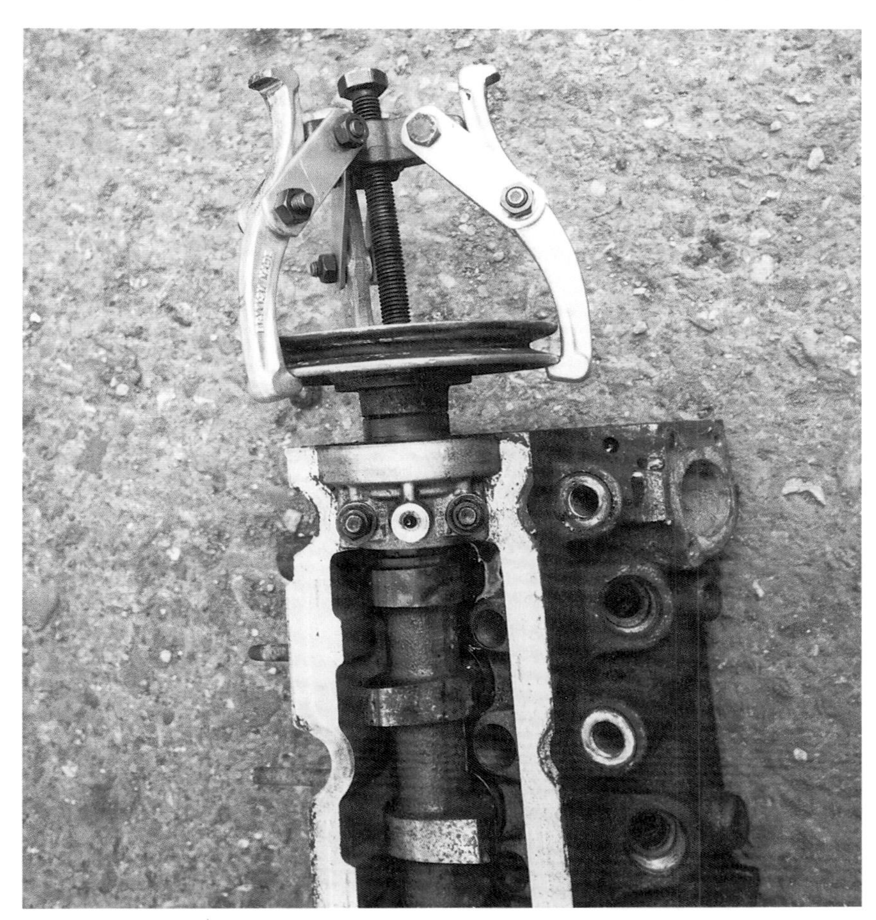

Fig. 3.13. To remove a component from a taper, undo the retaining nut and, if retained part will not yield to gentle taps around its periphery, use a gear-puller. Here a gear puller is being used to remove a camshaft pulley.

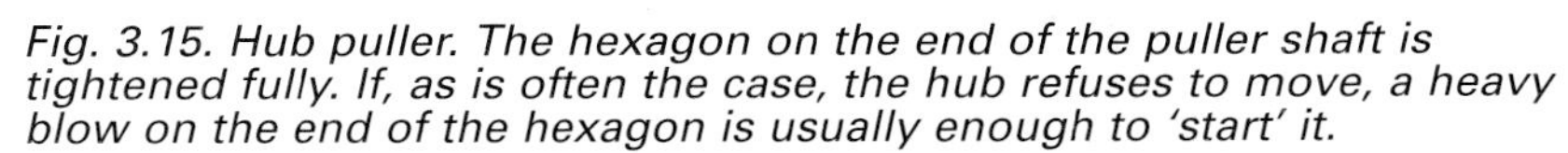

Fig. 3.15. Hub puller. The hexagon on the end of the puller shaft is tightened fully. If, as is often the case, the hub refuses to move, a heavy blow on the end of the hexagon is usually enough to 'start' it.

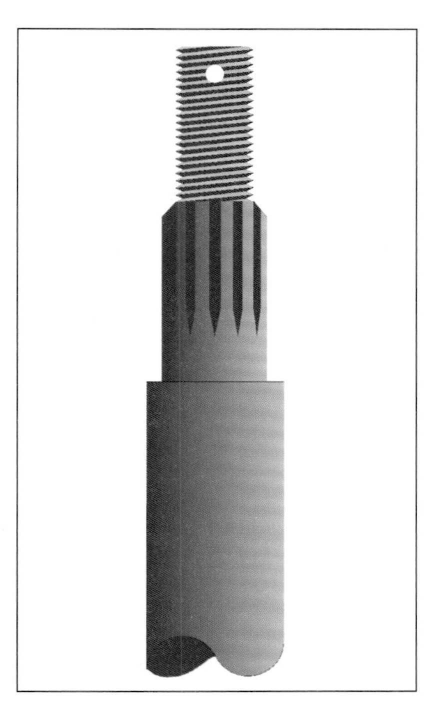

Fig. 3.14. Splines. Used on half-shafts (and other parts) to transmit motion and retain hubs. Remove split-pin and pull off hub – may need gentle persuasion or use of a puller.

Fig. 3.16. Clevis and pin. Used on brake rods/cables. Remove split-pin and pull/tap out clevis pin.

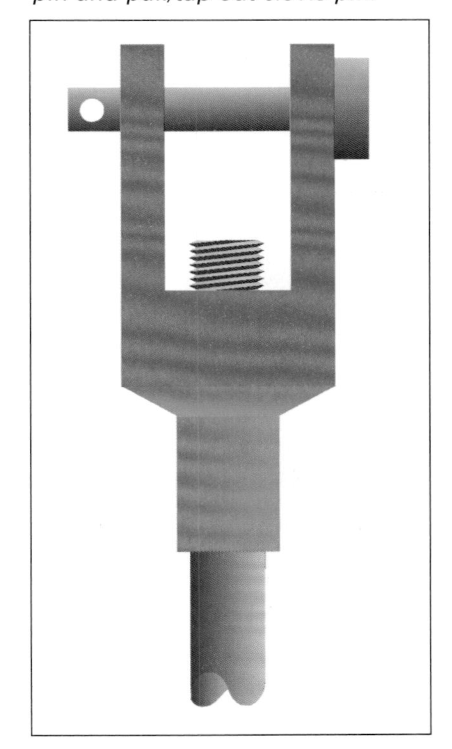

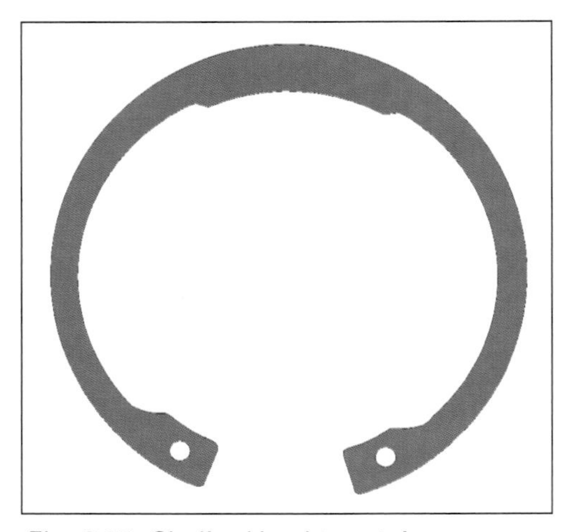

Fig. 3.17. Circlip. Used to retain rods/shafts. There are internal and external (illustrated) types.

Fig. 3.18. Use special circlip pliers and contract or expand circlip, as required, to clear groove in which it is fitted.

Fig. 3.19. Nut splitter. The splitter fits over the nut, and the chisel is advanced by turning the hexagon with a spanner or socket. Useful when you have clear access.

Fig. 3.20. Take lots of photographs and sketches from every angle. You will be surprised how useful they will prove to be.

SPARES AND OTHER SUPPLIES

When you start the building process you will need some new or replacement parts. There are specialist suppliers for instruments, seats, steering wheels and many of the more exotic components particularly suited to kit cars and specials. Look in the magazines for their advertisements, and send for their catalogues, which can make most enjoyable reading. If the donor car, or the subject of your restoration project is not too old, you may be able to buy replacement parts from agents or motor factors, some of whom can supply service parts for cars going back many years.

A good source of spares is a breaker's yard and, if you are missing a part, this is perhaps your first port of call. If you wish to replace a worn part, you will need to recognise the fact that similar components wear in similar ways, so all you can hope for is to find a part that has had less wear than yours. One-make car clubs realise this and often have batches of otherwise unobtainable parts made.

General suppliers of common parts, paint and equipment are to be found in every large town, and there are advertisements in the motoring magazines for many who specialise in mail order.

There are also autojumbles. If you are not already acquainted with them you should go along to one some time, as they are great fun and rank as a good day out. There are stalls that cover every aspect of motoring, and some of the larger ones may have complete restoration projects for sale. Even the smaller stalls have an enormous variety of mainly second-hand parts, so if you are looking for a difficult-to-find item you should certainly pay a visit. Discipline is required though, as there are so many goodies available. When I unpack after a visit to an autojumble I am always surprised at some of the items I have bought. If you can, take the old part with you to ensure an exact match. Also, make sure you take plenty of cash, and a number of plastic bags to hold the parts that you buy. If you can find a willing volunteer, it is convenient to have someone with you to carry the bags so that you can have both hands free to examine the stock – and towards the end of the day bags get heavy!

If you are really stuck for a part it can probably be reconditioned or a new one can be made, especially if it is a wearing part like a bush. If you have a rare car you may have to resort to having a part specially manufactured and the relevant owners' club can probably help with this.

As far as specialist engineering services are concerned, for crank-grinding, re-boring, surface grinding, milling and so on, every large town has at least one such firm that undertakes specific jobs or will machine parts or rebuild your engine for you. They also tend to know specialists in other areas, and can usually recommend firms for the work that they do not themselves undertake.

There are also specialists who supply fasteners like nuts and bolts, others who supply bushes and bearings and, of course, metal polishers and electro-platers. All you need do is look in *Yellow Pages*.

Chapter 4

The chassis

THE EVOLUTION OF CHASSIS DESIGN

The chassis forms the foundation on which a car is built and provides location for the running gear, engine and transmission. Early chassis, often of wood, consisted of two long side-pieces joined together by cross-members, rather like a bedstead, though usually described as 'ladder type'.

Later chassis were made of pressed steel, the Daimler Company in England being the first manufacturer to adopt this method, and were of channel section, tapering towards the ends with the front curved downwards to provide pick-up points for the front springs, and the back curved upwards over the rear axle to allow for its up-and-down motion. Cross-members were riveted or welded to the main members, and the engine helped to strengthen the front end.

Bodywork was separate from the chassis, usually wooden-framed (of ash), with steel, aluminium or fabric panels. The bodywork was bolted to the chassis, and this meant that body styles could be easily changed and that, on luxury cars, customers could order a body to their own design from the coachbuilder. As such, cars were provided by the manufacturer in chassis form only. It was not unusual for an owner who liked a particular body to have it taken off the existing chassis and have it mounted on a later one rather than buying a complete new car. This makes life easier for the

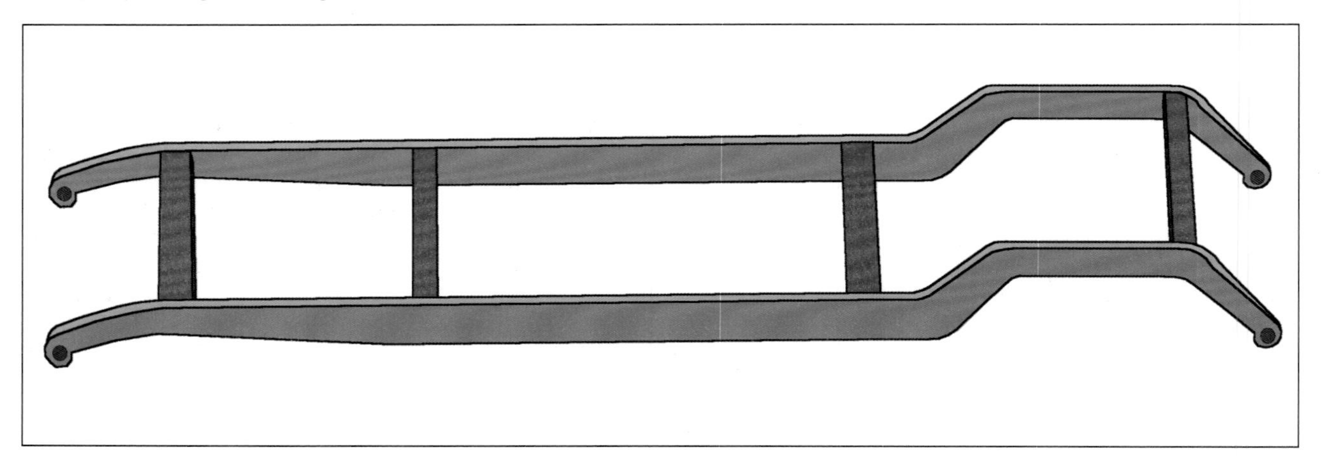

Fig. 4.1 A simple ladder frame.

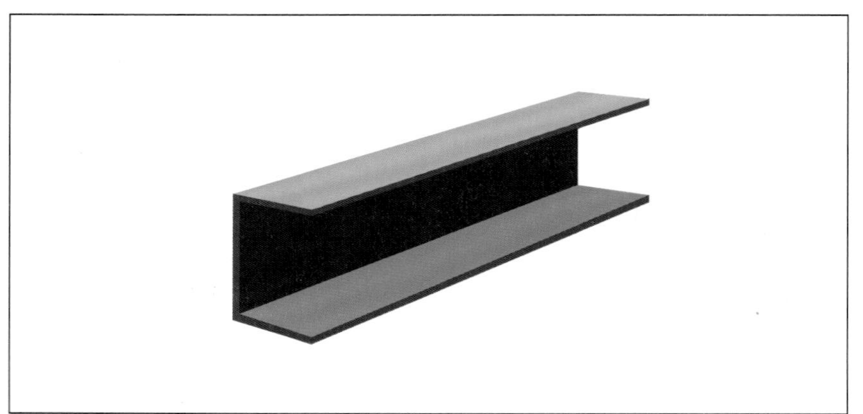

Fig. 4.2 Channel section.

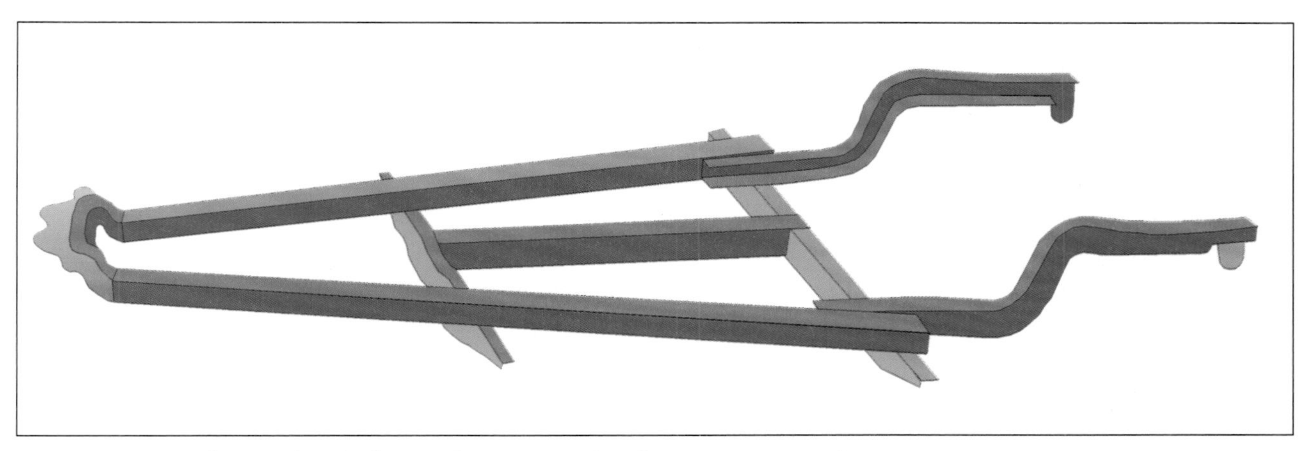

Fig. 4.3. Austin Seven chassis frame. Front mounting for transverse spring.

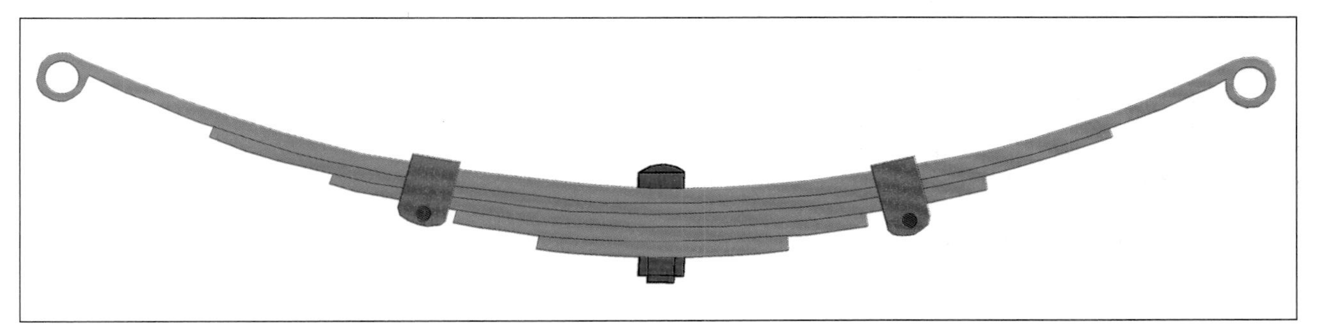

Fig. 4.4. A leaf spring.

restorer, as we shall see, since when rebuilding the car the body can be removed and worked on separately.

Until the late 1930s, with very few exceptions such as Lancia and Morgan, cars were fitted with leaf springs front and rear, usually four, one at each corner in line with the chassis, although the Austin Seven had three springs, the one at the front being transverse, and Fords managed with only two transverse springs as late as the 1950s.

Leaf springs, so called because they are made up of a number of separate leaves (often disparagingly referred to as 'cart springs') tend to give a firm, sometimes harsh, ride. To overcome this problem, designers usually produced chassis frames that were in some degree flexible in order to assist the springs.

This flexing of the chassis tended to affect the body, leading to creaks and groans from the body frame joints, and squeaks from the panels rubbing together. This tested coachbuilders' ingenuity in their efforts to overcome the problems, which were especially evident in open cars. Chassis flexing was not always good for the chassis itself either, and when rebuilding a car with a separate chassis the frame should always be closely inspected for cracks and loose rivets.

As cars became increasingly more powerful and sophisticated, so the need grew for improvement in the rigidity of the chassis frame, especially with the dawn of independent front suspension in place of the old beam axles. Various methods evolved for achieving the level of rigidity required to make independent front suspension effective, some chassis having deeper side-frame members joined by strong tubular cross-members, others having a strong cruciform structure in the centre of the frame which also helped to prevent the frame from 'lozenging'. Other designs had the channel-section side-members strengthened by being 'boxed'.

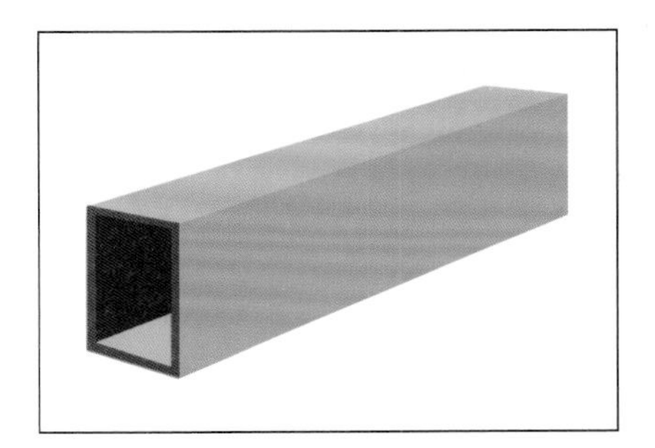

Fig. 4.5. Box section.

Some cars, like the 2CV Citroën, have a simple chassis frame which is completely enclosed by sheets of steel welded to the top and bottom.

Many alternatives to the pressed-steel, channel-section frame have been used. Morgans have traditionally had side-members of Z-section with the front suspension (always independent on a Morgan) mounted on a tubular cross-frame. Some manufacturers have used a

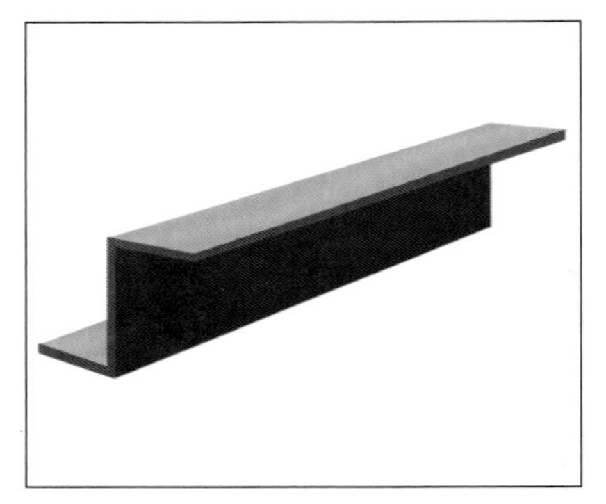

Fig. 4.6. 'Z' section – Morgan's favourite.

'backbone' chassis, varying from a single large diameter tube like the 1935 Mercedes, to a fabricated structure like the Reliant Scimitar or the Y-shaped Lotus Elan.

A fairly obvious alternative to the ordinary channel-section frame was the use of two longitudinal tubes, of reasonably substantial dimensions, united at each end by a fabricated structure to carry the suspension, and tubular cross-members. This design has been used by several manufacturers, notably AC when they adopted the Tojeiro design for the AC Ace and subsequently the Cobra.

In the 1960s the Coopers used the multi-tubular space-frame with great success, and Colin Chapman, who trained as a structural engineer, developed his own version for his Lotus Seven masterpiece. The Seven space-frame was designed to be light and rigid, and was fully triangulated with all loads in compression or tension, and with no bending moments. The frame provided location for all parts of the car and, in itself, formed the body frame. The original Chapman design has many derivatives, particularly amongst kit cars of the 'Seven' variety.

However, few cars built after the Second World War have a chassis frame. The pressure of mass production in the late 1920s in America gave rise to the introduction of the technique of pressing body panels out of mild steel sheets instead of forming

Fig. 4.7. A backbone chassis.

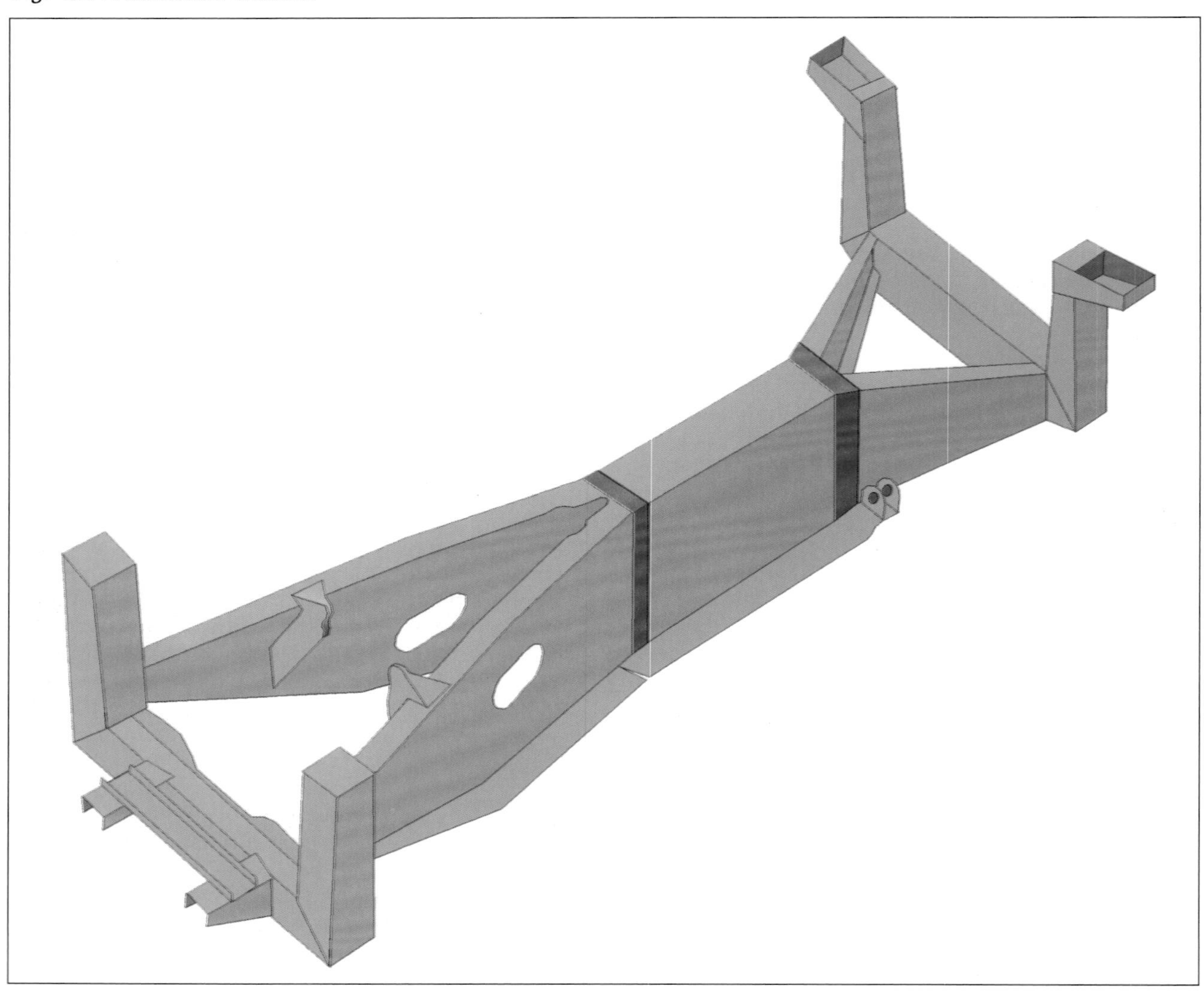

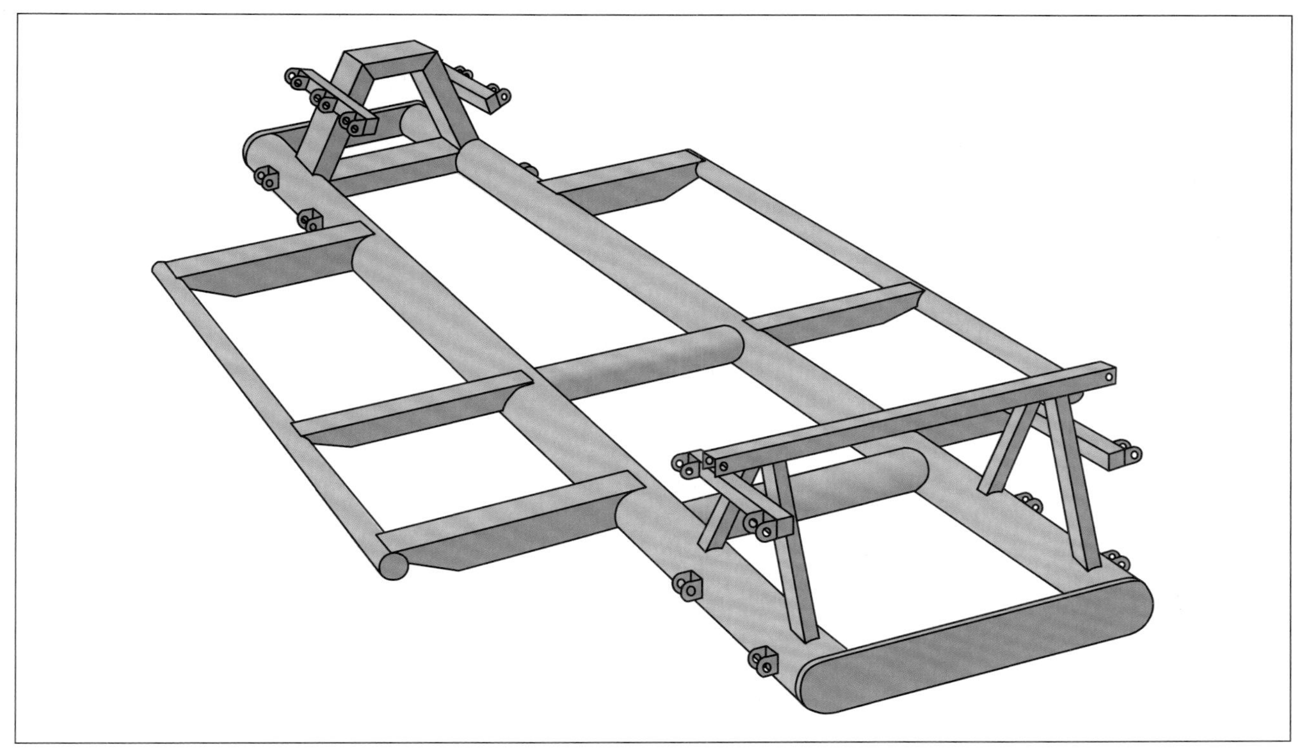

Fig. 4.8. A parallel tube chassis with outriggers and suspension mountings fitted.

them by hand using fabric or wood. This in turn led to the body panels being welded together to form a complete rigid structure without relying on a traditional framework to support them. This rigid structure forms a 'monocoque' or 'unitary structure' on which all the mechanical components – power train and suspension – are fitted (often on a subframe for convenience) and in which the seats and passenger accommodation are provided.

It is said that the perfect monocoque is an egg, or at least an egg-shaped structure. This may be so but, unlike an egg, a car needs openings to allow passengers to get in and out, and the provision of these destroys the inherent rigidity of the structure. However, all design is a compromise, and the difficulty is overcome by suitably reinforcing the structure to compensate for the openings.

The first British unitary-construction car was the Vauxhall in 1937, followed by Morris in 1938. Other manufacturers thereafter used the method with saloon cars, but open cars retained separate chassis (as some still do) until the arrival of the MGB in 1962, which was the first sports car designed as a unitary structure, not counting cars like the early Porsche which was developed from a saloon car (the VW Beetle). The monocoque, for all its production advantages, has the drawback of enormous initial cost when tooling up for a new body, which is the reason why manufacturers cling to one design for as long as possible with just occasional updating. It is also the reason why all the traditional coachbuilders, some of whom had

Fig. 4.9. A space-frame chassis.

been in existence for centuries, have gone out of business. And so the kit-car industry came into existence, so that the enthusiast could drive something more individual than the mass-produced car. The ladder chassis, often in very sophisticated form, is the basis of many kit cars.

DESIGNING A CHASSIS

Basic principles

When you have established the basic shape and dimensions of your car, the next step is to design the chassis, bearing in mind the need for strength, lightness and rigidity.

Fabricated Y-type chassis are difficult for the amateur to produce, and the traditional ladder-type is very flexible unless well braced. For a sports car, it may be worth constructing some form of space-frame built on traditional lines, particularly if you are good at welding. But perhaps the easiest type of chassis for the amateur to construct, or to have built, is the twin-tube chassis using either parallel round-section tubes or box-section material. Round tube of about 3in (75mm) diameter and $\frac{1}{8}$in (3.2mm) wall thickness, with cross-pieces front and rear fabricated from mild steel sections, and one or more transverse tubes, should give a sufficiently rigid structure. If you prefer box-section material, sections of say 40mm x 80mm x 3.2mm ($1\frac{5}{8}$in x $3\frac{1}{8}$in x $\frac{1}{8}$in) could be used, and can be doubled up side-by-side and seam-welded to increase chassis strength where needed, particularly in the middle of the sides where the weight of the driver and passenger is usually taken.

In both cases it should be remembered that the scuttle (the part of the car over the driver's legs that supports the windscreen) should be so designed as to increase the rigidity of the frame, and should be considered an integral part of it. In the days before unitary construction, chassis were usually complete with steering, dashboard, etc, and could be driven. The body formed only a cover for the passengers and machinery, and was not relied upon to add strength.

Build the frame on a flat surface, and check constantly that it is geometrically accurate. Be careful over the welding, and if in doubt have it inspected by a competent welder before you go any further. When you are satisfied that all is well and the joints have been fettled, the frame can be sprayed with a weld-through primer which will protect it but will allow brackets or other parts to be welded on later. Ideally you should assemble the completed chassis with all attachments first as a trial assembly, then take it to pieces for finishing and final painting.

If you have doubts about your ability to make a chassis yourself, remember that there are metal fabricators in most towns who spend their time cutting and welding steel sections. If you prepare a dimensioned drawing, they will quote you a price for making the chassis, which saves you the bother of buying the material and cutting and welding it yourself.

Pedal box and engine positioning

Before moving on from the chassis we need to consider two things which are best done at this stage;

Fig. 4.10. Pedal box (Ford).

Fig. 4.11. Ford pedal box fitted to space-frame chassis.

the positioning of the pedal box and the positioning of the engine. The pedal box is not necessarily a 'box', but comprises the cluster formed by the clutch, brake and accelerator (or throttle) pedals and the framework that attaches them to the car. If you do not consider the design of this area now, it can be very awkward later, which is why it should be counted as a part of the chassis. Much the easiest solution is to use the pedal assembly from the donor car, or one obtained from a breaker's yard, along with the brake master cylinder and, if the clutch is to be hydraulically operated, the clutch master cylinder. Beware of the servo, if there is one. If you are building a light sports car, you will probably find when it is on the road that it is over-braked anyway, and that the last thing you want is servo-assistance, as the brakes become very sensitive and in the wet tend to turn the car into a toboggan.

For many years nearly all production cars have had pendant pedals (VW excepted), that is pedals that are pivoted at the top. This is largely to make the hydraulic fluid reservoirs accessible, and there is a lot to be said for them as they come as a complete unit. However, race and rally cars often have bottom-hinged pedals that stick up from the floor – these are available, at a price, from the specialists. Bottom-hinged pedals provide a more natural action for the foot, which, resting on the floor, is also bottom-hinged and, therefore, moves in the same arc as the pedals. Bottom-hinged pedals are not difficult to make, but need to be robust in the interests of safety.

Pedal pads should be about 4–5in (100–125mm) apart, and of a height convenient to the size of your feet, since you operate them with the ball of your foot. You may have to experiment to establish the best vertical position for the brake master-cylinder push-rod to ensure that there is adequate leverage and travel. On my Locost there was a distance of about 2in (50mm) from the pedal pivot to the push-rod clevis.

Bottom-hinged accelerator and clutch pedals, if cable-operated, will need a segment welded to the bottom, below the pivot, to guide and operate the cable inners. Again, experiment to establish the size that will give full movement to the clutch and throttle. Be sure, when you couple up the cables and/or linkages, that all three pedals have a small amount of free movement before they begin to act on the components that they control.

Whichever type of pedal box you go for, try to make it self-contained so that it can be detached for servicing. If you are restoring a car or using a unit from a donor vehicle, check the pivots for wear. Some may require lubrication, but many have replaceable nylon bushes.

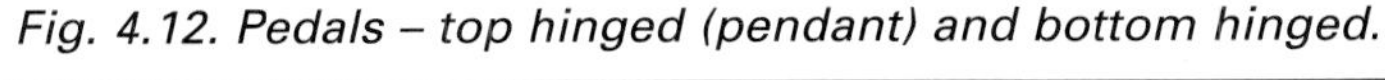

Fig. 4.12. Pedals – top hinged (pendant) and bottom hinged.

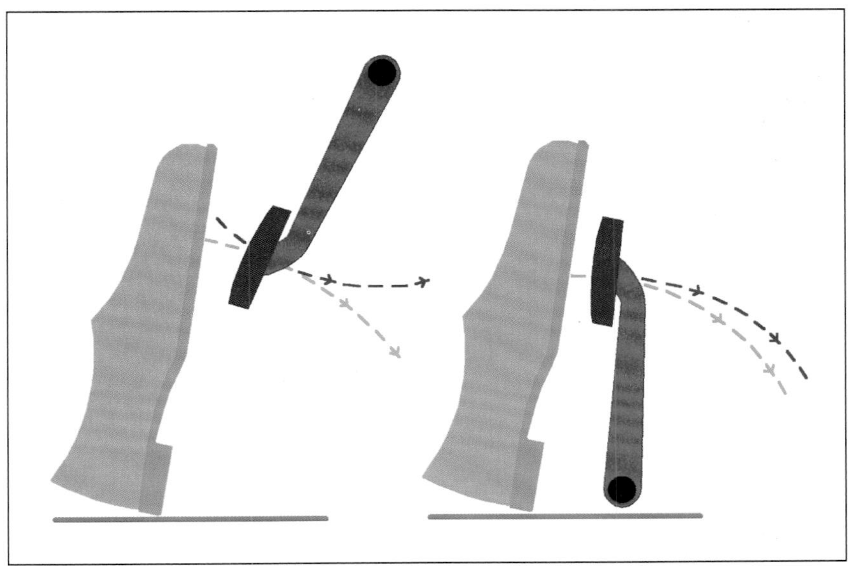

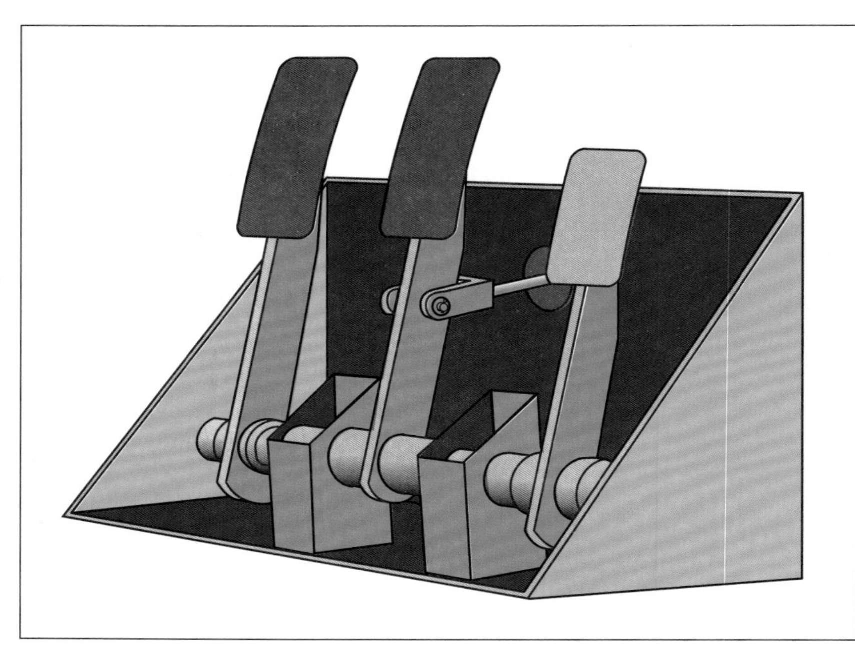

Fig. 4.13. A fabricated bottom-hinged pedal box.

Fig. 4.15. An engine mounting bracket with rubber bush.

Fig. 4.14. Bottom-hinged pedals fitted in a Locost.

Fig. 4.16. Another engine mounting in situ.

When you laid out your chassis dimensions, you will have chalked round the engine and gearbox to get some idea of their position; you now need to position the units accurately. If the engine is to be at the front of the car, it needs to be located as far back as possible, and you should have it in its complete state when you undertake this, bearing in mind that the starter motor may protrude, and also allowing for ease of access. You will want the engine to be mounted as low as possible to keep the centre of gravity low, but not so low that the sump is in danger of hitting the road. On a sports car you may not have a lot of ground clearance, so ideally keep the bottom of the sump not more than say 1in (25mm) lower than the bottom of the chassis. You can establish this by sitting the engine on the floor and positioning the chassis over it on blocks of suitable height. Making sure that you have got enough clearance, and that the engine is in line with the centre-line of the chassis, you can mark the position for the engine-mounting brackets and measure their height. It is no bad plan to make a cardboard pattern from which you can make the real thing in metal when you are satisfied that all is well with the dimensions and angles. Depending on your chassis design, you may find that you need additional engine bearers, or a subframe, on which to mount the brackets.

On a front-engined, rear-wheel-drive car, the combined engine and gearbox assembly is usually mounted at three points, one on either side of the engine, and one under the gearbox or attached to the gearbox sides. You will have to make provision for the gearbox mounting on a suitable cross-member of the chassis frame.

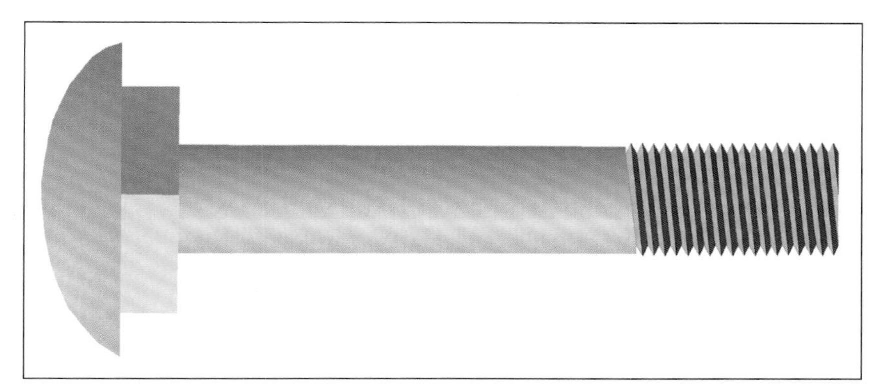

Fig. 4.17. A coach bolt.

INSPECTING AND RESTORING A CHASSIS

If you are intending to use an existing chassis, or are rebuilding a car, then you will be concerned with renovation rather than manufacture. You will need to remove and store out of harm's way all the detachable parts of the car so that you are left with only the body shell before you remove this from the chassis.

If components like lamps, mirrors and the windscreen frame are detachable, take special care of them, as they may be irreplaceable. Plan to lift the body off towards the rear, if you are leaving the bulkhead fixed to the chassis at this stage, making sure that you have enough space above it for clearance.

Wooden-framed bodies are held to the chassis by means of coach bolts. These have large heads with a square underneath which, when tightened, bites into the wood of the sill board to stop the bolt turning. What happens, of course, is that after years of exposure to the elements the nuts rust on the bolts, and the wood in contact with it rots, so that the whole assembly turns when you put a spanner on the nut – a problem not helped by the fact that some of the bolts are often difficult to reach.

It is sometimes possible to saw a slot in the bolt head with a hacksaw so that it may be held with a screwdriver, or to cut or file two parallel flats to grip with a spanner. If this does not work you may be able to chisel the nut off, or split it. If not, you will have to saw the bolt off by wedging a screwdriver between the sill and chassis and holding the hacksaw blade in a pad saw handle. (You now vow to use coach bolts welded to small metal plates, with countersunk holes for wood screws in them, when you come to reassemble the body.)

Bodies are heavy and awkward to handle if they are large, so you will have to recruit some help when lifting the body from the chassis. Make sure that everyone knows what is supposed to be happening.

The vulnerable part of the body at this stage is the sill boards under the door openings, if they are at all weak, lifting the body at front and rear can easily result in breaking at the opening, and you will finish up with two half-bodies rather than one complete one. It is advisable to support the body under the sill boards when lifting if from the chassis.

Store the body in a safe place. If it has to live outside, place it on bearers to lift it off the ground and cover it with a plastic sheet, well tied down so that it will not flap and tear in the wind.

You can now strip the chassis of all attachments – suspension, brakes, steering, engine and so on – not forgetting the petrol tank, pipes and clips. Now clean the chassis thoroughly, removing all paint and rust using a wire brush in an electric drill, and examine it for damage. This is perhaps the most unpleasant part of the restoration, but do remember to wear protective goggles and gloves, as it is a dirty job with much rust, grit and possibly the odd bit of wire from the brush flying about. If you can afford it, you can have the whole chassis shot blasted, but make sure that it is painted immediately afterwards.

Some damage to the chassis

Fig. 4.18. Support the body under the sill boards (arrowed) when removing it from the chassis.

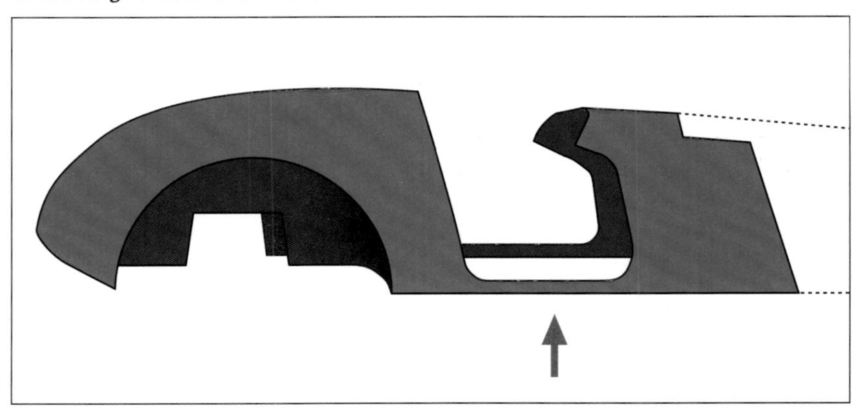

may have been apparent before you took the car to pieces. I once bought an impressive pre-war roadster and, from the position of the doors and the fact that they would not open, it could be seen the chassis had cracked on both sides. However, I did not bargain for the fact that it had rusted through in no less than seven places!

If the doors have irregular gaps, or the bonnet does not fit, or the wheel arch clearance looks dodgy, it is very likely that the chassis frame needs attention.

Put the chassis frame on blocks or axle stands, measure it diagonally from corner to corner, and check that the sides are parallel or symmetrical. If the frame is 'lozenged' or 'banana'd', or the geometry is out in any other way, you are likely to need the services of a professional, though bent side members can often be straightened by being pushed or pulled by means of jacks, a chain and some stout pieces of timber or RSJs (rolled steel joists). The local bodyshop will have hydraulic rams and other equipment for straightening accident-damaged cars, and will doubtless be able to help.

Cracks tend to occur at stress points such as mounting points for springs, or the engine and cross-member attachment points, and any cracks found will need welding.

On a car with leaf springs, if the spring hangers have rubber bushes, they are likely to be of the type that have a hardened-steel sleeve with a rubber insert and a mild steel housing. These are often worn or damaged and need replacing. They are a tight fit in the bracket or hanger, and if you cannot drive them out with a drift of suitable diameter, or pull them out with a length of studding and a bush, the best way of removing them is by burning the rubber out (never mind the smell) and threading a hacksaw blade in the hole. The outer sleeve can then be sawn through and tapped out. New bushes can be tapped into place or drawn in with studding.

To finish the frame you can have it powder-coated, or paint it yourself. Two coats of 'Rust Stop', or one of the many other preparations designed to inhibit rust and prime metal surfaces, followed by the finishing paint in the colour of your choice, will look good and will give excellent protection.

If rust has eaten through the chassis metal, or damage necessitates replacement, cut the relevant section out and butt-weld in a new section ('V'-shaped ends will give a greater area of weld) – your local metal fabricator will 'fold' you a new piece. Reinforcing plates should generally be avoided, except perhaps in the middle sections of the side-members, since as explained earlier, a degree of flexibility is usually designed into the ladder-type frame, and reinforcing plates tend to prevent this and may lead to new cracks elsewhere.

If the chassis is designed for independent suspension, it should be rigid enough not to need reinforcement, as it should not flex and therefore cause fractures, although it can be reinforced if necessary. With a multi-tubular type frame any damaged tubes should be cut out and replaced with tubing of the same section and gauge.

INSPECTING AND RESTORING A MONOCOQUE

If the car you are restoring is of monocoque construction, you cannot of course remove the body from the chassis, but the preparations, inspection and some of the repairs are similar to those already mentioned. To make life a bit easier, before you start work on the car use a hose pipe or, preferably a high pressure water jet, and clean off all the mud, loose rust and 'gunge' from under the wheel arches and anywhere else you can reach; this will make inspection much easier and will result in less wire brushing.

Position the car where you can work on it easily (if you have any choice in the matter!) and strip it of all external fittings, bumpers, lights and so on. Jack the car up as high as you can to make working under the wings as comfortable as possible, put it on axle stands, and remove the wheels. You can now begin the inspection.

You are looking for rust, damage and any previous repairs. While you should inspect every inch of the car, with a good light to help you, you will need to concentrate on the areas usually affected by rust. If you have joined the appropriate club, you can find out where these areas are by asking, and you may have read articles in the motoring magazines on your particular model. In general they are the places that have the most contact with road dirt, mud and salt, and many cars have built-in mud traps that collect wet mud and let it gently rust its way through the metal. Inspect under the front wings, especially around the headlight mountings and the suspension mounting points, where fractures sometimes occur, and if the car has MacPherson struts, check that the tops of the turrets are sound. Inspect the sills, which are usually an essential part of the structure and frequently rot, and the rear wheel arches. Jacking points, if welded on, often rot, sometimes affecting the surrounding floor areas, and spare wheel wells in the boot can collect water as their drainage arrangements become blocked. If it is difficult to assess the condition of the metal because of underseal, paint, or surface rust, tap the suspected area with a small hammer (beloved by the MoT inspector) which will quickly tell you whether the metal is sound or not.

Externally, rust can be easily identified from bubbling paint or more obvious signs. Door bottoms, wing edges, boot lid edges, and windscreen and door pillars should all be examined carefully not only for rust, but for filler that has been used to repair rust areas and has been painted over.

Look over the various parts of the suspension carefully. Shock absorbers need replacing if there are any signs of leaks, and spring seats can rust, especially the bottom ones which sometimes hold water and wet mud. Most accident damage takes place at the front of cars, so both the suspension parts and the main structure of the car need careful inspection for damage and repaired damage.

Much use is made of rubber bushes in modern suspension systems, and it is essential for safety reasons, as well as for good handling, that these are in a satisfactory condition. Carefully inspect the ends of struts, lower and trailing arms, anti-roll bars and any other suspension members for fatigue and wear. A large tyre lever or other substantial lever is a help in trying to assess the condition of suspension bushes, as it can be used to attempt to prise joints apart. Renewal of these bushes is usually as described previously for cars with a conventional chassis, but modern bushes rarely have outer metal sleeves. A coating of washing-up liquid will help to draw new bushes into place when refitting.

If there are signs of damage to the monocoque structure, you can check by dropping a plumb-line from the centre of the hubs (with the steering in the straight-ahead position), and marking their position on the garage floor. The diagonals between the marks on the floor (corresponding to the hub positions) can be measured and should be equal. A very few cars have a shorter wheelbase on one side than the other because of the configuration of their rear torsion bar suspension systems, so you will have to make allowance for this. (When working abroad I once took delivery of a new car, and was alarmed when, after several hundred miles, irregular tyre wear at the rear made me measure the wheelbase on each side, only to find that it was over an inch (25mm) less on the offside. Since it had a live rear axle this was a puzzle until it was revealed that the car had been dropped heavily on being off-loaded, which had bent the rear axle. The agents rebuilt the axle with a new casing, but using the original internal components, with the result that it whined faintly for a long time until the gears were run-in to their new positions.)

After any repairs have been made, the areas under the wings, the sills, door bottoms and anywhere else you can reach should be painted with rust-proofing paint and undersealed or coated with Waxoyl or similar preparation.

THE KIT-CAR CHASSIS

Kit car builders will receive a chassis specifically designed for the body and running gear of the car of their choice, probably already painted or powder-coated with all brackets fitted, and can proceed straight away with the build.

Chapter 5

Suspension

CHOICE OF SYSTEM

If you are building a special, there is plenty of scope for choosing the type of suspension system your car will have. There are plenty of models from which to choose as, over the years, designers have tried almost every conceivable layout. Suspension design is highly complex, and you will do well to stick to a well-tried system rather than letting your imagination run riot. Inevitably, some systems are better than others, and some are best left alone. Swinging axles, front or rear, are not a good idea, as they do odd, unpredictable things to the road-holding. Strangely enough, it is respected German manufacturers who, since the 1930s, have used swinging axles at the rear. Auto-Union, VW, Mercedes and Porsche all used this system, and for many years persisted in developing and refining (as Porsche still do) a fundamentally unsatisfactory system.

Minis and some Citroëns have their own quite different suspension systems, both very effective for the cars for which they were intended (and in the case of the Citroën oleo-pneumatic system, for Rolls-Royce too). The Citroën type requires a pressure pump and hydraulic accumulator and is not easily adapted to other cars likely to be built by the amateur, so will not be dealt with here. If you are restoring a car fitted with one of these systems, you will certainly need the specific data from the workshop manual.

One of the easiest ways to deal with suspension is to lift it direct from another car, especially if your special is a front-wheel-drive type. Many cars have the front suspension (and steering), and sometimes the rear, mounted on a subframe of some sort that is in turn attached to the body of the car, from which it can be unbolted, complete with all components. Obviously, your chassis needs to be designed with this in mind so that the dimensions and pick-up points are correct. All that is then necessary is to clean and restore the components, and you have an instant, well-designed commercial assembly front and rear. The front and rear assemblies need not come from the same type of vehicle, so you have a wide choice of systems available to you.

Of course, you need to choose sensibly. There is no point in fitting, say, Jaguar subframes and suspension to a light two-seater of modest power, if only because of the weight and complexity, similarly it is unwise to use Mini subframes if you intend to build a large and powerful touring car. The donor vehicle needs to bear some relationship to the size, weight and power of the car you are building.

In the 1960s, Triumph produced its range of Herald and Spitfire cars with independent suspension all round. The rear suspension was by swing-axle (later modified) and not very satisfactory, and the front used wishbones, and coil springs over telescopic shock absorbers, a system which was very effective and was used commercially on some low-production cars, kit cars and by many amateur builders. If you can find the front end of a Triumph, it will do very well for your special.

The main problem with making your own front suspension, apart from getting the geometry right,

Fig. 5.1. A beam axle.

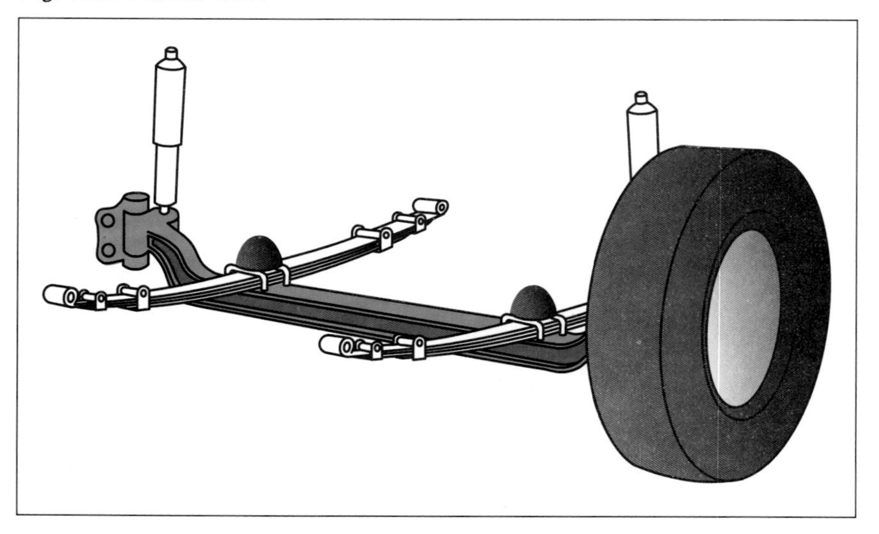

lies in the 'upright' or 'hub carrier'. This is the part that carries the stub axle for the road wheel, and the connections for the suspension and steering. As the upright must be very strong, it is usually a forging, accurately machined to provide the necessary housings, and strong enough to take road shocks, braking stress and the gyroscopic effects of a heavy road wheel revolving at speed when the steering wheel is turned – it is not easy to make. Many modern cars have MacPherson strut suspension which in itself forms the upright, and although this is not much use to the amateur suspension constructor who needs a separate upright, it is useful in itself if it is not too tall for your special. Fortunately the Ford Cortina has an excellent and very usable upright (and disc brake) that gets us out of trouble. If you mate this to wishbones you will have a very effective front suspension.

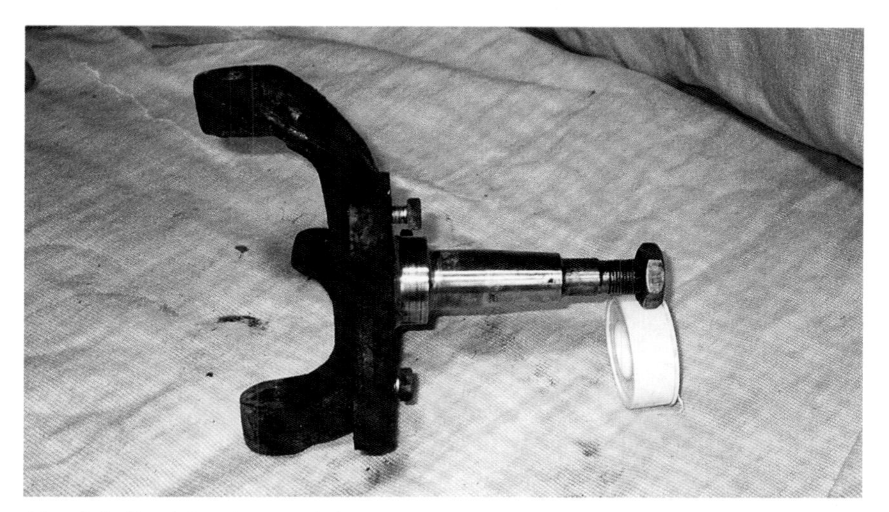

Fig. 5.2. Ford Cortina upright.

Fig. 5.3. Lower wishbone with upright.

As far as the rear suspension is concerned, many of us are content with a live rear axle, suspended by coil springs with telescopic shock absorbers, and controlled by radius rods and a Panhard rod for lateral location. Since Colin Chapman's day, this has become a classic used by most 'Seven' look-alikes.

If you fancy independent rear suspension, the problem of finding a suitable 'upright' arises, as encountered with the front suspension. A visit to a breaker's yard will offer a variety of solutions, but again we can turn to Ford and use the Sierra units (and differential). You can either use Sierra wishbones or make your own, replicating the measurements and geometry.

As far as springs and shock absorbers are concerned, there is little to match the 'coil over' units (coil springs surrounding telescopic shock absorbers) that are offered by a number of manufacturers. These tend to be expensive – especially those that have adjustable springs and damper controls, as these can be 'tuned' to the use and ride-height of the vehicle – though second-hand units are often available at autojumbles. If you buy second-hand, check that the shock absorbers are not leaking oil, and go armed with a note of the dimensions that you require, such as the 'free-length' of the assembly, which is the uncompressed distance between the centres of the mounting points, and the diameter and poundage (ie, the strength) of the spring required. For a typical light sports car, the front springs should be about 200lb and the rear springs should be about 160lb–180lb for normal road use.

Kit-car builders will either be supplied with complete suspension units, or will take them off the donor car.

INSPECTING AND RESTORING LEAF SPRINGS

The first use of springs on horse-drawn carriages must have been in search of improved comfort – solid wheels, however large, on axles bolted rigidly to the body could not have afforded much comfort on the rutted tracks then used as roads, even at two or three miles per hour. The eventual improvement in road building, with the aid of vehicles sprung not only for comfort but also for roadholding, made increased speeds possible, and in the late eighteenth century journeys by coach, with relays of horses, meant that distances of

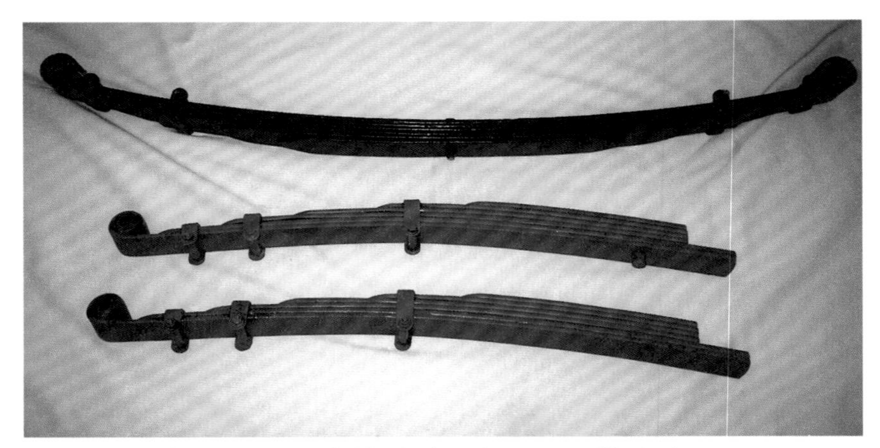

Fig. 5.4. Leaf springs – half elliptical and quarter elliptical.

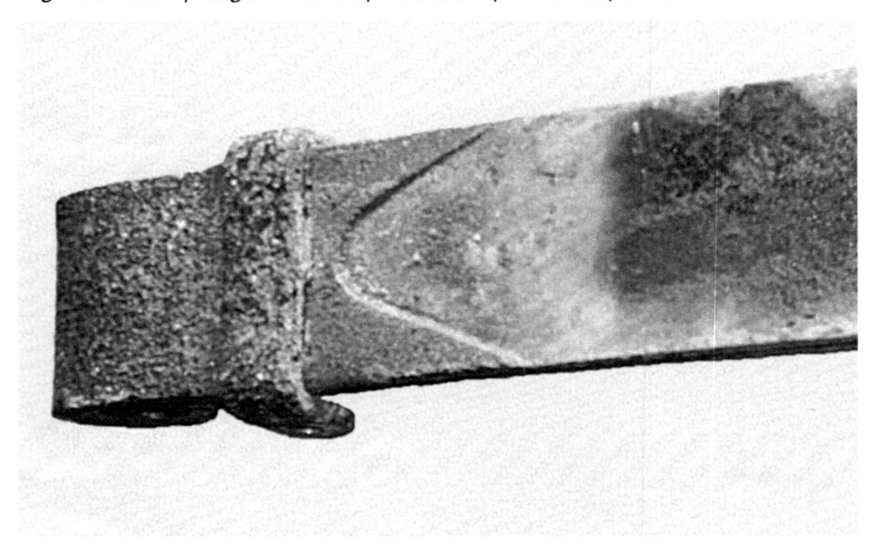

Fig. 5.5. Wear on a leaf spring.

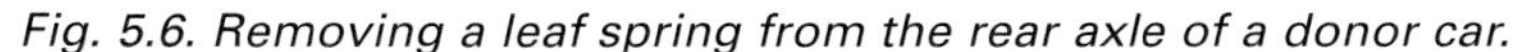

Fig. 5.6. Removing a leaf spring from the rear axle of a donor car.

over a hundred miles a day could be covered.

Springs, therefore, were available when the first cars were made (though the first car, a Daimler three-wheeler in 1885, did not use them), and nearly all cars used 'leaf' springs. It was not long – 1910 – before Morgan, like Lancia, appeared on the scene with coil springs for its sliding-pillar type of front suspension, but virtually all other manufacturers continued with leaf springs until the almost universal adoption of independent front suspension in the late 1940s.

Similarly, nearly all manufacturers used beam front axles until just before the Second World War, and some continued after it. Rear axles were 'live' and transmitted the power to the rear wheels which drove the vehicle.

Leaf springs were useful as they have a built-in damping effect because of the friction between the leaves. If, like Rolls-Royce springs, the leaf springs were long, supple and had their surfaces ground and grooved so that lubricant could be fed to them under pressure, and were then encased in leather to keep the dirt out and the lubricant in, they could be very good indeed.

The majority of manufacturers did none of these things, with the result that as the various leaves flex with the vertical movement of the car, and especially when the car leans over under cornering, they rub against each other and eventually wear adjacent leaves before cracking.

To recondition leaf springs, the springs should be removed from the car and taken apart by withdrawing the central bolt that holds the leaves together, then releasing the clamps that locate the leaves laterally. Clamp the spring in a vice so that the central bolt is not in tension, and undo the bolt. Rather than the normal hexagon, the bolt is likely to have a conical head that helps to locate the assembly in the spring seat on the axle.

Remove the bolts from the clamps. Because the bolts are often badly rusted, and frequently break, they will need replacement. De-grease and de-rust the leaves, and examine them for cracks and wear. Any leaves that are badly indented will have to be replaced, but if the wear is not too deep the leaves can often be made serviceable again by carefully grinding their surfaces flat.

When reassembling, smear the leaves with a molybdenum disulphide grease, such as 'Molyslip', or a copper-impregnated grease like 'Coppaslip', clamp the assembly in the vice and refit the centre bolt. The clamps may need remaking – a simple matter of drilling and bending strip steel which should be a good fit over the leaves and, with the tubular spacer round the bolt, just long enough to allow the bolt to clamp effectively.

Springs are held to the chassis by means of a bolt through the eye of the upper spring fitting into a spring hanger mounted rigidly to the chassis (usually at the front) at one end, and to a shackle at the other end which pivots on the chassis frame. A few cars, such as some MGs and Morgans, omit the shackle and grind the end of the main leaf of the spring so that it will slide between two phosphor-bronze blocks, thereby giving better lateral location.

The bolts or 'pins' run in bushes which usually consist of an inner hardened metal sleeve encased in thick rubber, which in some cases is itself surrounded by another metal sleeve. The bushes are often a very tight fit, and if you are unable to tap them out with a hammer and drift, the best way of removing them is by burning the rubber out and threading a hacksaw blade in the hole. The outer sleeve can then be sawn through and tapped out. New bushes can be tapped into place or drawn in with studding. Replacement bushes of the 'Metalastik' or 'Silentbloc' variety are usually available from bearing specialists.

Wear on the pins is perhaps more difficult to deal with, especially if you have an older car for which replacements are not available, though one-make car clubs often have batches made. If you have a lathe, you will be able to turn up a set for yourself out of suitable material; if not, you will have to commission a set from your local engineering shop. Some older cars, and some of the later and more expensive ones, had solid bronze bushes instead of the rubber type. These are normally a push-fit into the eyes and are easily removed. Again, if none are available they can be easily turned up and reamed to size.

Fig. 5.7. A grease nipple (arrowed) on a leaf spring shackle bush.

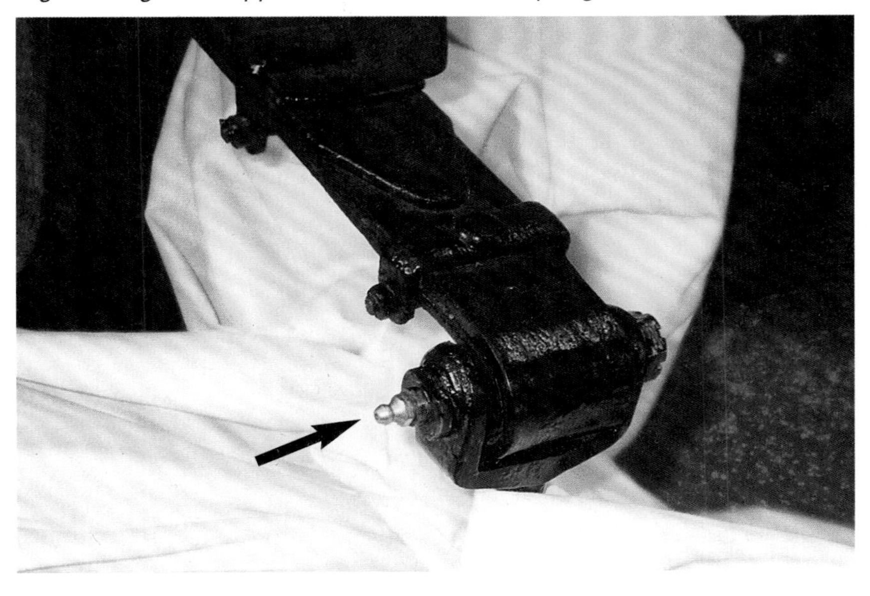

The pins depend on adequate lubrication for their effectiveness, so do not forget to drill them and fit grease nipples. Make sure that the locking device that secures the pin, whether split-pin, cotter or self-locking nut, is effective.

Shackle pins and bushes are the connection between the car and its suspension. You cannot expect either precise steering or good handling (or comfort!) if there is a lot of 'slop' in them.

Beam axles and rear axles are normally clamped to the springs by two large U-clamps – the head of the centre spring bolt fitting into the pad over which they are clamped. Two nuts to each leg (the second tightened against the first and so locking it) are normally fitted.

INDEPENDENT FRONT SUSPENSION

In the late 1930s, some car manufacturers started fitting their products with independent front suspension (IFS) to improve ride comfort and road holding, and a wide variety of designs evolved. *Fig. 5.8* shows the geometric principles on which some of them worked. Transverse leaf springs were used in some of the designs, while cars as diverse as the VW Beetle, Morris 1000, and Aston Martin used torsion bars. These are long steel bars which are anchored to the suspension at one end and to the chassis at the other, and twist when up and down movement takes place at the road wheel. In due course, longer wheel travel became desirable and torsion bars gave way to ordinary spiral springs – which are, in fact, torsion bars wound in cylindrical form – as the straight variety could not conveniently be made long enough to provide the desired movement. Many firms were, of course, already using coil springs.

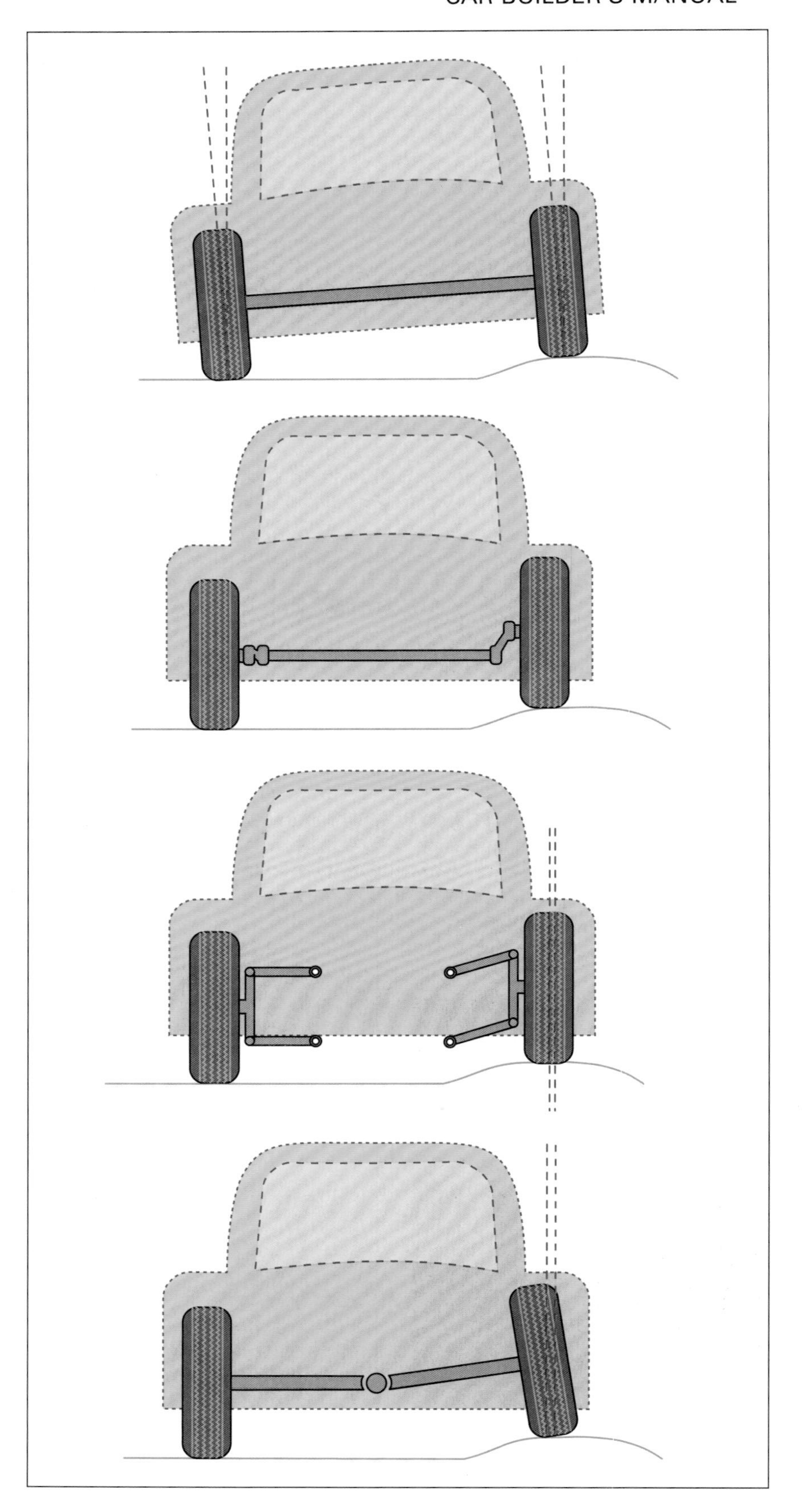

Fig. 5.8. Behaviour of suspension when encountering an irregular surface.

a. Beam axle.

b. Trailing (or leading) arm.

c. Equal length wishbones.

d. Swing axle.

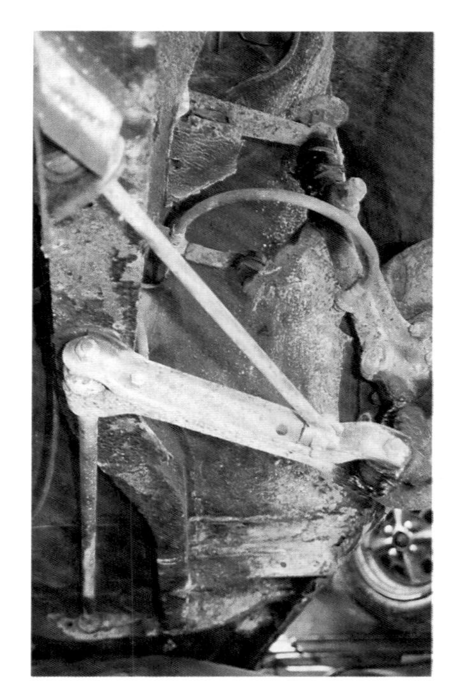

Fig. 5.9. Torsion bar front suspension. The torsion bar runs from the lower suspension member to a chassis cross-member.

Fig. 5.10. Triumph front suspension.

Early designs tended to use at least one wishbone-shaped suspension member, the two inner ends being pivoted to the chassis and the outer end to the 'upright' on which the wheel is mounted. A few used double wishbones, top and bottom, a system that takes a lot of beating and is currently proving increasingly popular for production cars as well as sports cars. Some, like those used by Rolls-Royce, MG (on the 'B') and other BL products used upper wishbones which formed the lever arm of a shock absorber.

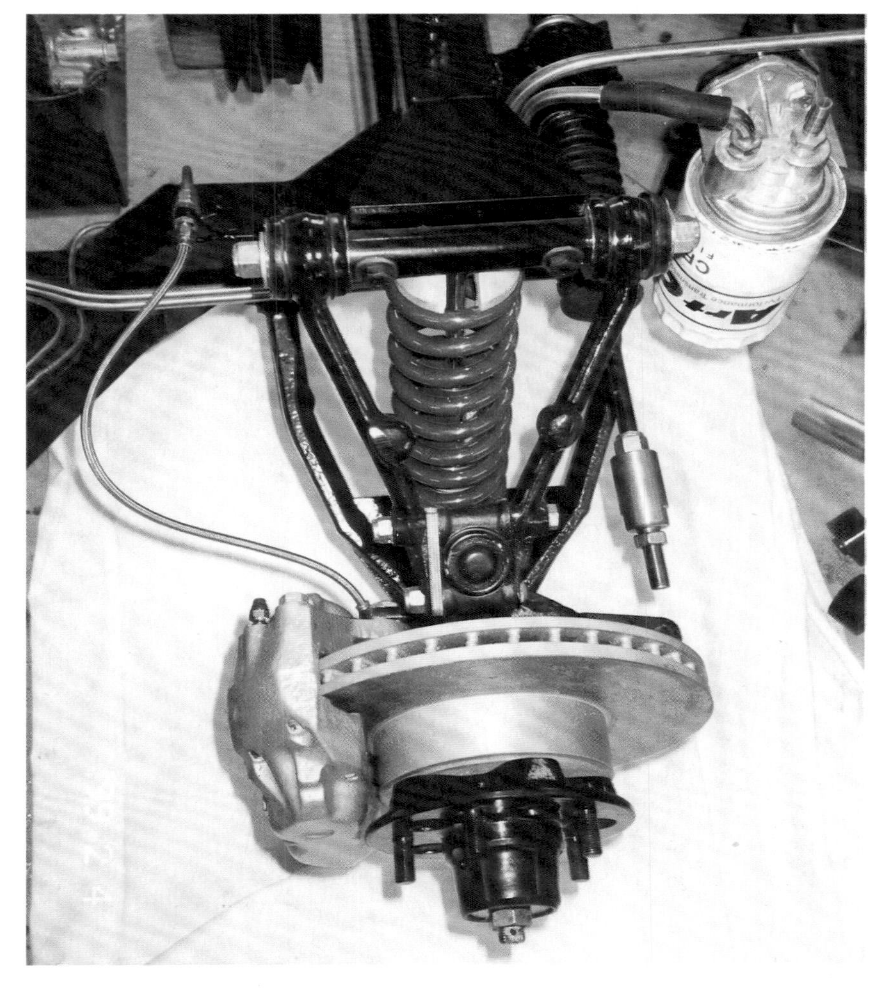

Fig. 5.11. Jaguar front suspension. Note how similar the design is to the Triumph. The Jaguar, being a much faster and heavier car, has forged rather than pressed wishbones.

Fig. 5.12. An upright and disc assembly in situ with wishbone suspension.

Independent suspension contains more moving joints than beam-type suspension systems, and restoration consists largely of ensuring that the various pins and bushes which form the pivots are in good condition, and checking the condition of springs and shock absorbers. The springs and shock absorbers are particularly important. Springs can crack or settle, so if the height of one side of the car is greater than the other, check the spring on the low side. If you need to replace a spring, ensure that you get the right one as springs on the driver's side are occasionally slightly stronger than those on the passenger's side. As already mentioned, hydraulic shock absorbers often show their age by leaking. If they are of the telescopic variety, they cannot normally be serviced so new ones should be fitted. If in any doubt about their efficiency, disconnect one end and compress and extend the piston, moving it through its full range of movement. If the piston moves freely with no or little resistance it is useless.

If you had a chance to drive the car before starting the restoration or overhaul, you will have some idea of the condition of the suspension from the 'feel' of the front end when on the road, and from any crashes and bangs when driving over uneven surfaces. Looking at the wear on the tyres will also give an indication as to the condition of the suspension components.

Start the checking procedure by jacking-up the front end of the car or chassis, and placing it securely on suitable stands. Axle stands are cheap enough to buy and, unlike a pile of bricks, do not suddenly crumble when you are underneath the car. With the wheels removed and the grease and dirt cleaned off, examine the suspension for accident damage and cracks. You may need to remove the spring in order to test the play in the pivots, and for this you may need a spring compressor. Coil springs are extremely powerful and can be very dangerous if not dealt with properly and with caution. Using tyre levers to compress them, and wire or lengths of string to hold them compressed, is just not good enough. Spring compressors are easily available from any accessory shop and **must** be used.

Fig. 5.13. An exploded drawing of the system shown in Fig. 5.12. (Courtesy Ron Champion)

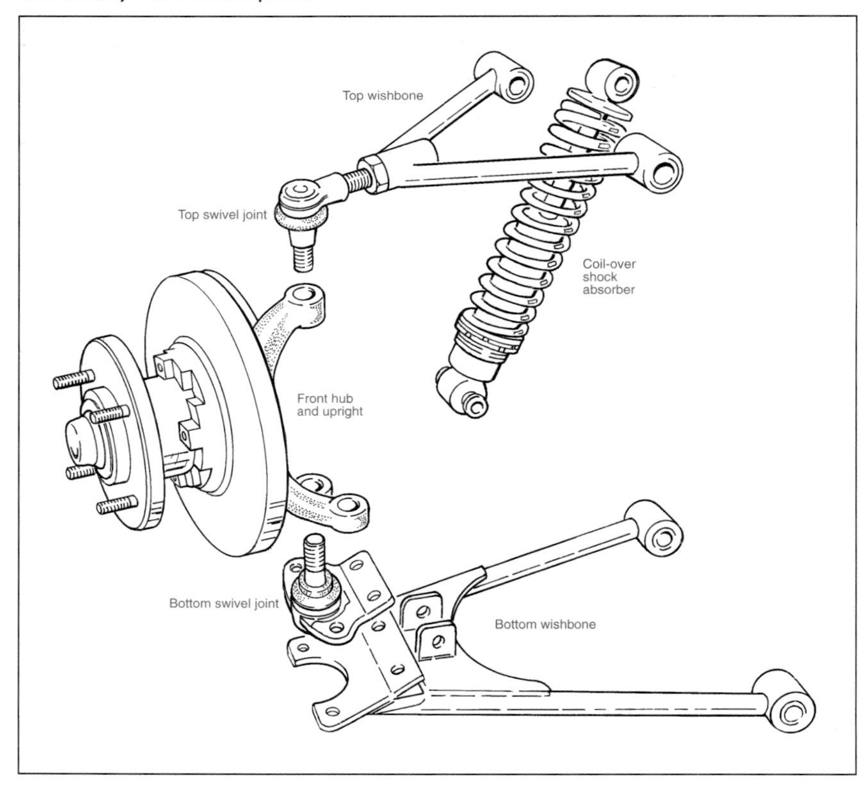

Fig. 5.14. A coil spring compressor in action. This is a particularly safe design, as the arms have additional hooks which are tightened and prevent the unit from being dislodged when in use.

deal with it on the bench. The judicious application of heat from a gas torch often eases things by breaking the bond caused by rust or corrosion. Always take suitable fire precautions when using a gas torch.

If you have to use force, make sure that you are applying it to the right part, and if driving out a bush, ensure that the drift is of the correct diameter. Being a coward, I normally wear industrial gloves when undertaking these operations. Skinned knuckles are painful and not improved by the application of an ointment composed of old grease and road grit. Eye protection should always be worn when undertaking such operations.

Many cars built in the last 30 years use the MacPherson-strut type of suspension, as this is relatively cheap and, as it has no upper wishbone, is relatively compact.

As the mounting points are widely spaced, steering accuracy is not unduly affected by the rubber mountings incorporated for the sake of quietness and damping of road-induced vibration. With this type of suspension there is usually

Fig. 5.15. A MacPherson strut.

With the springs and shock absorbers disconnected, test the freedom of movement of the suspension members by pushing and pulling them sideways. If there is any movement, new bushes and, possibly, pins will be required. As with leaf springs, bushes may be either bronze or sleeved rubber – the presence or absence of grease nipples will usually indicate which sort are fitted. If a hydraulic shock absorber is used, and it is found to be worn or faulty, you will have to obtain a replacement unit as these cannot normally be rebuilt, except by specialists.

Access is often limited, and parts are sometimes reluctant to yield to normal means of persuasion, especially if rusted together. Whenever possible, remove the unit completely and

Fig. 5.16. Complete Ford Fiesta front sub-assembly, engine, drive train and suspension. Here the mounting points are outlined in yellow, and these need to be measured from the bodyshell.

Fig. 5.17. Ford Sierra front sub-assembly, comprising suspension and steering rack.

little that needs doing to repair it in normal service. The bottom links (track control arms) have replaceable rubber bushes, as do any anti-roll bar attachments which should be checked and changed if necessary. The struts contain, or are composed of, the telescopic shock absorbers, which can fail and are replaceable, as is the strut top bearing, which should also be checked.

REAR SUSPENSION

Rear suspension usually falls into one of three categories; live-axle, where the drive is transmitted to the rear wheels through the axle casing; dead-axle, usually just a tube or beam which merely carries the wheels, the drive being to the front wheels; and independent rear suspension. If the rear suspension consists of a live-axle suspended on leaf springs, this is usually straightforward and the details given previously concerning leaf springs apply, but many rear axles are suspended on coil springs. Unlike leaf springs, which are rigid enough laterally to resist sideways movement, a coil spring is very undisciplined and can move in any direction. A coil spring therefore needs restraining in such a way that it is free to move up and down, but not sideways or fore-and-aft (especially under braking and acceleration). The axle is therefore restrained by struts or linkages of various types, which are used to control sideways and fore-and-aft forces. These links are anchored at one end to the chassis or body frame and to the axle at the other, almost always by rubber bushes or 'doughnuts'. The links should be inspected for damage (rare, except after an accident), and the bushes for wear – replacement being the cure. As always, check that the nuts and bolts attaching the various parts are secure.

If you drove the car, you may have noted not only strange noises from the rear suspension, especially under braking and acceleration, but also a phenomenon known as 'rear steer', which occurs on opening or closing the throttle or on braking, and is caused by movement of the rear axle relative to the car. It has the effect of pushing the front of the car off course, making a slight but noticeable correction of the steering necessary. This is often accompanied by an audible 'clonk' from the rear, and points immediately to failed bushes (or worse) which needs attention both for safety's sake and the MoT test.

Independent rear suspension (IRS) is now almost universal, especially on vehicles with front-wheel-drive, but is also fitted to most rear-wheel-drive production cars such as Mercedes and BMWs. Rear-engined cars, like the VW Beetle, have always had independent rear suspension, of course.

Independent rear suspension is often very similar in layout to independent front suspension,

Fig. 5.18. The rear suspension sub-assembly from a Ford Fiesta.

Fig. 5.19. The rear suspension from a Ford Sierra. Note that this is independent and carries the differential and drive shafts.

without the complication of the steering but, on rear-wheel-drive cars, with provision of drive to the rear wheels. Since space permits, long trailing arms are also often used. On a rear-wheel-drive car with a front-mounted engine, the differential is a separate unit bolted to the chassis (usually via rubber bushes), whereas a rear-mounted engine will have the differential built into the engine/gearbox assembly.

The same considerations apply to IRS as to IFS; wear takes place on the moving parts, such as the pins, bushes and shock absorbers, and again the usual remedy is replacement, but check that the mountings have not come adrift. If the car has had accident damage or hard usage, the fixtures may have torn or rusted away.

SHOCK ABSORBERS (DAMPERS)

If suspension consisted only of springs, cars would rapidly become uncontrollable at quite low speeds, and difficult to steer, since a spring, once deflected, does not move just the once before regaining its normal position, but oscillates with diminishing movement. To prevent, or at least to curb this oscillation, shock absorbers (or dampers) are used. These are now nearly always of the telescopic type, in which oil is forced through a small hole by means of a piston working in a cylinder, one end being attached to the suspension and the other to the chassis. Before manufacturers arrived at this solution many other types were tried.

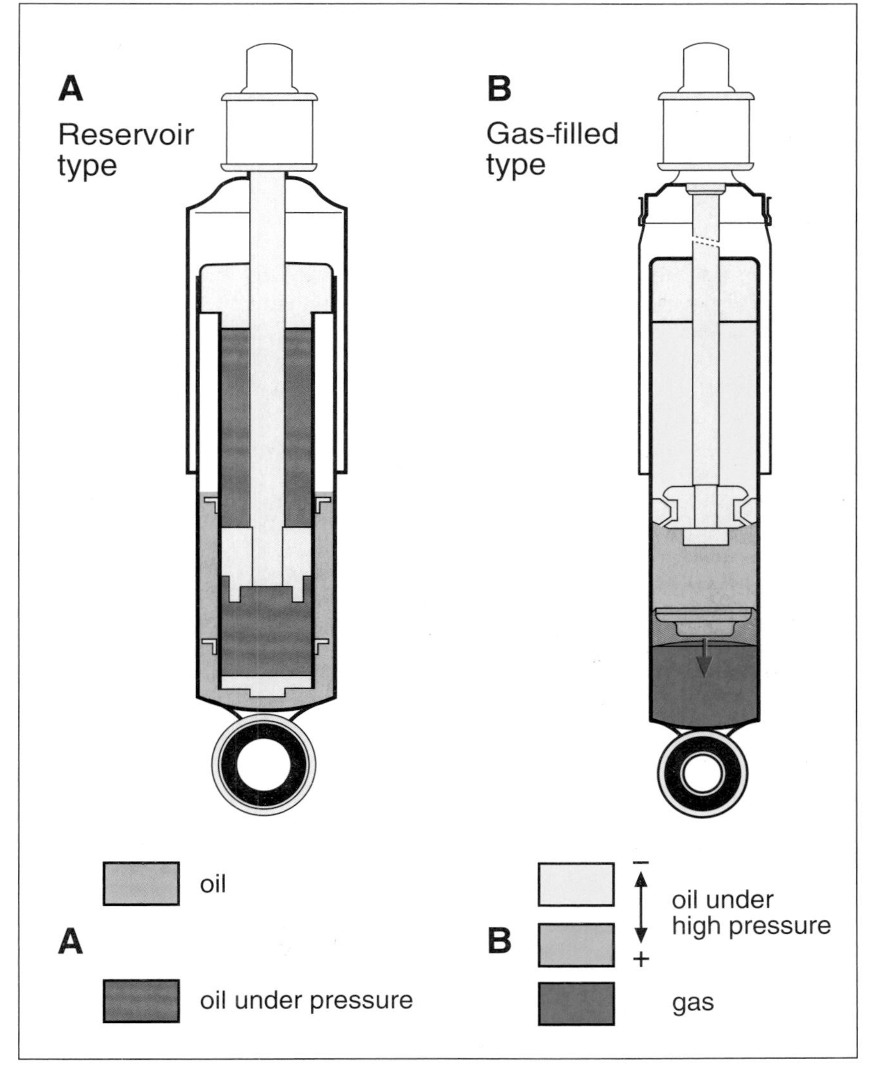

Fig. 5.20. Cross-sectional views showing the differences between the reservoir-type and the gas-filled type of shock absorber. (Koni)

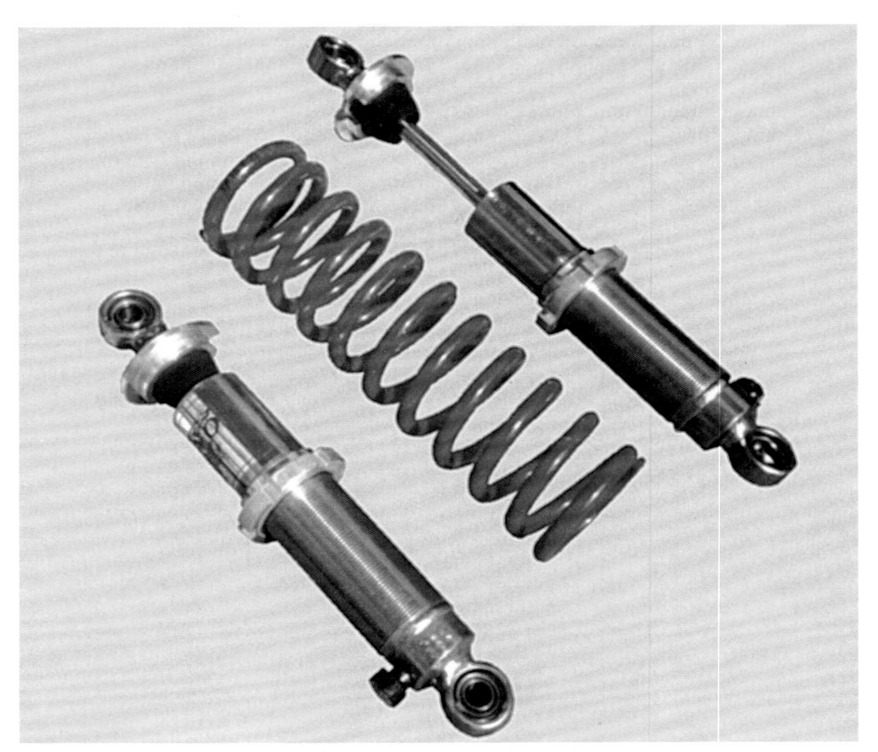

Fig. 5.21. Coil spring and shock absorbers. Coil springs are available with different strengths, marked on the top in lb/kg. The shock absorbers are adjustable for hard or soft ride, and they are threaded so that the ride height of the car can be adjusted.

Some telescopic shock absorbers are described as being 'gas filled'. When the piston in the shock absorber moves, it displaces oil through the valve, but because of the need to make room for the oil displaced by the piston rod, ordinary telescopic shock absorbers have a reservoir around their periphery. This means that they can only be used in an upright or, at best, in a slightly sloping position. To make it possible to use a hydraulic shock absorber at any angle, or even upside down, gas-filled shock absorbers have been developed. These have a gas-filled chamber separated from the hydraulic fluid by a diaphragm which compresses the gas when the hydraulic fluid is displaced.

As already mentioned, British Leyland, amongst others, used on many of its cars shock absorbers which effectively incorporated wishbones. Some types of dampers can be topped up with the appropriate fluid. If you have these, check that there is oil in them up to the correct level. If not, top them up and test them by hand – they should need steady pressure to move them, since they are sealed. If there is no, or little, resistance, or if there is evidence of leakage, then the shock absorber will have to be renewed, as it is a specialist job to rebuild them. Cars with this sort of shock absorber sometimes need the suspension set at a predetermined height, usually by means of simple distance pieces, before the various fastenings are fully tightened, and reference to the appropriate manual or club should be made for the correct information.

Another very popular form of shock absorber, especially on sports cars, was the Andre-Hartford friction type, in which two sets of arms, attached respectively to the suspension and chassis, are clamped together by a single bolt that compresses the arms between friction discs. The number of arms and discs depends on the weight of the car, and some of the more expensive cars had a hydraulic mechanism by which the driver could vary the amount of compression, while travelling, to compensate for speed and road surface. On the more ordinary cars it was necessary to set the amount of friction by tightening the central bolt. Obviously, this could not be done on the move and it was left to

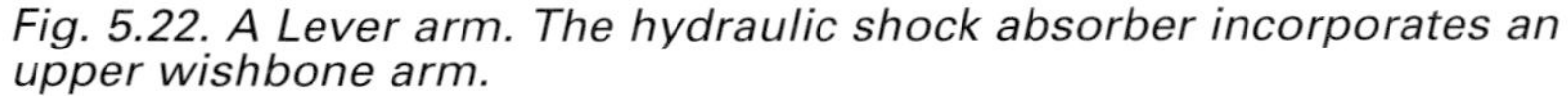

Fig. 5.22. A Lever arm. The hydraulic shock absorber incorporates an upper wishbone arm.

the driver to sort out his preferred setting using a spanner. The friction discs consist, strangely, of wood (box) clamped in between thin brass plates. To service this type of shock absorber, note the relative positions of the various parts, and withdraw the central bolt, which will allow the components to come apart from the middle. The discs are replaceable but not, unfortunately, the bushes in the ends of the arms, so these will have to be sent to a specialist if they are badly worn. The car must be on its wheels and at its normal ride height and weight (driver and some fuel) before the mounting bolts are tightened. All four friction bolts should be tightened equally. You can then carry out final adjustment front and rear by trial and error when on the road.

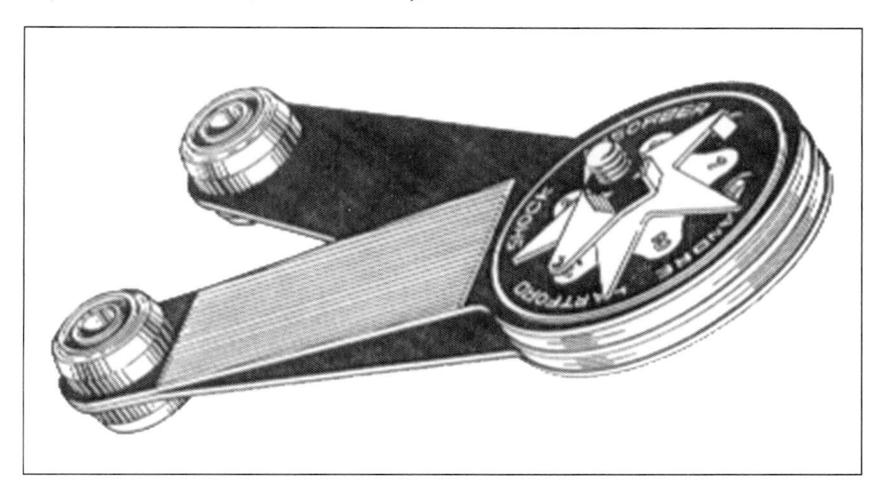

Fig. 5.23. An Andre-Hartford shock absorber.

Fig. 5.24. A cross-sectional view showing the components of an Andre-Hartford shock absorber.

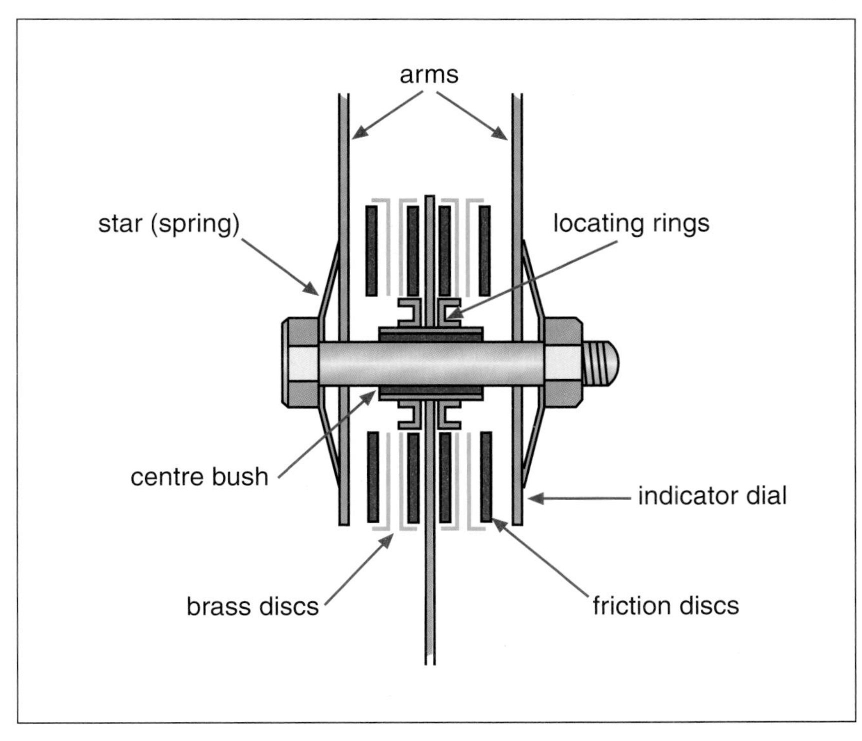

WHEELS

If you are restoring a car, it is likely that you will wish to keep the original wheels and refurbish them. Whatever type – pressed-steel, wire or alloy – if you can afford it, have them shot- or bead-blasted to clean off any rust so that you can examine them in detail to assess their condition. Wire wheels can be rebuilt by specialists, who will fit new spokes, or even rims, to your hubs. Pressed-steel wheels, if damaged at the rim (through excessive 'kerbing') should be renewed, but any small cracks can be welded. Alloy wheels, if damaged, should be discarded, but if in good condition can be polished and painted. As alloy wheels are often protected with a coating of clear lacquer, this must first be removed by using a preparation such as 'Nitromors', obtainable from paint suppliers and motor accessory shops.

If you wish to replace pressed-steel wheels with alloys, of which there is a very wide choice new or second-hand from a breaker or autojumble, you may decide to go up one size in diameter in the interest of better traction and appearance (without incurring a weight penalty), provided there is room under the mudguards or wheel arches.

Be sure when buying alloy wheels that they will fit your hubs. Not only should they have the right number of holes for the wheel studs (or bolts), but they must be spaced on the same 'pitch circle diameter' (pcd), which is the circle passing through the centre of the studs (or bolts). The easiest way to ensure this is to make a cardboard template and take it with you when you go to look at wheels, so that you can lay it on a wheel to see whether the holes match. (If you are buying new wheels, the supplier will advise you.) Try to obtain the wheel nuts or bolts that go with the wheels, as they may be different from the ones that you already have, and specific to the

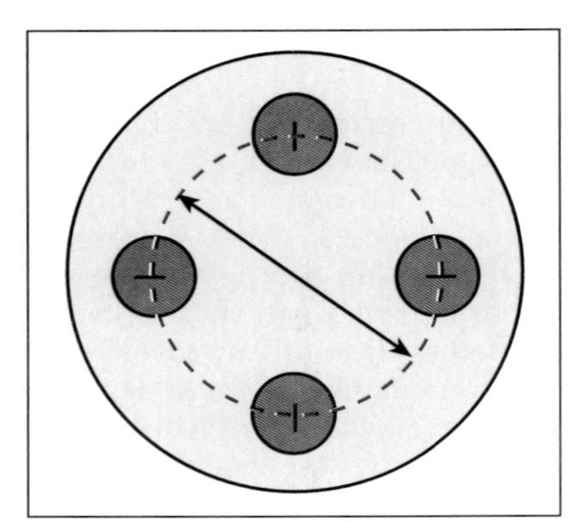

Fig. 5.25. Pitch circle diameter (PCD).

wheels. In some cases, wheel nuts or bolts can be expensive to buy separately; a set of new ones can be as expensive as a set of second-hand wheels.

It is also important to buy wheels with the right 'offset'. This is the distance between the centre-line of the wheel and its mounting face. Too much offset one way will probably mean that the tyres rub on the bodywork, especially at the front on full lock, and too much the other way will make them extend beyond the wheel arches and not only look silly but have a surprising and unnerving effect on steering.

As usual, choose what is appropriate to the type of car you are building. Some years ago there was a spate of activity in the rebuilding of Mk VI Bentleys into retro-look sports cars. Some looked quite good, but the majority were spoilt by having wheels that were too small – presumably wire wheels of appropriate size were no longer available.

Tyres will naturally have to match the wheels. Again there is a very wide choice, but you must bear in mind the use that the car will have. Tyres for a small tourer of modest performance will cost much less than high-speed rubber. Specials are often much lighter than production cars, so you will be able to run on lower pressures. Bear in mind that too much rubber on the road can lead to aquaplaning in the wet.

Tyres are your only link with the road and must, therefore, be at least adequate both in condition and type. Do not forget the spare which you may need one day.

Fig. 5.26. Wheel offset.

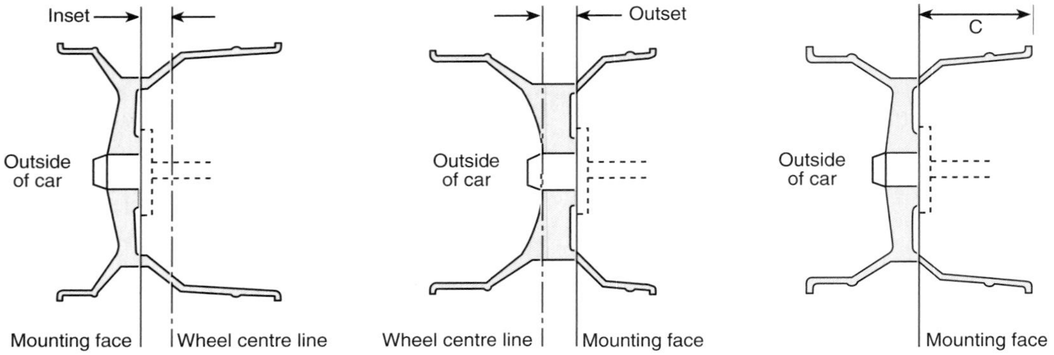

Inset is calculated by measuring *in* from the hub face to the wheel centre line.

Outset is calculated by measuring *out* from the hub face to the wheel centre line.

The 'C' dimension is the measurement from the wheel mounting face to the edge of the inside rim.

Chapter 6

Steering

INSPECTING AND RESTORING STEERING COMPONENTS

Conversion of the rotary motion of the steering into the reciprocating motion needed to push and pull the front wheels to steer the car can be achieved by several different types of mechanism, each enclosed in a 'steering box' at the lower end of the steering column, which is usually clamped to the chassis or subframe. From the steering box, motion is transmitted to the road wheels by means of rods (usually tubular) with joints that allow for suspension and steering movement.

Steering systems of this kind are prone to wear which, because of the geometry involved, is greatly accentuated in its effect at the steering wheel. The MoT test allows up to 3in (75mm) free movement at the steering wheel, although the actual amount of wear in the system may be almost unnoticeable. If this amount of free-play seems excessive, it is worth remembering that before MoT testing was introduced there were many vehicles on the road that had very considerable amounts of free-play in the steering, the drivers having become used to it and not being conscious of anything out of the ordinary.

Because steering geometry tends to exaggerate faults and wear in the components, it is essential to eliminate as much play from the system as possible, paying attention to the steering box, steering joints and king-pins or swivels.

Start by checking the mounting of the steering box itself. On older cars with separate chassis frames, the steering box mountings are often bolted to the top flange of the chassis, which 'gives' a little in reaction to the effort imparted when the steering wheel is turned. If you find this happening, the mounting should be reinforced at the point where it flexes. Alternatively, the relevant chassis member could be boxed, or long mounting bolts could be used (fitted with spacers between the chassis flanges) passing through both top and bottom chassis flanges. On monocoque structures the steering box may be firmly mounted on a subframe, attached to special lugs on a spaceframe, or may be mounted on the bulkhead, and nothing needs to be done apart from checking the security of its fastenings.

Some steering boxes incorporate the facility to compensate for wear by means of an adjustment which

Fig. 6.1. Steering rack clamps.

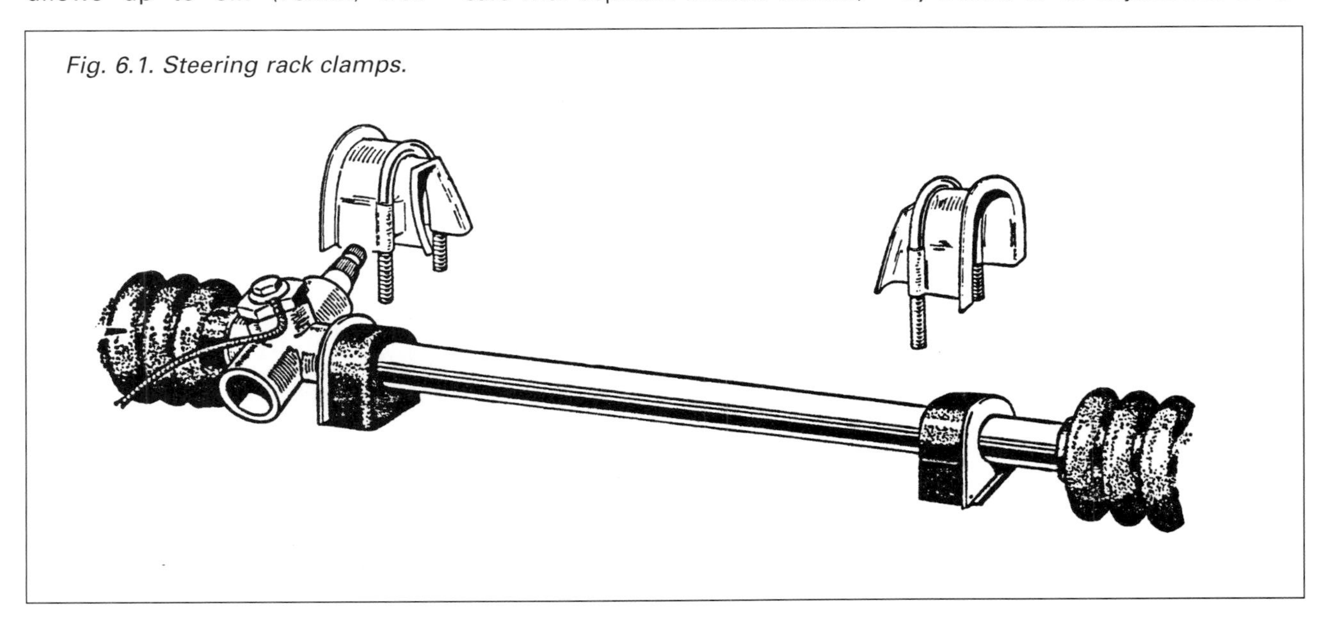

Fig. 6.2. Steering rack clamped in position.

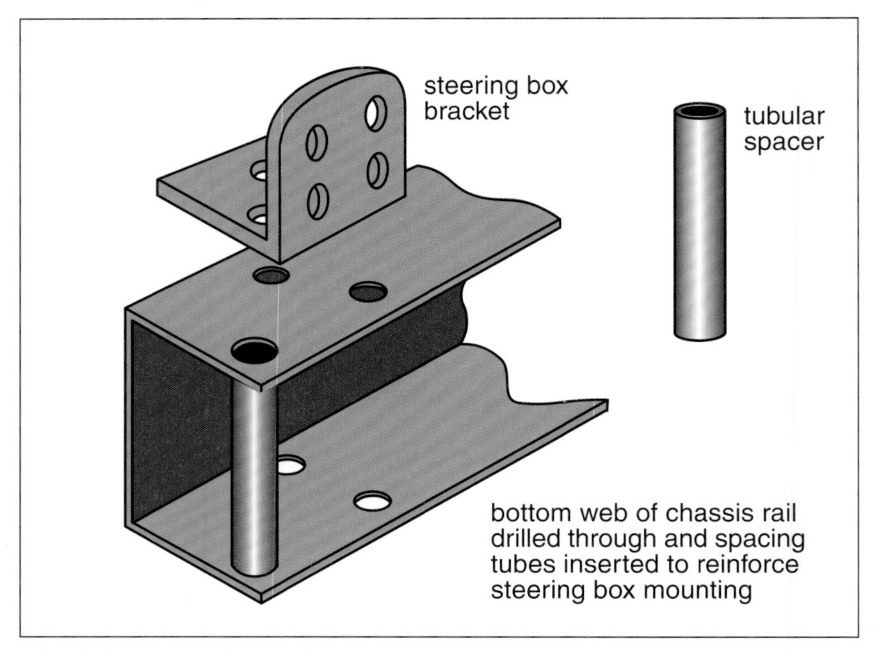

Fig. 6.3. Steering box reinforcement.

brings the moving parts closer together, and on the worm-and-nut variety of steering box, wear may be eradicated by the fitting of a new 'nut' (actually a bronze screwed sleeve) available from a specialist. These systems were in use with beam axles (and still are with specialist vehicles), but with the introduction of independent front suspension, rack-and-pinion steering was gradually adopted as it greatly simplifies things and reduces the number of joints necessary.

Check, also, that there is no up-and-down movement in the column itself. This is sometimes adjustable at the top bearing, or it may be possible to add shims at the bottom to take up any play.

To check the steering system itself, jack up the front of the car and place it securely on stands. With the aid of an assistant to turn the steering wheel, check each of the track-rod ends for wear. On older vehicles, these are usually spring-loaded – a ball-end being clamped between two bronze pads. They can often be screwed up tighter to take up any play. While you are working on this type of track-rod end, make sure it is well greased. Modern track-rod ends are of similar construction, but are normally sealed and therefore not adjustable.

The hub carrier and brake assembly is pivoted by means of king pins, or swivels, on some types of independent suspension. These must have no play in them whatsoever, and should be tested, with the wheel in place and without load on it, by pushing and pulling at the top and bottom of the wheel. If there is wear, the pin must be removed and new bushes fitted, and the pin should be renewed if it shows signs of being scored or grooved. Alternatively, the swivel itself can be renewed.

King pins are often held in place by cotter pins which are removed

Fig. 6.4. Stub axle and brake assembly pivoted by means of a king pin.

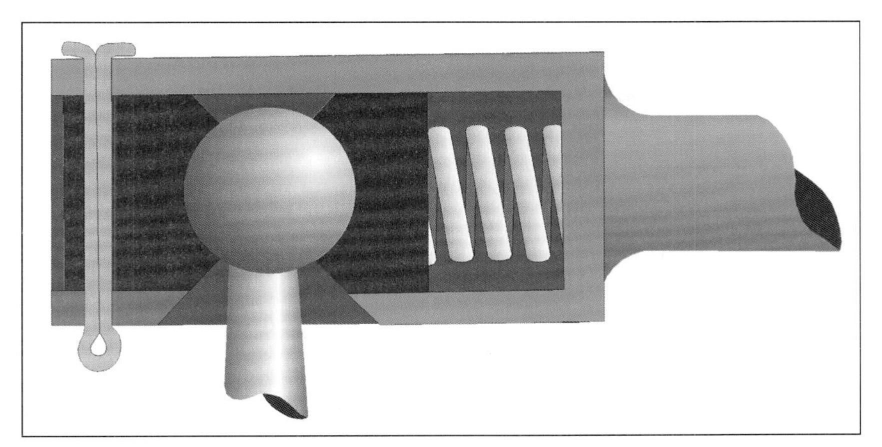

Fig. 6.5. A track rod end.

by unscrewing the retaining nut and tapping the pin out. Because of its shape, a cotter pin will only fit one way round. Be careful to note the locations of the 'washers' that surround the king pin top and bottom, in between the hub carrier (or 'upright'), and the suspension member. The washers at the top are hardened thrust washers, which take the weight of the car, and should always be refitted in the correct order (greased). The bottom washers are spacers. The king-pin housings often have domed covers top and bottom to close them off and keep the lubricant in. The covers fit into grooves, and after refitting should be tapped gently on top of the dome to flatten them and press them into the grooves.

Track-rod ends, and other steering joints, are held in place by means of a short tapered shaft (usually fitted to a balljoint) with a threaded end; a nut pulls the tapered shaft tight into its housing and secures it. After many years of service these joints are often reluctant to come apart. If you want to reuse the unit, do not attempt to disconnect the joint by removing the nut and hitting the screwed end with a hammer, as this will damage the thread. Special balljoint splitters are available which are inserted between the taper and its housing, and screwed to press them apart, or alternatively a tapered fork can be tapped in between the two components to separate them. These are useful tools but, if you have enough room, a strong hammer-blow on the side of the housing, with a second large hammer or other solid piece of metal held against the opposite side, is often effective in springing the two pieces apart. These joints usually have a rubber gaiter over the large end of the taper, which is used to retain the grease in the balljoint, and to keep dirt and moisture out. If the joint is to be reused, take care not to damage the rubber gaiter when separating the components.

RACK-AND-PINION STEERING

Most independent front suspension systems use rack-and-pinion steering systems, which are much more precise and effective than other types. The rack is clamped across the front of the car, usually in rubber mountings which should be checked for tightness from time to time. The two ends of the rack are fitted with track rods, which are universally jointed and encased in rubber gaiters to protect them and retain their lubricant, while keeping the abrasive road dirt out. The outer ends of the track rods are fitted with the track-rod ends. With this system there should be no free-play at the steering wheel. If there is, suspect wear in the track-rod ends, but note that some racks are adjustable to permit the pinion to be engaged more deeply with the rack in order to take up any wear that may have occurred.

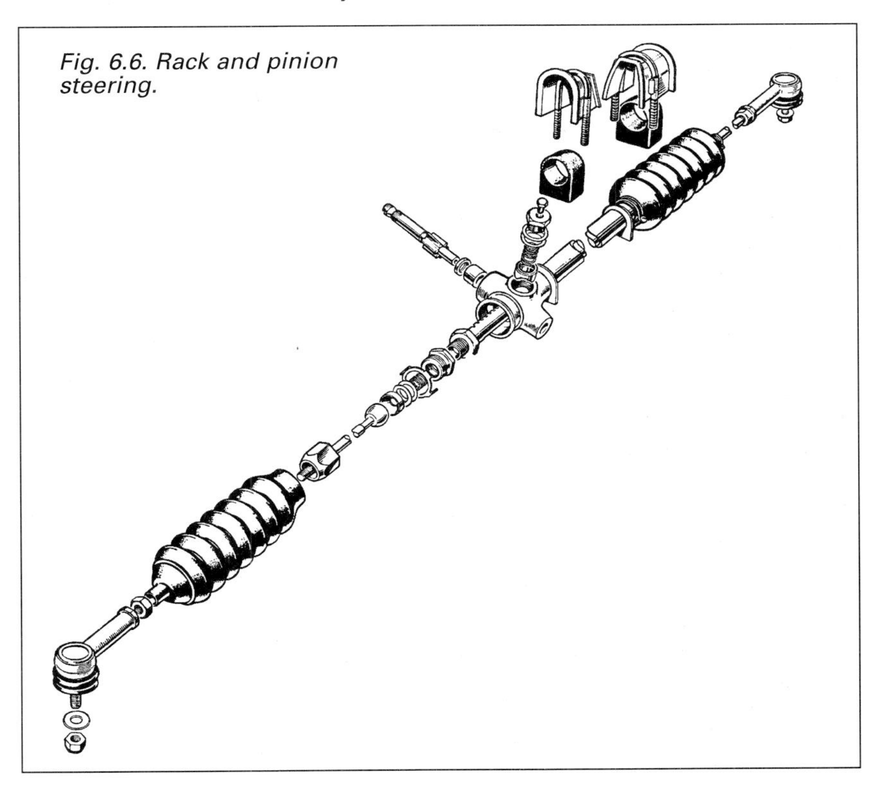

Fig. 6.6. Rack and pinion steering.

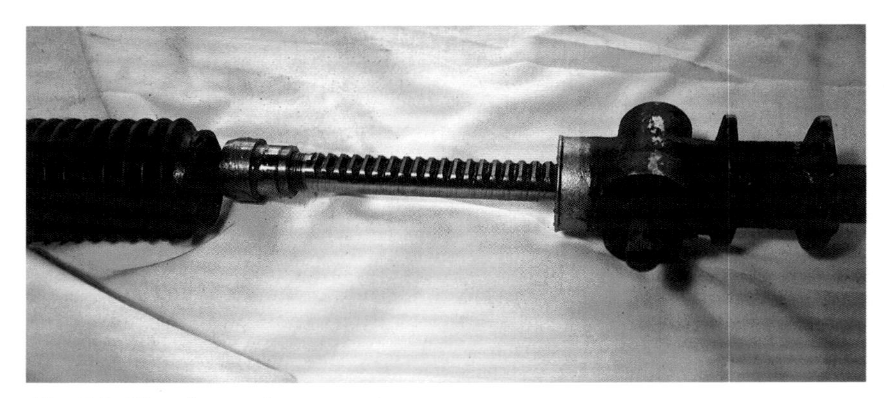

Fig. 6.7. Steering rack exposed.

Track-rod ends are threaded so that the correct 'tracking' of the wheels may be achieved by screwing them in or out of the track rods equally at each end. Some racks have grease nipples for lubrication, but most are filled with a specified quantity of oil or grease; the maintenance or workshop manual will give details.

Builders of specials will need to choose a rack suitable for the width of their chassis, and with track-rod ends that have the same taper as that on the uprights into which they fit, so it makes sense to use the rack and the uprights from the same car. The total distance between the track-rod ends can be altered to some extent by screwing them in or out of the track rods, provided there is enough thread for them to be secure and to leave some adjustment for tracking. More major alterations in overall width can be made by cutting the track rods and shortening or lengthening them by welding close-fitting seamless steel tube in between the cut portions. Extreme care must be taken when doing this, as if a track rod breaks when driving, the ability to steer will be lost.

Racks are available in different ratios. Large and heavy vehicles, especially without power steering, have a low ratio which means that more revolutions of the steering wheel are required from lock-to-lock than cars with a high ratio. A small, light sports car will need a ratio of about 3:1 or 3½:1.

POWER-STEERING SYSTEMS

Power-steering systems usually have a hydraulic ram that acts on the rack when a valve opens, and are always of the 'fail-safe' variety, which means that they only *assist* the driver's effort, so that if the power steering fails the manual system remains, though more than usual effort will be required.

Light cars do not require this extra assistance, but larger and heavier cars, particularly on wide tyres, are less tiring to drive and to park if power is available. To give better 'feel' to the steering, some systems are proportional and assist more at slow speeds than when travelling fast.

All power-steering systems need a pump and a hydraulic fluid reservoir. The pump is usually driven via a belt from the engine's crankshaft. If you decide to fit a power-steering system, you can do no better than to retain the complete original system from the donor car, rather than mixing and matching components.

STEERING GEOMETRY

To make your car respond precisely, steer comfortably, and to minimise tyre wear there is some very important geometry which must be observed, starting with the Ackermann angle. When a car turns a corner, the outer wheels

Fig. 6.8. When a car turns a corner, the outer wheels have to turn about a greater radius than the inner wheels.

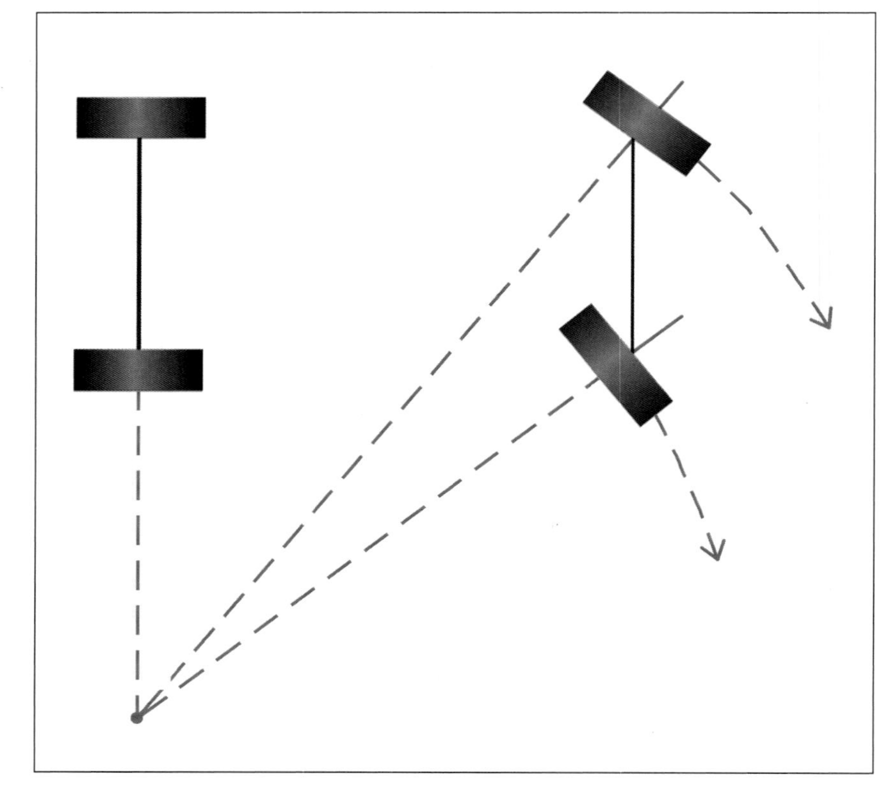

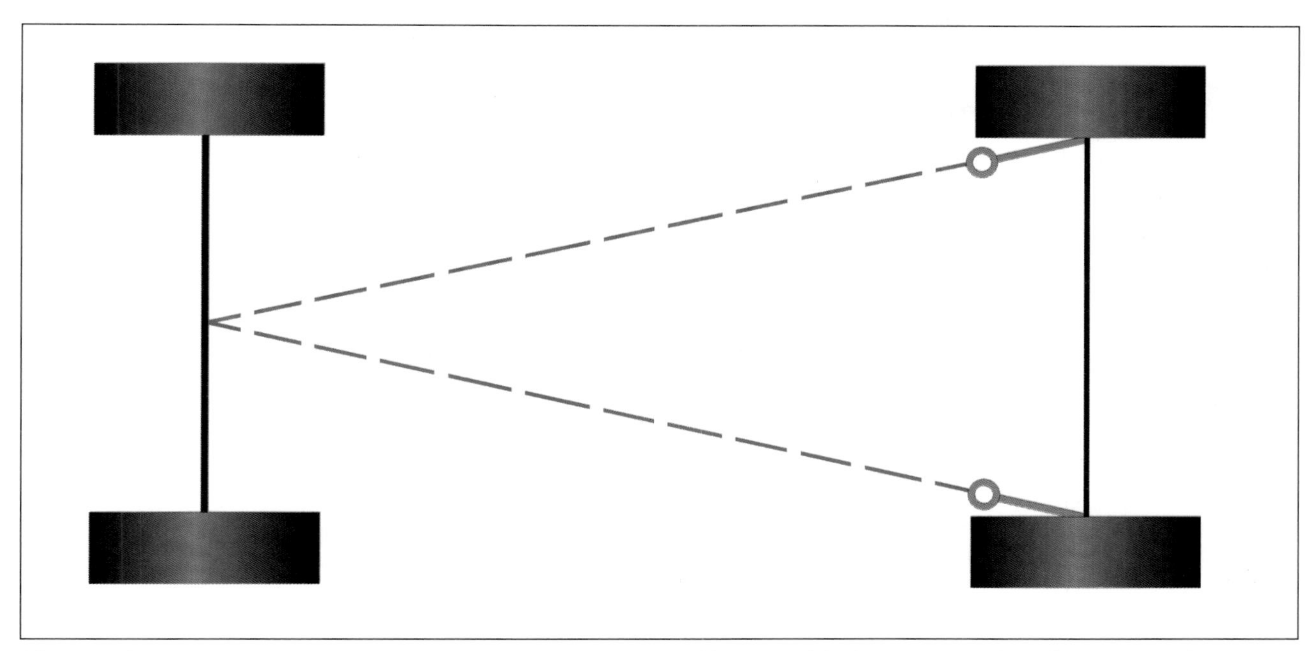

Fig. 6.9. Ackermann steering geometry – the steering arms line up with the centre-point of the rear axle.

have to turn about a radius which is greater than the radius turned by the inner wheels, as shown in the *Fig. 6.8.* The two radii must intersect somewhere on the line of the back axle. This is achieved by ensuring that the steering arms on the front uprights line up with the centre-point of the rear axle. Modern designs place this point of intersection behind the back axle for very fast cars. We can compromise by putting it somewhere between the back axle and a car's length behind it.

'Camber' is the angle that the top of a roadwheel leans outwards (positive camber) or inwards (negative camber) from the vertical, when viewed from the front or rear of the car. If you are using the front suspension from a donor, the camber angle may be suitable for the car you are building, but factors such as differences in weight, wheel base, tyres etc, may require a different setting. The best course of action is to set the camber at zero, that is with the wheels upright, and wait and see how the car behaves on the road. You can fine-tune the camber angle once you get a feel for how the car handles.

Fig. 6.10. Camber angle. Positive camber shown.

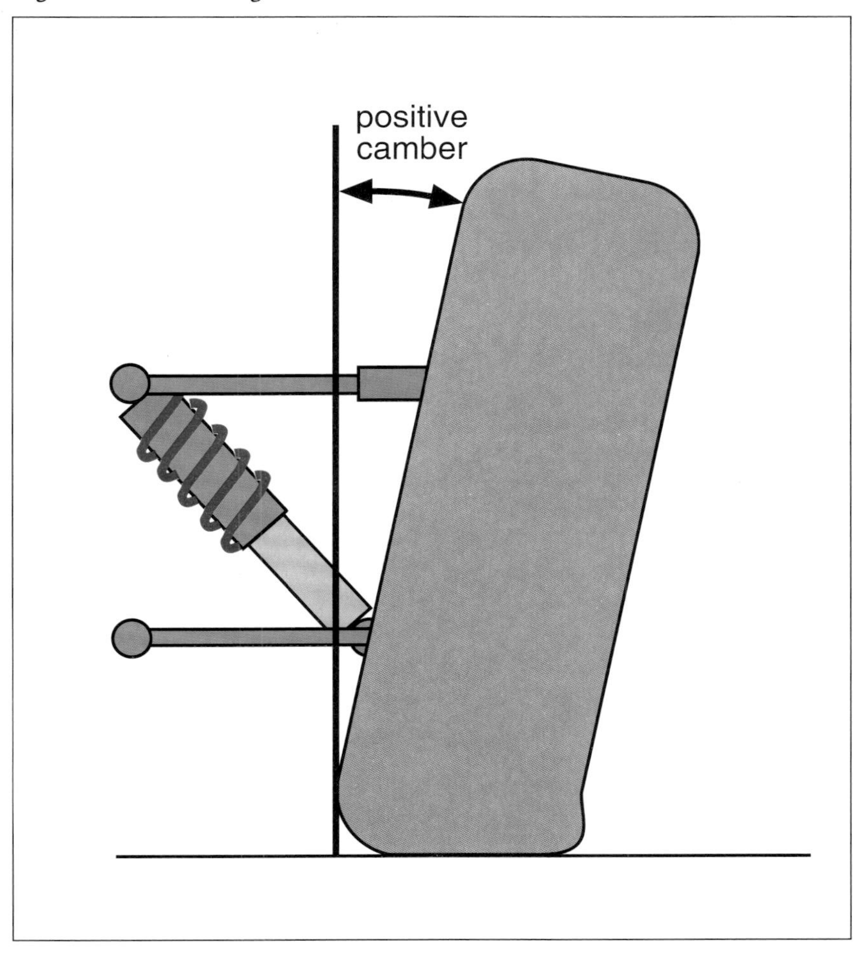

Fig. 6.11. Camber adjustment on this design is easy. The upper wishbone is detached from the suspension upright, the locknut is slackened and the balljoint screwed in or out as necessary.

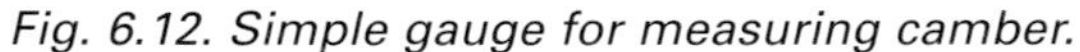

Fig. 6.12. Simple gauge for measuring camber.

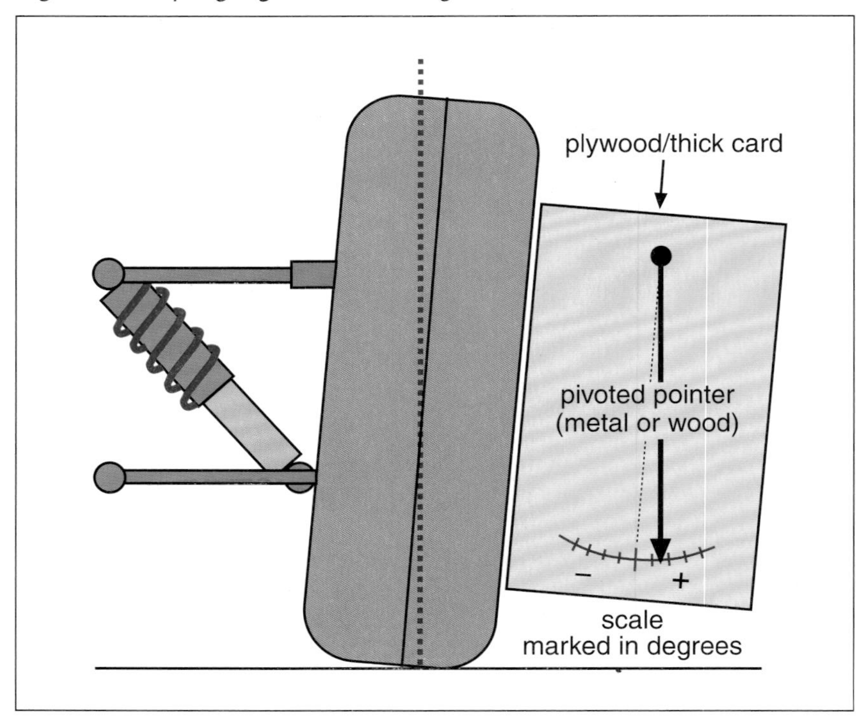

To lighten the steering effort, and to help the front wheels return to the straight-ahead position after cornering, the pivot (king pin or swivel) for each front wheel is usually inclined backwards at the top (when viewed from the side of the car), so that a line drawn through the pivot axis (steering axis) projects down to the ground ahead of a vertical line drawn through the centre of the roadwheel. This angle between the steering axis and the vertical line drawn through the centre of the roadwheel is known as castor angle, as it has the same effect as the castor wheels on a trolley. Depending on the car, somewhere between 2 degrees and 4 degrees of castor should be sufficient, though some cars have more (a 'Locost' has 5 degrees and an AC Cobra replica 6 degrees). Again, once you have driven the car you can make the necessary

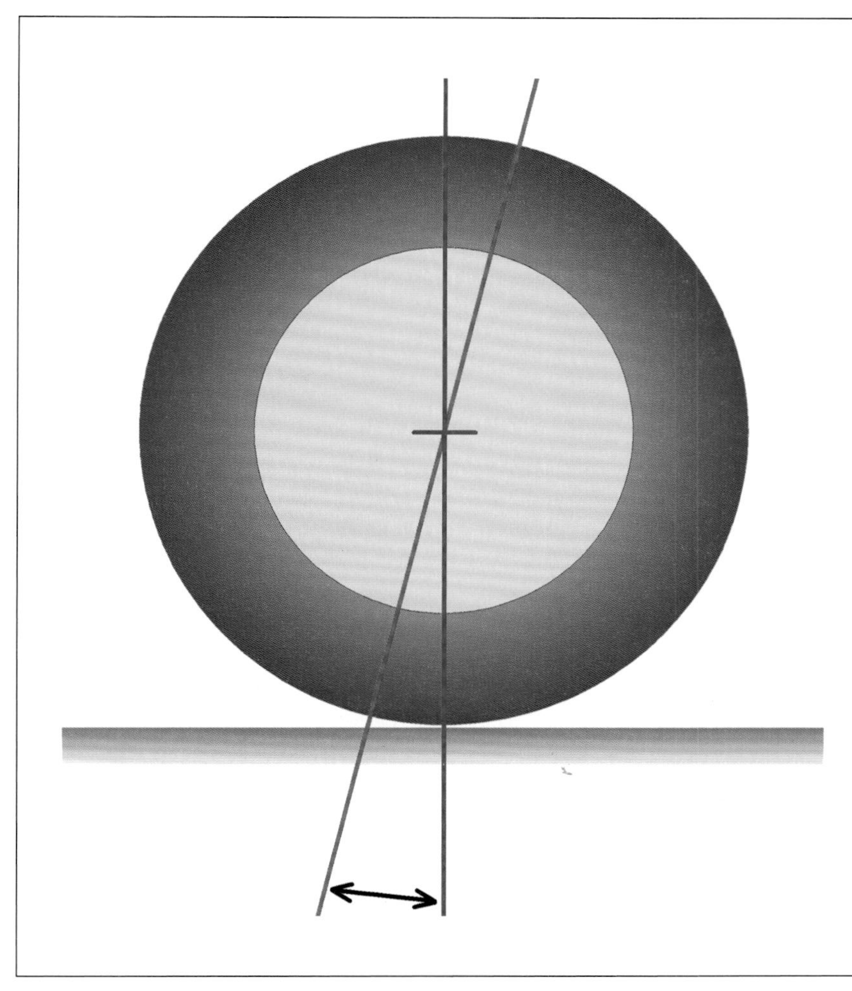

Fig. 6.13. Castor angle.

adjustments to give you nicely weighted steering.

Finally, there is 'toe'. Toe is the difference, viewed from above, between lines drawn through the centres of the roadwheels and the car's centreline. Toe-in is when the roadwheels point inwards, towards each other, at the front. Toe-out is when the wheels splay outwards from each other at the front. Rear-wheel-drive cars tend to have a small amount of toe-in, whereas on front-wheel-drive cars there is normally a small amount of toe-out, as the torque from the driven wheels tends to force the wheels inwards at the front.

Measuring these angles and dimensions accurately is sometimes difficult for the amateur, but most tyre-fitting establishments have equipment for measuring wheel alignment and can make the necessary adjustments for you. Even small adjustments can transform the handling of your car and increase immeasurably the pleasure of driving it.

Fig. 6.14. Toe angle. Toe-in shown.

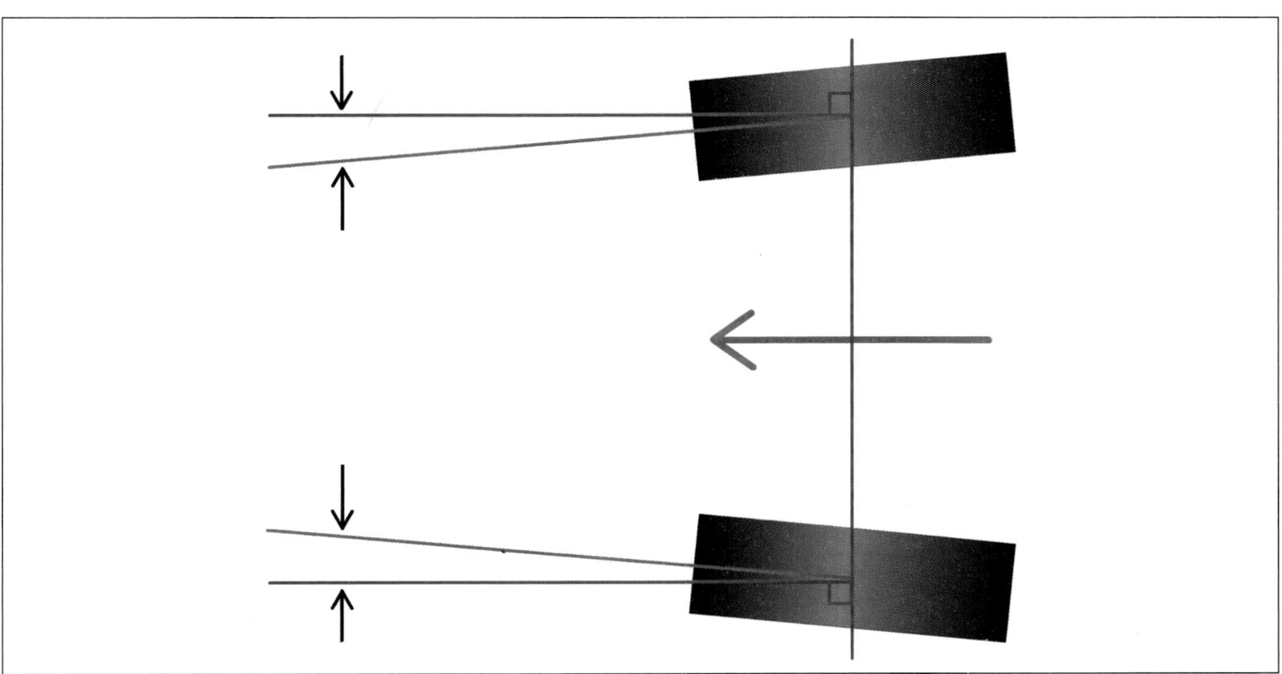

Fig. 6.15. Adjusting the toe angle. The locknut at the track-rod end is slackened and the track rod gripped with a Mole wrench or similar. Turning this screws the rod-end inwards or outwards depending on rotation. Both sides are adjusted equally with the steering wheel centred.

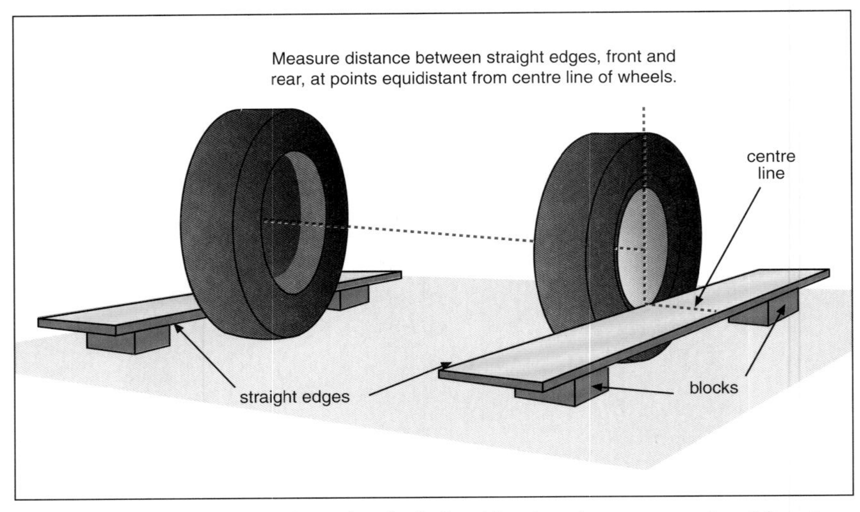

Fig. 6.16. An improvised method of checking/setting toe angle of front wheels. The straight edges should be pushed flat against the wheel rims.

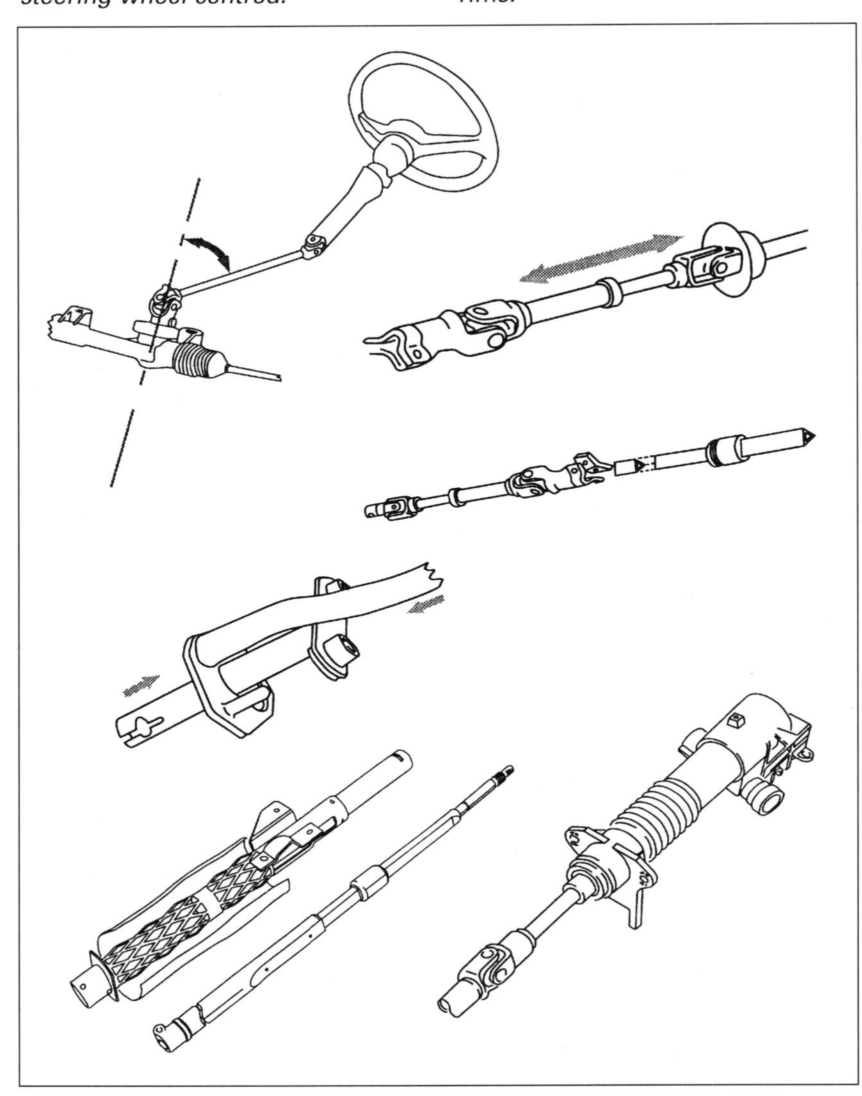

STEERING COLUMN

The steering column links the steering wheel to the steering box by means of one or more universal joints. The sensible thing is to visit a breaker's yard and pick up a complete steering column so that you can convert it to your own needs, bearing in mind the recommendations in the Single Vehicle Approval (SVA) regulations to ensure that it will be safe.

Always ensure that the steering column top mounting is secure at the scuttle. Nothing is worse in moments of stress, when you may be clutching the wheel with considerable force, than to find that you are supporting it rather than the reverse.

Steering wheels really set off the cockpit or car interior, and there is an amazing variety from which to choose in accessory shops, catalogues and autojumbles. Make sure that the hub supplied with the steering wheel will fit your column (adaptors are usually available to suit most columns), and that the wheel will conform to the SVA requirements – many older ones with holes in the spokes will not.

Fig. 6.17. Different steering column layouts showing safety systems. (Courtesy SVA Vehicle Inspectorate.)

Chapter 7

Brakes

THE EVOLUTION OF BRAKING SYSTEMS

With a few exceptions, motor manufacturers in the early days concentrated on making cars run reliably, and the development of effective braking systems seems to have been long delayed. It is true that right up to the beginning of the Second World War the volume of traffic was very low, as were the speeds attained by the ordinary motorist, so the need for brakes as efficient as ours are today may not have been so apparent. But, even then, there were emergencies to be met with and steep hills to descend – to the smell of burning brake linings in the usually tiny and inefficient drums.

The attitude of many manufacturers could be summed up by the retort made by Ettore Bugatti to one of his customers who had complained of poor brakes: 'We make our cars to go, not stop!'

This is a pity because it means that some older cars, which are otherwise a pleasure to drive, have their overall performance spoiled by the fact that their brakes are inadequate in modern traffic conditions. Anyone restoring an elderly car, or thinking of using its chassis for a special, should be aware of such shortcomings and should think seriously of ways to improve the brakes. Modern linings are a big help – you should specify 'soft' linings if the brakes are cable- or rod-operated – but a conversion to a hydraulic system, with servo if the car is fast or heavy, should be considered. Many older cars have had hydraulic braking systems fitted later in their existence and, unless the car is extremely rare, few would be critical of such a sensible modification.

Over the years many different types of braking systems have been used and, until about 1920, most cars had to make do with brakes on the rear wheels only. It was feared that brakes on the front wheels would affect the steering, but faster and heavier cars, together with different road conditions, soon made brakes on all wheels essential.

When front brakes were fitted, some of them were largely ineffective, like those fitted to the Austin Seven which started life with them but, because of poor design, had a reverse servo action which tended to decrease rather than increase braking effort the harder the pedal was pressed. It also took some time before manufacturers decided that front and rear brakes should all be operated by the brake pedal rather than having those at the back worked by the handbrake and those at the front by the pedal. Those operated by the handbrake were usually more powerful because of the greater leverage it was possible to exert, but since the more efficient use of braking effort is at the front wheels, this did little to improve the overall braking.

Brake operation was by cable, sometimes exposed and running over pulleys, like Bugatti and Riley, or more often running within a flexible conduit. As an alternative to cables, rods were frequently used and sometimes a combination of both, as in many modern handbrake systems.

In the 1920s the first hydraulic systems appeared. Hydraulic braking systems operate by using what is in effect a pump – the master cylinder – operated by the brake pedal to pressurise the hydraulic fluid. The fluid is pressurised in small bore pipes that are, in turn, connected to smaller 'pumps' at each wheel that, under the pressure of the fluid, expand the brake shoes outwards against the brake drum or, on disc brakes, squeeze the disc between friction pads.

One of the great benefits of the hydraulic system is that as pressure is equal throughout the system, the same pressure is applied to each brake. One of the problems with rods and cables was trying to equalise the pressure in order to achieve straight-line braking, and many compensation devices were developed for this purpose. However, it took a long time before all manufacturers converted to full hydraulics, Rolls-Royce perhaps being the last in 1955, though it has to be said that their brakes were always superb.

Although the greatest automotive genius of all, Dr Fred Lanchester, patented disc brakes in 1902, drum brakes remained the norm until Jaguar first used discs (developed from the aircraft industry), and many modern cars still have a mix of brakes, discs on the front where most of the braking takes place and drums on the rear. Unless the car is a high-performance machine, this is a good combination since drums are more effective than discs at slower speeds and it is easier and more effective to fit a parking brake system to drum brakes.

As already mentioned, disc brakes have friction pads that actually grip the rotating disc, whereas drum brakes have semi-circular 'shoes' that are lined with friction material and are pressed against the inside of the drum. This is where most wear takes place, and it is here that the work of refurbishing a braking system should start.

DRUM BRAKES

The inside surface of the drum should be inspected for wear. Drums are often unevenly worn, as grit tends to become embedded in the surface of the soft friction linings and scores the working surface of the drum. If scoring is at all noticeable it must be removed by being turned down on a lathe, or ground out. You might make some impression on it with emery cloth by hand, but turning in a lathe will ensure concentricity and parallelism.

If you are able to turn the drum, do not rely on the concentricity of the lathe chuck, but turn up a mandrel on which the drum can be fitted, relying on the concentricity of the diameter that registers with the hub. Note before you start that there is a minimum permissible wall thickness which is often marked on the drum itself or is given in the workshop manual for the car. If the drum will not clean up within the permissible limit you will have to find a replacement.

Next, turn your attention to the backplates with the shoe operating mechanism, shoes and linings. Remove the shoe steady springs by pressing down on the cap with a pair of pliers and twisting through 90 degrees, or by sliding the springs out, as applicable (see *Fig. 7.2*). Note the positions of the pull-off springs and carefully remove the shoes by easing them out of the anchoring and actuating slots at each end, if necessary unhooking them from the pull-off springs. I have a simple tool, bought many years ago, which makes this easy. In lieu of this an adjustable spanner is very helpful.

Remove and clean the various parts, being careful not to breathe

Fig. 7.1. Removing scoring in a brake drum by turning in a lathe. A trued mandrel is essential.

Fig. 7.2. Two types of brake shoe steady springs.

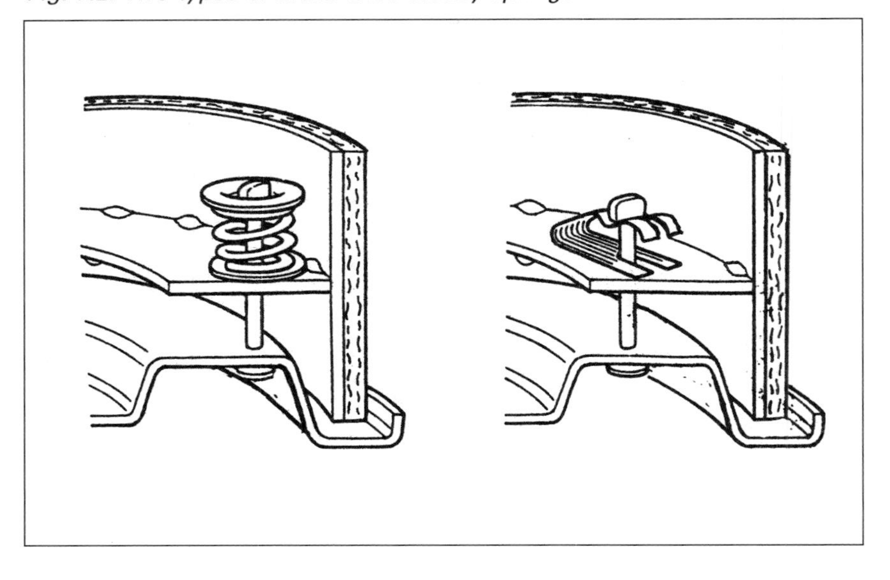

Fig. 7.3. Removing brake shoes. The shoe is eased out of the wheel cylinder and the spring is then removed.

Fig. 7.4. Special brake shoe removal tool in use.

in the asbestos dust from the shoes. Methylated spirits are useful for cleaning hydraulic parts. If the linings are at all worn, it is worthwhile replacing them while they are stripped down. Linings are usually bonded to shoes, but on older cars they were riveted with soft copper rivets. If your linings are riveted, remember to buy the rivets as well. Riveting is easy, but take care not to compress the rivet too much or it will fracture the lining which is quite brittle.

Select a rod with a diameter about the same as that of the rivet head, to act as an anvil, and clamp the rod in a vice. Starting at the middle rivets, hold the assembly with the rivet head on the rod end, and expand the hollow end of the rivet with a centre punch, tapping it gently with a light hammer until it holds firmly. Work outwards from the middle, and chamfer the ends of the linings with a file, remembering not to breathe in the dust (a suitable dust mask should always be worn when carrying out this work).

Check the pull-off springs and replace them if they are damaged –

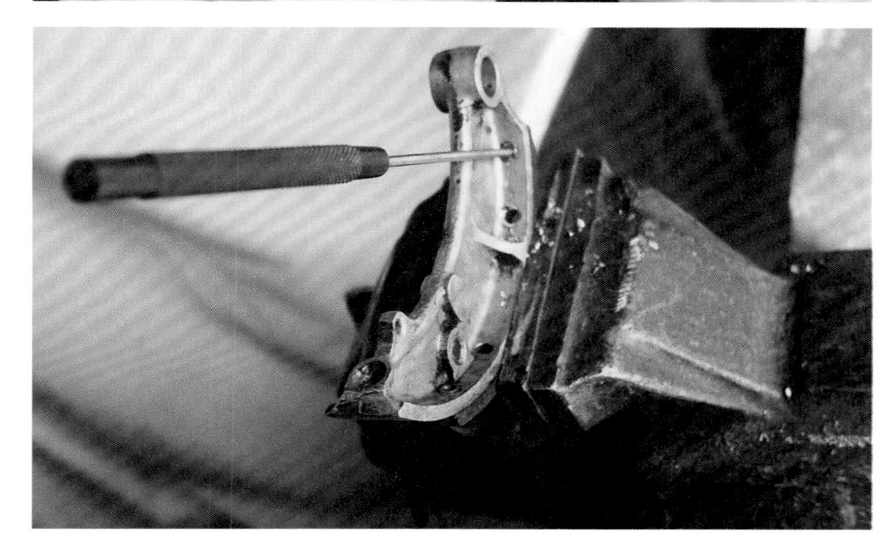

Fig. 7.5. Removing the rivets securing the lining to a brake shoe.

Fig. 7.6. The new lining and hollow rivets.

Fig. 7.7. A rivet and lining supported ready for fitting to the shoe.

Fig. 7.8. Expanding the rivet.

if the shoes have been renewed often the springs tend to suffer. The pins in the shoe steady springs are often rusted, but replacements can be bought. Overhaul kits for the popular makes of drum brakes are easily obtainable. Hydraulic wheel cylinders that are seized or damaged should be renewed, along with their seals. Wheel cylinder overhaul kits are cheap enough, and new seals should be used whatever the condition of the old ones.

While you have got the wheel cylinders off, check the bleed nipples. These often seem to suffer from rust and misuse that destroys the 'flats' on them, making them impossible to undo with a spanner. Unscrew the nipple, using a vice to hold it if necessary, and replace it with a new one. Special brake pipe/bleed nipple spanners are available which will help to avoid damage when unscrewing the nipples in the future.

Build up the backplate, and fit the new rubbers to the wheel cylinder, lubricating them with brake fluid. Use 'brake grease' sparingly on the various parts that touch, such as the shoe ends, and the surfaces of the shoes which bear against the backplates. Make sure that the shoe adjusters can be turned, but leave them in the fully 'off' position otherwise you will have difficulty refitting the drum.

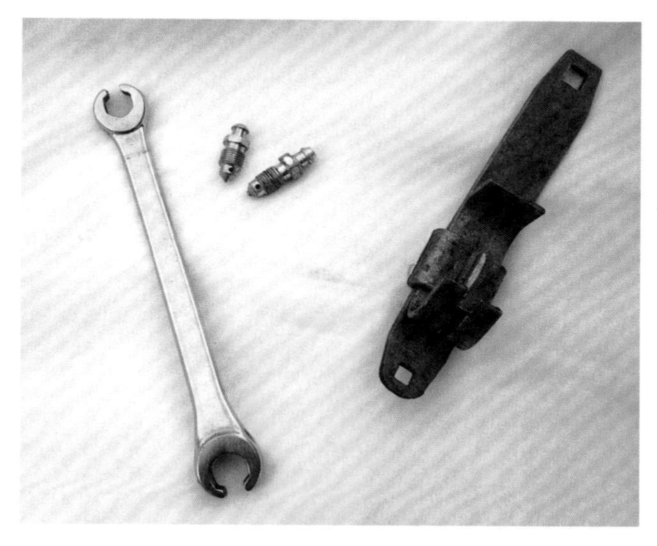

Fig. 7.9 (top left). Bleed nipples, correct spanner for nipples and unions and special brake shoe removing tool.

Fig. 7.10 (top right). New wheel cylinder fitted to rear brake, with the handbrake operating mechanism visible, and the adjuster (at the bottom) rebuilt.

Fig. 7.11 (middle left). Girling type brake adjuster. Screwing in the central screw with the squared end forces the two pistons apart. The brake shoe ends fit into the slots in the pistons and are held there by the springs.

Fig. 7.12 (middle right). The Girling rear wheel brake cylinders are free to slide in the back plate and are held in position by the two spring 'horseshoe' clips.

Fig. 7.13 (bottom right). Shoes refitted with springs in position.

DISC BRAKES

Disc brakes have their friction pads mounted in calipers. The pads are designed to be easily replaceable and are often secured by long pins or split pins to prevent them coming loose. The pads slide inwards towards the disc under pressure from the pistons. There are normally two pistons, but performance cars may have four or more. Many modern cars now have disc brakes with sliding calipers, and these have a single cylinder and piston assembly, mounted on rails in such a way that as the piston pushes one pad towards the disc, the caliper moves in reaction to the piston, pulling the opposite pad towards the disc.

Each caliper piston operates within a cylinder, with a rubber seal fitted to a groove in the piston to prevent the loss of fluid. A rubber dust cover is fitted between the end of the cylinder and the piston to keep out dirt and moisture. As the area of the piston that bears on the pad is exposed, it tends to suffer from corrosion, especially if it has been unused for any length of time, and the dust seal may be affected.

Before removing the pads, make sure that there is enough room in the fluid reservoir to accommodate the fluid which will be pushed up into it when you ease the pistons back into their cylinders ready for fitting new pads. The pads should be pushed outwards, away from the disc, using the proper tool or a wedge-shaped alternative. If the brakes are seized, or are leaking, it will be necessary to remove the caliper by undoing the bolts holding it to its mounting, and the hydraulic hose will have to be disconnected. With a proper tool, or a wedge-shaped alternative, ease the pistons all the way back into the caliper body ready for fitting the new pads.

If you need to overhaul a caliper, bear in mind that pistons are often difficult to remove. There are special removal tools on the market, but a blast of high-pressure air applied to the caliper fluid inlet will often force a piston out which, together with its cylinder, can be cleaned up and new seals fitted. If the caliper has more than one piston, the overhauled piston can be refitted and clamped in place temporarily whilst a blast of air is tried again to push out the remaining piston(s).

If you do not have access to a compressed air supply, reconnect the caliper to the hydraulic system, and try to pump the piston out using the brake pedal. Alternatively, in desperate situations, connect a grease gun to the caliper fluid inlet and pump the grease gun to force the piston out. If this method is used, you will then have to ensure that every trace of grease is removed by washing the piston and cylinder in white spirit or other degreasing agent before drying with a lint-free cloth and coating the components with hydraulic fluid.

There is usually a groove at the outer end of the piston in which the dust seal sits. Gentle use of a screwdriver in this groove will sometimes prise the piston out, but more often it breaks a piece out of the very narrow ridge. If this happens you will have to replace the whole caliper which, if new, can be expensive.

The surfaces of pistons and cylinders should be shiny and without scoring, and there should be no bright, polished patches which are caused by the two surfaces rubbing together.

When refitting a piston, fit a new seal (or seals), lubricate the piston and cylinder with brake fluid, then slide the piston, solid end first, into the cylinder as far as it will go, and fit a new dust seal. If the caliper bleed nipple has been maltreated, fit a new one.

When refitting the caliper, replace the securing bolt locking plates, if fitted, or coat the threads of the securing bolts with thread-locking compound.

If you are restoring a car, check the condition of the brake pipes and make sure that they are well clipped up to the chassis and are not damaged. Inspect the flexible

Fig. 7.14. Assembled disc brake caliper and pads.

Fig. 7.15. Caliper components – caliper, piston, piston seal and dust seal.

Fig. 7.16. Caliper piston refitted and dust seal about to be fitted. Lubricate well with brake fluid.

Fig. 7.17. A simple brake (or clutch) master cylinder with piston and pushrod assemblies removed. It has only a single outlet and so would not gain SVA approval if used as a brake master cylinder on a newly built car.

hoses minutely, and if they show signs of leaking or cracking, renew them. Now is also the time to check and if necessary renew the brake-light switch, if it is fitted in the brake piping.

MASTER CYLINDER

The master cylinder, and servo if fitted, come next. Many cheaper cars had a very simple master cylinder that operated all four brakes from one cylinder outlet. These work perfectly adequately, but if there is a leak anywhere in the system, all the brakes will fail. To prevent this, many manufacturers fitted a 'tandem' (dual-circuit) system which, in effect, consists of two simple cylinders fitted end-to-end within one unit. A tandem master cylinder has two reservoirs (usually one single chamber divided into two) and two fluid outlets, which allows two braking circuits to be operated independently. On a dual-circuit system, the system is split front and rear on many older cars (one circuit operating the front brakes and the other operating the rear brakes) or, on most modern cars the system is split diagonally (each circuit operating one front and the diagonally opposite rear brake). The dual-circuit system is safer than a single-circuit system, since any failure will normally affect one part of the system only and should leave two brakes operative.

Before dismantling a master cylinder, it should be well cleaned externally. Piston assemblies are usually held in place by a circlip in the end of the cylinder, often under a rubber gaiter. When this is taken out the piston(s), springs and seals can be removed. Keep all components in order, and make a note of the way they are assembled. Clean the bore of the cylinder and make sure that it is not scored, and if all is well lubricate it and reassemble with new parts. Overhaul kits are available for most popular types of master cylinder, and for some modern master cylinders, new piston assemblies are supplied, complete with seals, in cartridge form.

SERVO

Some cars are fitted with a brake 'servo', which is easily identified, as it is a large drum attached either to the master cylinder itself or, if separate, piped to it. The purpose of a servo is to increase the braking effort over that exerted by the driver when the pedal is depressed, thus calling for less effort on the driver's part. With fast or heavy cars this is important, particularly if the car is equipped with disc brakes, as these need more pressure than drum brakes, which are to some extent self-energising. Nearly all servos, except those on Rolls-Royces and Bentleys, which are mechanical, are vacuum-operated via a connection to the inlet manifold, and can provide an effort of up to about 30psi (2kg/sq cm). The vacuum is supplied through a one-way valve fitted in the pipe connecting the manifold to the servo, and the valve should be checked to ensure that it is working properly. If the valve is removed, it should be possible to blow through it in one direction, but not the other.

If you were able to drive the donor vehicle you will know whether the brakes were heavy or light to operate, and therefore whether the servo was working or not. If the servo does not appear to be working, be suspicious first of the connection to the inlet manifold, which is normally via a flexible rubber or plastic tube, and examine this for leaks or cracks. Check also that the servo body is not corroded or pierced in any way, since it must be airtight to enable it to work.

Fig. 7.18. Brake servo. Note dual master cylinder with separate pipes for front and rear brakes.

As mentioned earlier, if you are building a light sports car (and specials are usually lighter than a production car) you are unlikely to need a servo, even with disc brakes. If in doubt, first try the car without, then add a servo later if you think you need one.

BRAKE PIPES

Brake pipes are made of copper or plated steel, usually of $^3/_{16}$in (5mm) diameter, which is strong enough to resist the pressures of over 200psi (14 kg/sq cm) that can occur

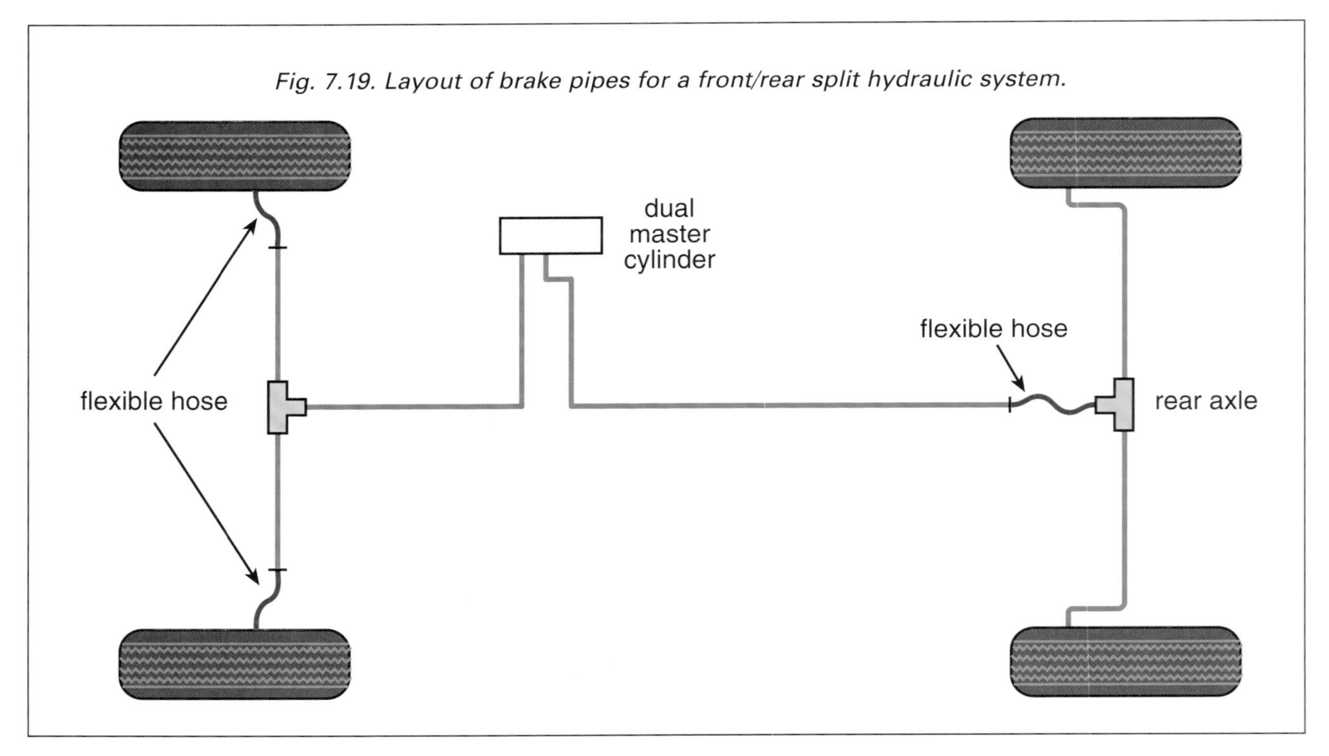

Fig. 7.19. Layout of brake pipes for a front/rear split hydraulic system.

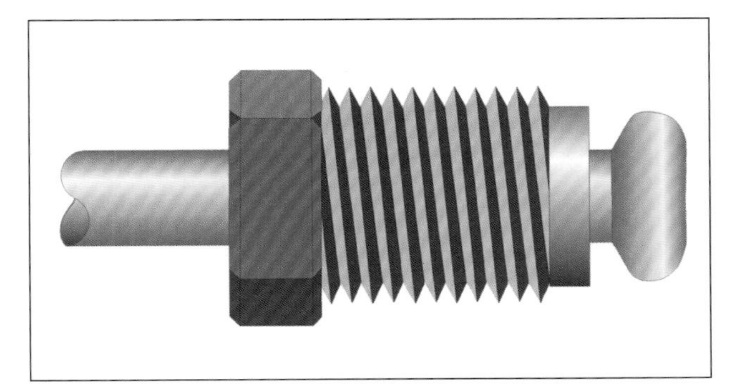

Fig. 7.20. Male brake pipe fitting with single flare on pipe end.

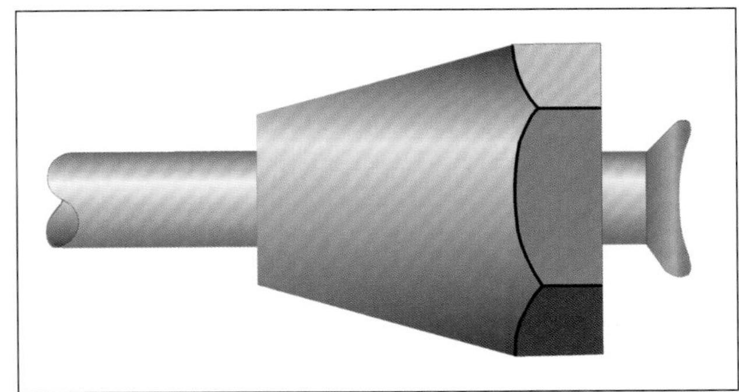

Fig. 7.21. Female brake pipe fitting with double flare.

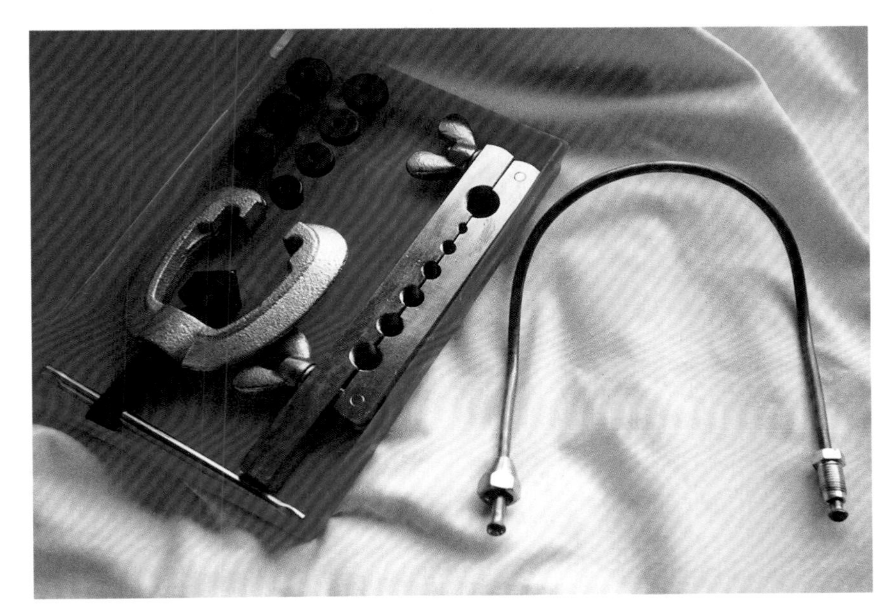

Fig. 7.22. Brake pipe flaring tool kit.

when panic braking. Together with the necessary fittings, brake piping is available from accessory shops in coils, one coil being sufficient for the average car. A special tool is needed to 'flare' the ends of the pipes for the fittings. If you measure the lengths of the pipes required, and specify the fittings, the accessory shop should be able to make up a set of pipes for you. A typical layout, using a dual master cylinder, is shown in *Fig. 7.19*.

Note that there are two types of fitting, each requiring different preparation of the pipe ends. One accepts a single flare see *Fig. 7.20*, while the other requires the pipe end to have a double flare, see *Fig. 7.21*. The type of flare used must suit the component to which the pipe is being connected.

Three flexible hoses are required (possibly four if you have independent rear suspension), one for each front wheel and one for the rear axle or crossbeam. The inboard ends of the hoses must be securely fixed to the chassis by means of small brackets or to the, preferably reinforced, bodywork.

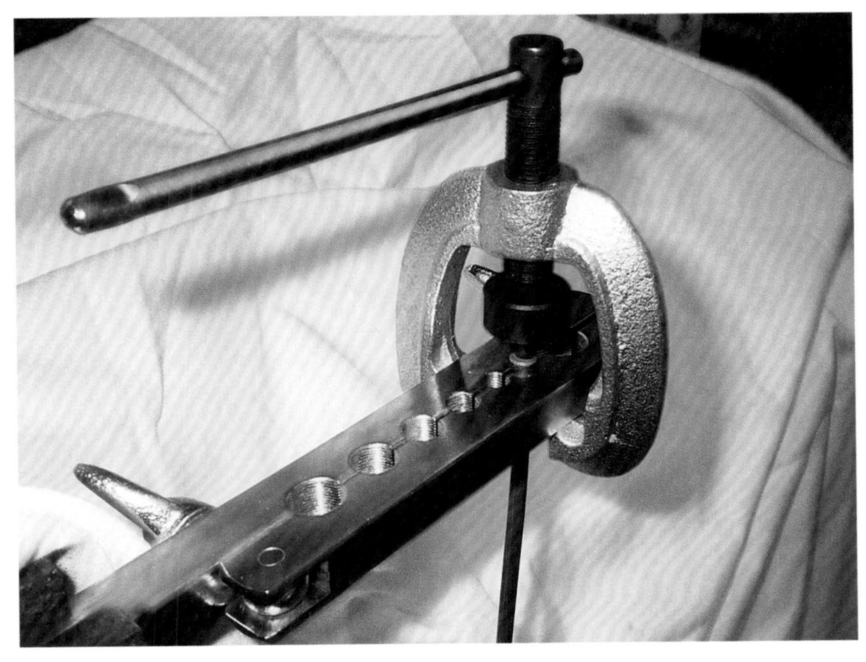

Fig. 7.23. Flaring tool in use.

Fig. 7.24. Reinforced bodywork for flexible hose.

Fig. 7.25. Pipe-bending former.

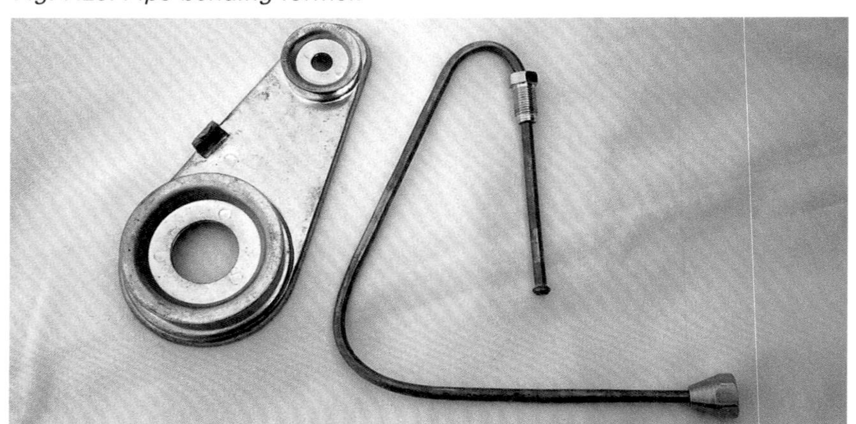

Most master cylinders have an integral fluid reservoir, but if necessary for reasons of accessibility, a separate reservoir can be mounted elsewhere and piped to the master cylinder.

On older cars, the stop-light switch may be pressure-activated and may be screwed on to the end of the master cylinder, or a separate switch may be screwed into the pipe connector. On more modern cars the switch is usually activated directly by the brake pedal.

Brake piping bends easily by hand, but if you want a bend with a small radius it is best formed with a special pipe bender, or at least round a former of the correct radius.

Pipes should be securely fixed to the chassis or body to prevent vibration and damage, using plastic P-clips or rubber-insulated metal clips at intervals of not more than 300mm. If possible, run the brake pipes inside the body rather than outside so that they do not suffer road knocks or corrosion.

Fig. 7.26. Typical neat brake pipe layout.

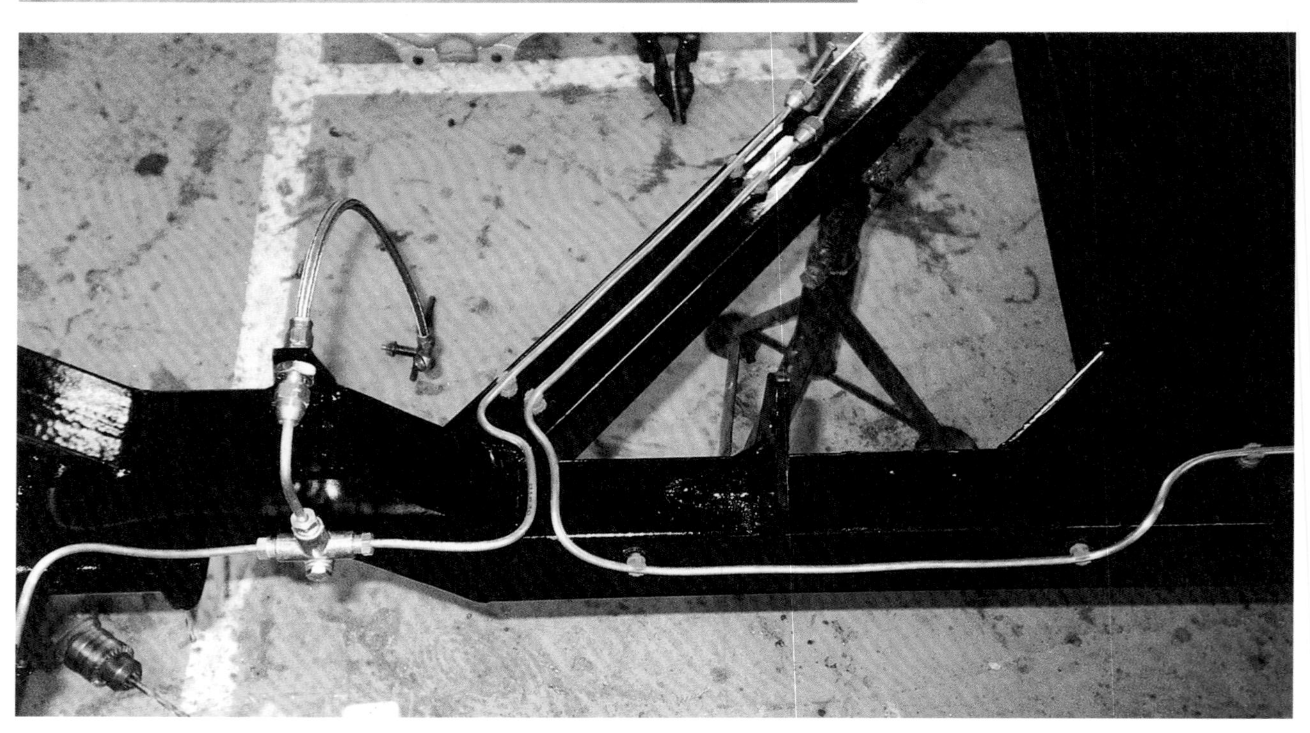

FILLING AND BLEEDING A BRAKE HYDRAULIC SYSTEM

When the braking system is complete, if drum brakes are fitted, adjust the shoes (if the adjustment is manual) so that they are close to the drum. You will now need to fill the hydraulic system with fluid, and 'bleed' it to ensure that it is free of air which, being compressible, will give a 'squidgy' feel to the pedal and make braking unpredictable.

Fill the reservoir with brake fluid and, with an assistant to keep the reservoir replenished, attach a piece of pipe to the bleed nipple on the brake furthest away from the master cylinder. Immerse the end of the pipe in a clean jam jar containing brake fluid (make sure that the end of the pipe remains immersed in fluid at all times during the procedure), and unscrew the bleed nipple by about one turn. Ask your assistant to push the brake pedal down slowly and then hold it at the bottom of its travel, while you watch the fluid as it comes out of the pipe into the jar. Initially, the fluid will be mixed with a stream of air bubbles, but after a time these will diminish. Ask your assistant to keep the pedal depressed while you close the bleed nipple. Once the bleed nipple is closed, your assistant can release the pedal. This operation should be repeated until there are no air bubbles visible in the jar, tightening the bleed nipple before the pedal is released each time. The whole procedure should be repeated on the other three brakes, working first from that which is furthest away, and therefore has the longest pipe.

There are two other methods of bleeding which do not require an assistant. The first uses a bleed pipe with a non-return valve in it. The pipe is connected to the bleed nipple, the other end being placed in a suitable receptacle to catch the escaping fluid. The nipple is opened and the operator then pumps the brake pedal up and down slowly until no air bubbles are visible in the fluid entering the receptacle. Once no more air bubbles are visible, the nipple is tightened and the next brake is dealt with. It is all too easy when using this method to forget to keep the fluid reservoir topped up!

The other method of bleeding is more sophisticated. A receptacle is filled with fluid and connected to the top of the reservoir, and is then pressurised by air, usually from the spare tyre. All that is then necessary is to open each bleed nipple in turn until the fluid flows with an absence of air bubbles.

Brake fluid should not be reused. It is hygroscopic (it attracts moisture), so must be carefully stored in a sealed container. Brake fluid is an efficient paint stripper so must not be allowed to drip on to painted surfaces.

MECHANICALLY OPERATED BRAKES

Brakes operated by means of rods and cables are similar to hydraulically operated brakes as far as drums and shoes are concerned, but instead of the shoes being operated by a piston under hydraulic pressure, the pressure on the pedal and movement of the rods or cables is converted into the appropriate motion by different means. Either a cam, or a lever may be used or, perhaps best of all, the Girling system which consists of a wedge with rollers between the shoe ends. Because of its efficiency and the light pressures required on the brake pedal, the Girling system was very popular.

The mechanism operating the brake shoes is easy to understand when the drum is removed. Freedom of action is important, but any undue wear needs taking up, and moderate lubrication with brake grease of parts in contact is essential. Note that in some systems, especially the Girling and Bendix, the shoe-expanding mechanism is not bolted rigidly to the backplate but is intended to 'float' under braking and wheel rotation, when it achieves a servo effect.

Cables are useful because they are flexible and rattle-free, but are prone to rust and seizure if not adequately lubricated, and not all have grease nipples for this purpose. If seized or reluctant to move, replace the cables.

Rods should be rust free, especially at the screwed ends, and the clevis pin must be a good fit in the clevis forks – except in the case of the Girling system which had a 'free' fit (the pin being treated as a roller) – and well lubricated with molybdenum grease.

The bugbear with mechanically operated brakes was always one of compensation – ensuring that all brakes operated equally and pulled the car up in a straight line. Attention should therefore be paid to the efficiency of whatever compensating arrangements exist. The compensator components should be free to move and entirely without lost motion. Their levers and any other levers in the system should normally be positioned so that motion starts just before the 'upright' position of the lever is reached, otherwise the full travel and leverage will not be available.

HANDBRAKE

Handbrakes, which sometimes seem to be a bit of an afterthought, depend on rods and/or cables for their actuation, and the foregoing remarks apply to them also. Ensure that the handbrake ratchet teeth in the lever quadrant are not badly worn – if they are it may be possible to sharpen them with a file. As a guide, the handbrake should be adjusted so that it begins to operate on the third 'click' of the ratchet.

If you are building a kit car or special, consider carefully the position of the handbrake. On small sports cars you may find that if the lever is mounted in the traditional place, on the transmission tunnel, it can be too high and consequently difficult to operate. Consider repositioning the lever at the side of the tunnel where it does not conflict with the gear lever, or mount it under the scuttle.

Chapter 8

Engine

THE EVOLUTION OF PETROL ENGINES

In the early days of motoring the engine was the most fallible part of a car (apart from the tyres). If you travelled any real distance without major trouble you wrote to *The Times* about it, but as materials gradually improved and designers became more experienced it was not too long before engines became quite reliable in themselves, though they needed frequent attention and oil changes. Before anti-freeze became common, it was necessary to drain the cooling system if it was likely to freeze overnight, and then fill it up again with hot water the next morning if you expected an easy start. This was particularly important when there were no self-starters and engines had to be cranked by hand to start them.

When mass production began and parts became standardised, replacement became easier, but mechanics needed more manual skills then than now in order to make parts and 'fit' bearings, and not all engines were built to be easily repairable. The pre-Second World War Ford 8 engine was meant to be renewed about every 20,000 to 25,000 miles (32,000 to 40,000km). If it was not renewed it wore out rapidly, thus obeying Henry Ford's dictum that: 'Cars should not need repairing but should wear out like a bar of soap.' It was difficult even to adjust the tappets on this Ford side-valve engine, since no means of adjustment was provided, the common practice being to grind the end of the valve stem if the clearance was too small, or braze a bit on to it if too large. Of course, fitting a new engine was not expensive on a car that cost only £100 new.

One of the normal service routines was the decarbonisation of the cylinder head and piston crowns about every 10,000 miles (16,000km), and the grinding-in of valves. Garages thrived on 'decokes', and it was almost the first thing that the amateur mechanic learnt to do. The majority of engines had side valves, so taking the cylinder head off was easy, though the valves themselves could be a bit of a fiddle to replace. The deposits of carbon built up on the cylinder head and pistons rapidly because of the impurities in the petrol and oils then available. Enormous improvements took place in the 1950s, with the introduction of detergent oil and petrol additives that quickly made the need for decarbonising a thing of the past. Engines started to last for considerable mileages with only schedule servicing, so that at least 100,000 miles (160,000km) are now expected of most engines.

Major overhauls of engines as a routine are no longer required, and it is now the bodywork of a car that tends to be troublesome. Nowadays, body-rot is usually the reason for a car being taken off the road and being scrapped. This is good news for the special builder, as the likelihood is that if you buy a second-hand car the engine will have had reasonable maintenance and will be in usable condition, or can easily and cheaply be made serviceable.

A very wide variety of engines is available from which the special builder can choose. The restorer will presumably stick with the original, but the special builder is free to consider front- or rear-wheel-drive, size, weight, power output and all the other factors, such as valve operation and carburation or fuel injection, that make it all so interesting. A chart showing some of these factors in relation to the more common engines available is given opposite.

These details can serve as a guide only, since there were so many changes made in production. With the exception of the Wankel rotary type of engine, all engines work on the same basic principle, and are similarly constructed. Almost all car engines now employ the four-stroke cycle (commonly known as 'suck-squeeze-bang-blow'), which is properly known as the Otto cycle. The two-stroke principle, or Clarke cycle, is rarely used for modern car engines, but you come across it in a sophisticated form in motorcycles, and in a less sophisticated form in garden machinery.

The four-stroke engine consists of one or more cylinders, closed at one end by the cylinder head. Each cylinder contains a piston which is a close fit in the cylinder and is free to travel up and down within it (rather like a bicycle pump). Each piston is joined by means of a connecting rod to the crankshaft, which converts the reciprocating motion of the piston into rotary

Make	Valve actuation	Cyls	Capacity litres	Output bhp	Carbs/inj	Notes
Ford Kent	OHV push rods	4	1.1–1.8 2.0–2.5	41–84	Single, twin choke carb and tuneable.	Very popular, engines. Simple
Ford CVH	Single OHC	4	1.6–1.8	59–64kw	Injection	Good engine, plentiful
BMC B series	OHV push rods	4/6	1.2–1.5 1.6–1.8	30–75	SU carb(s)	Sturdy, tuneable, fairly heavy
VW Beetle	OHV push rods	4	1.3–1.6	44–50	Carb(s)	Reliable, air cooled
Rover V8	OHV push rods	8	3.5–4.0	From 130	Carbs/inj	Light, powerful, tuneable, plentiful
Jaguar XK	2 OHC	6	3.8	150	Carbs SU	Classic looks, powerful plentiful
Coventry Climax derivatives (Imp, Talbot)	1 OHC	4	1.0	40	Stromberg carb	Light, small, compact
Vauxhall	2 OHC	4	1.4–2.0	86–150	Inj	2.0 very popular
Ford Zetec	2 OHC	4	1.6–2.0	80–140	Inj	Light, powerful
Rover K series	2 OHC	4	1.1–1.8	50–150	Inj	Excellent, highly tuneable

motion, in a similar manner to the pedal crank of a bicycle.

The first of the four strokes is the induction stroke (suck) when the piston slides down the cylinder and sucks in a mixture of petrol and air (about one part of petrol to 16 parts of air) through the inlet valve, which opens for this purpose. The next stroke is the compression stroke (squeeze) when, with the valves closed, the mixture is compressed as the piston travels up the cylinder. The third, or firing stroke (bang), happens because the compressed petrol/air mixture is ignited by the electrical spark produced at the sparking plug. This, in fact, causes an explosion, and the burning gas expands rapidly, forcing the only moveable thing, the piston, down the cylinder, thus causing the crankshaft and flywheel to revolve. This in turn forces the piston back up the cylinder when the exhaust valve opens and the spent gas is expelled (blown) through the exhaust pipe. The whole cycle then starts all over again.

Early cars had just the one cylinder (as do many motorcycles still), but it was soon realised that this was inflexible and rough, so engines were built with 2, 3, 4, 6, 8, 12 and 16 cylinders, and in recent years it has become quite common for cars to have 5-cylinder engines, and occasionally 10.

The only common car in current use with a two-cylinder engine is the 2CV Citroën. 16-cylinder engines were always rare, and of the rest, 4-cylinder engines are by far the most common, followed by 6s and then by 8s. Five-cylinder engines are used by several German manufacturers, having first been introduced by Audi, and 10-cylinder engines are used exclusively, with the exception of Chrysler, in some racing cars. Most engines have their cylinders positioned in a straight line, but some, like those used in 2CVs, VW Beetles, some Alfa Romeos, and Subarus, have horizontally opposed cylinders ('flat' or 'boxer'), and many six, and nearly all 8-cylinder engines have their cylinders positioned in two banks in a V-formation.

CHOOSING AN ENGINE

In choosing an engine you will need to consider the type of car you are building, the performance you expect, and what the chassis can handle. If you want a large car, there is no point putting a small engine in it, even for the sake of economy, because it will have to work so hard it will not be economical. If you plan a sports car, you need to resist the temptation to fit the most powerful engine possible as, apart from the strength of the chassis frame itself, weight, space, drive components, cost of insurance, and your own capabilities all have to be taken into consideration if a well-balanced, well-engineered and usable car is to result.

If you already have a donor car and were able to drive it, you will know something about the state of the engine and whether there are any untoward noises coming from it. If the engine runs well and does not leak oil or water then, on the basis that 'if it's not broken don't mend it', a good clean and a coat of paint will look after the outside, while an oil change and fine tuning should put it in a serviceable state.

If you buying the engine from a breaker or other source, they may be able to tell you whether it was a 'runner' when it came in, and they may be able to demonstrate the fact. If not, look it over carefully to make sure that there is no obvious damage and, with the aid of a large adjustable spanner on the crankshaft pulley nut or bolt, turn the engine to make sure that it is not 'seized'.

There is no point in buying a seized engine unless it is in some way very special, as the reasons for its seizure cannot be discovered until it is stripped, and it may be very expensive to put right.

INSPECTING AN ENGINE FOR OBVIOUS SIGNS OF WEAR

In any case, if you have any doubt about the condition of the engine, then it is worthwhile taking the head and sump off and looking inside. Drain the oil, clean the engine externally and mount it on a bench if, like most of us, you do not possess an engine stand. Remove any ancillaries, such as the carburettor or fuel injection system components, the distributor (where fitted) and any pipes, in case they get damaged, then remove the rocker cover. If the engine has overhead camshafts, you will have to remove the belt(s) or chain(s) driving them, but before you do, check that there are timing marks on the various pulleys or gears so that you can reassemble and time the engine correctly (see pages 78 and 79).

Undo the cylinder head retaining bolts or nuts and then take off the head itself. This can at times be difficult, as the head can become firmly stuck to the block through corrosion, especially when the head is retained by studs and nuts instead of bolts. Often there are two lips cast into the side of the head, under which you can gently tap a block of wood to break the seal. A more drastic method is to tap a knife blade into the gasket at several points in order to 'start' the head, but take great care not to mark the mating faces. Once the head has moved, gentle tapping with a soft-faced mallet should remove it. (On big engines, when the going got tough, it was quite common to attach the head to a hoist and lift it against the full weight of the car.) If the head is really stubborn and the engine is a valuable one, you may have to leave the head on until you have taken the sump off and removed the crankshaft and pistons, when lengths of wood can be inserted in the bores and tapped against the lower face of the head in turn. In this case, ensure that all cylinder head securing bolts or nuts have been removed first, and take care not to damage the valves.

The piston crowns and cylinders can now be seen. Turn the crankshaft if you can and, as each piston reaches the bottom of its stroke, you can inspect the condition of the bores (the walls of the cylinder). These should be smooth and without scoring. If the bores are scored, it is because of lack of lubrication, or because something has broken and caused the damage. If one or more bore is damaged like this you can have the engine rebored and new pistons fitted, if it is valuable, or go back to the breaker's for another one in the hope that it might be better.

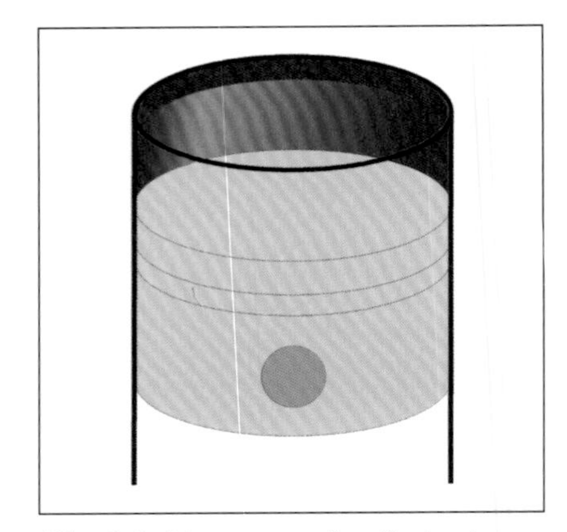

Fig. 8.1. Lip at top of cylinder bore.

If the bores appear to be all right, check the wear by feeling at the top of the bore to see whether there is a 'lip'. This is, in fact, the original bore that is not in contact with the piston rings and therefore is unworn. The presence of a lip denotes some wear, the more pronounced, the higher the mileage. If the lip is slight, ignore it; if moderate, fit new piston rings; if

Fig. 8.2. Crankshaft assembly with sump removed. The gauze filter at bottom left is for the oil pump pick-up.

really noticeable then a rebore will be needed. If you decide to fit new rings, you will need to get rid of the lip in case it fouls the upper ring when the piston is at top dead centre. Special tools are available for this purpose, but the edge of a broken piston ring used as a scraper can be quite effective.

Having set your mind at rest about the condition of the cylinders and, by implication, the pistons and rings, carefully remove any built-up carbon deposits on the piston crown with a blunt scraper, trying not to scratch the metal, and also clean the face of the block, ensuring that the debris does not fall into the cylinders or the water jackets.

Attention can now be turned to the crankshaft and bearings. Undo the bolts or screws holding the sump to the block and remove it carefully. Grasp the big end of each connecting rod in turn and push and pull it firmly up and down to see whether there is any movement between the connecting rod big-end and the crankshaft journal. There should be no noticeable play, but note that a limited amount of side-play is permissible. If the big-ends seem to be in good order you should be safe in assuming that the main bearings also are, but if you are keen you can take off the main bearing caps and inspect both the bearings and the crankshaft journals. The bearings should be an even matt-grey in colour, without any scoring, and the journal should be bright and polished. If not, the crankshaft will have to be removed, ground and undersize bearing shells fitted. If the shells show 'signs of flaking (exfoliation) they must be renewed, and you will have to measure the journal with a micrometer to determine its size. (You cannot assume that the crankshaft is of standard size as it may already have been ground.)

Fig. 8.3. A main bearing cap with a shell bearing. The lip at the top of the shell fits into a recess in the housing.

Fig. 8.4. Bearing shells. The pair of main bearing shells on the left have been starved of oil and the lining has begun to 'pick up'. The big-end bearing shell on the right has also been starved of oil and has been run for much longer than the main bearing shells as it has not only lost all of its lining but has also been hammered out of shape.

Fig. 8.5. Crankshaft removed, with two main bearing caps.

Fig. 8.6. Checking the crankshaft endfloat using a feeler gauge.

You should also check the endfloat of the crankshaft. This is the longitudinal movement of the crankshaft which can measured using a feeler gauge. A feeler gauge consists of a number of leaves of thin steel, each of different thickness, measured in thousandths of an inch or in millimetres (their sizes etched on them). Several leaves of the gauge may be used in combination. To measure the crankshaft endfloat, push the crankshaft fully forwards or backwards in the crankcase, then insert the feeler gauge between the end face of the appropriate crankshaft thrust washer, and the crankshaft web (the thrust washers are usually fitted either side of one of the main bearing locations, or are sometimes incorporated with the main bearing shells). Read off the thickness of the feeler gauge leaves inserted, and add them together to give the amount of crankshaft endfloat. The permissible amount can be found in the workshop manual, and if the endfloat measured is significantly different from the amount specified, the thrust washers, which control the play, will need replacing. Thrust washers are often situated at the centre or rear main bearing, but may be positioned at the 2nd or 4th main bearing on engines with five main bearings. Some modern engines do not have separate washers, the thrust washers being incorporated in a main bearing shell.

When reassembling, squirt oil liberally on to all the contact surfaces, and check that the bearing caps fit snugly and that oil holes line up. Renew the tab washers (where applicable) and bolts or nuts, and tighten these down to the correct value, as specified in the manual, using a torque wrench.

Where applicable, lock the bolts with the tabs, and on completion turn the crankshaft to ensure that it is not binding. Clean out the sump and oil pump pick-up pipe gauze, then fit a new sump gasket and seals (as applicable), noting from the old one how it should be done, and refit the sump. Note that on some engines the sump may be sealed to the cylinder block using sealant instead of a gasket.

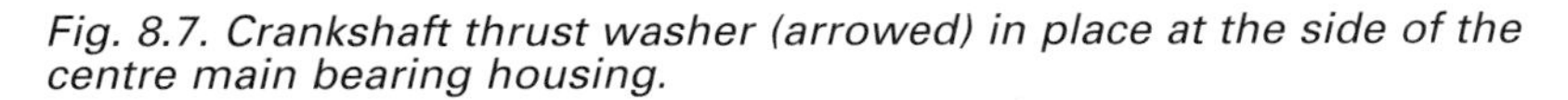

Fig. 8.7. Crankshaft thrust washer (arrowed) in place at the side of the centre main bearing housing.

OVERHAULING THE CYLINDER HEAD AND VALVES

While the cylinder head is off, it is worth checking the valves and springs, and decarbonising the combustion chambers.

Some cars, like Fiats and Jaguars, do not have rockers, and the cams themselves bear directly on to the valves via inverted 'bucket' tappets. The valve clearances are adjusted by adding

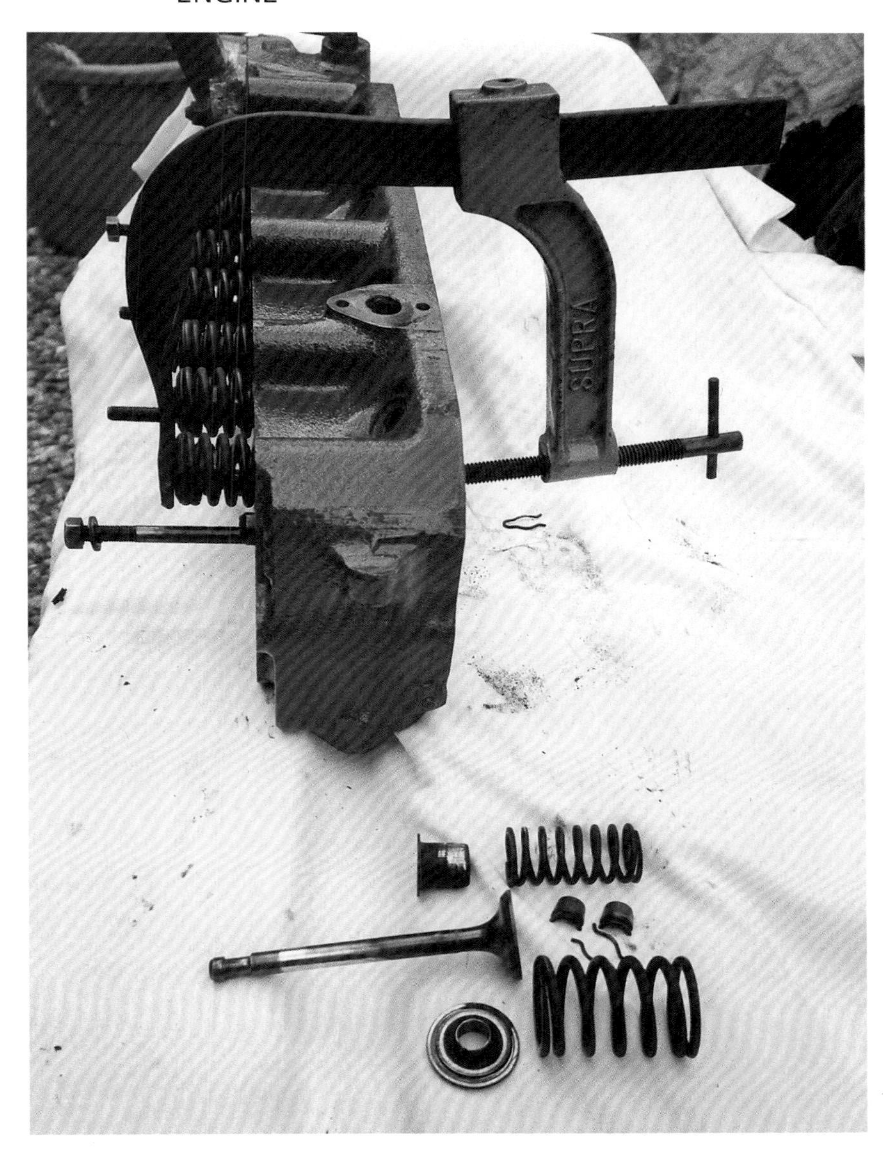

Fig. 8.8. Removing valves with a spring compressor.

or removing shims of varying thickness. On engines with bucket tappets, before removing the camshaft you need to measure the gap between the top of the bucket tappet and the cam lobe, using a feeler gauge. Note the clearances so that you can make any corrections easily before refitting the camshaft, and keep each valve's shim or shims identified so that they can be refitted in their original locations if necessary.

Many modern cars have hydraulic tappets, which cannot be adjusted. Hydraulic tappets take up the valve clearance automatically, and work using engine oil pressure. For this reason, hydraulic tappets may be noisy when an engine is first started up after overhaul.

Remove the camshaft(s) and/or rocker gear, and where applicable the bucket tappets and any shims, then remove the valves. If bucket tappets and shims are fitted, they should be stored in their correct order (if hydraulic self-adjusting tappets are fitted, they should be stored upright in an oil bath). The valves should be placed in a rack in correct order – an upturned shoe box with a line of holes pierced in it will do. Remove the valves by depressing each spring using a spring compressor until you can take out the split collets (or other means of securing the spring), then slide the valves out. If valve stem oil seals are fitted (these are usually fitted to the top face of the cylinder head to prevent oil from passing from the rocker cover into the combustion chambers), they should be removed, and new ones should be fitted before refitting the valves. The seat on which each valve closes, and the valve itself, should have an uninterrupted

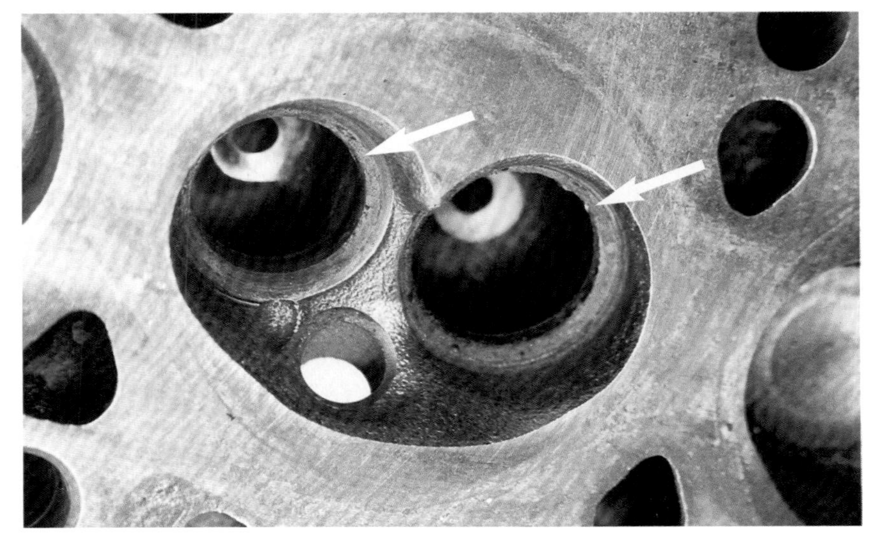

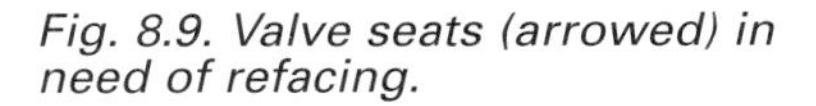

Fig. 8.9. Valve seats (arrowed) in need of refacing.

Fig. 8.10. Valve refitted with new oil seal (arrowed) in position.

Fig. 8.11. Valve-grinding tool in action.

surface of light grey, and there should be no sideways play between the valve stem and its guide.

If the valve or valve seat is pitted, then the valve must be ground in. Valve grinding is done by smearing the seat with a small quantity of fine grinding-in paste, available in small tins from accessory shops, and rotating the valve backwards and forwards in light contact with its seat. A special tool, which consists of a rubber sucker on a wooden handle to hold between the palms of the hands, can be used to rotate the valve. After a few seconds, remove the valve and wipe it and the seat clean with a cloth soaked in paraffin. This will get rid of the paste so that you can examine the mating faces. Stop grinding as soon as you have an unbroken ring of light grey metal on both valve and seat, and clean well with the cloth and paraffin to ensure that all traces of the paste are removed.

If valve grinding has been done many times before, the valve seat may be recessed and the head of the valve may be too thin to be serviceable, in which case both must be renewed. Valve seats are usually shrunk into place, and renewal is a job for the engine specialist. If your engine was designed to run on 4-star petrol and you want to convert it to unleaded, now is the time to have the exhaust valve seats changed. If the valve guides are at all worn, they can be renewed at the same time.

Check the cylinder block mating face of the head with a straight-edge to ensure that it has not warped. If it has, you will need to ask an engine specialist to skim it for you, if this is possible. Not all heads can be skimmed, and you will need to check the manufacturer's recommendations to see if, and by how much, this can be done.

Fig. 8.12. The refinished valves and seats.

Where applicable fit new valve stem oil seals, then refit the valves and their springs – new springs if the engine has been standing for a long time (note that some engines have more than one spring per valve).

Use a new head gasket, and bolt the head back on the block. Bear in mind that on many modern engines, new bolts must be used when refitting the cylinder head. The cylinder head bolts or nuts must be tightened evenly in the correct sequence, and a diagram will be given in the workshop manual, together with the torque values for the bolts or nuts. These are tightened to the specified value with a torque wrench, tightening them a little at a time in order not to crack the head. If there is no diagram, then start in the middle and work in a spiral pattern.

If the engine has bucket tappets and shims, or hydraulic self-adjusting tappets, the tappets (and shims, where applicable) should be coated with oil, and then refitted in their original positions.

If you are carrying out a complete overhaul, you should look at the rocker bushes, if the engine is equipped with rockers, and ensure that they are in good condition. If the camshaft or shafts lie in the head, you will be able to examine their bearings, but before doing so check the arrangements for adjusting the tappets.

The camshaft(s) and/or rocker gear can now be refitted. On overhead camshaft engines, refit the timing-belt or chain, making sure that you have the timing correct and that the tensioning device is in working order. On engines with timing belts, it is advisable to fit a new belt, as if a belt breaks whilst the engine is running it can cause serious damage. Where applicable, check the valve clearance adjustment as recommended in the workshop manual, then refit the rocker cover using a new seal. Clean the engine down with white spirit and paint it. Special engine paint, which is heat and oil resistant, is available in a range of colours.

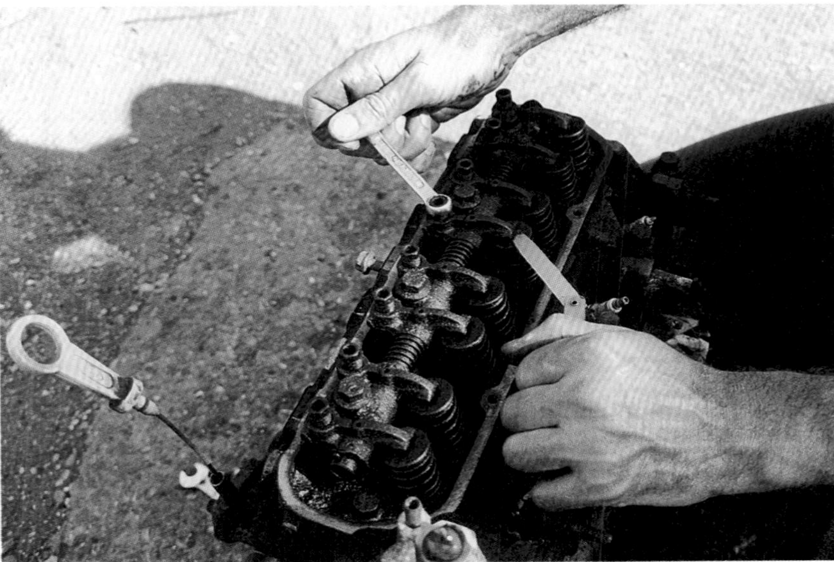

Fig. 8.13. Adjusting the tappets on an OHV engine.

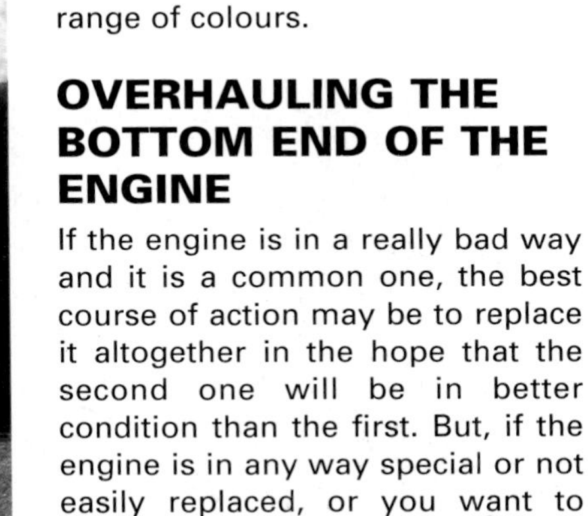

OVERHAULING THE BOTTOM END OF THE ENGINE

If the engine is in a really bad way and it is a common one, the best course of action may be to replace it altogether in the hope that the second one will be in better condition than the first. But, if the engine is in any way special or not easily replaced, or you want to keep the car strictly original, then a complete rebuild will be necessary.

Start as detailed previously, but remove all the ancillaries, the clutch and flywheel, crankshaft, connecting rods and pistons. Do not remove the timing belt or chain, or the timing gears, until you have made sure that you can refit them in exactly their original locations, so that the crankshaft and camshaft(s) are in the same relationship with one another (this is vital to ensure that the correct camshaft timing is maintained). Nearly all engines have some system of marking the components for this purpose. On engines with a camshaft in the crankcase, the chain sprockets are usually marked, either with dots on the teeth or other marks which need to be in exact alignment. On engines

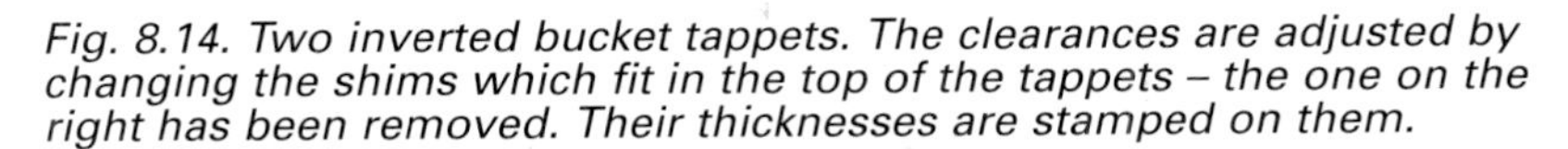

Fig. 8.14. Two inverted bucket tappets. The clearances are adjusted by changing the shims which fit in the top of the tappets – the one on the right has been removed. Their thicknesses are stamped on them.

Fig. 8.15. The timing chain and tensioning device (arrowed), in this case spring-loaded.

with timing belts or chains for overhead camshafts there should be marks on the pulleys or sprockets that coincide with marks on the adjacent castings or casings. These marks are usually designed to coincide when the crankshaft is positioned at TDC on No 1 cylinder.

If no marks are present, then you will need to rotate the engine until No 1 piston is at TDC on the firing stroke, and make your own marks using centre-punch dots or paint. Once satisfied about this you can remove whatever drives the camshaft(s), and the camshaft itself if in the block. If you are working on an overhead camshaft engine, then you will deal with camshaft removal when working on the head.

The rest of the block can now be dismantled. Undo the bolts or nuts holding the connecting rod big-end bearing caps, then lift the bearing caps from the crankshaft journals, first checking to see whether they have identification marks or not. If not, make alignment marks between the bearing caps and rods, and always make sure that the bearing shells are kept in order so that, if they are to be re-used, they can be refitted in their original locations.

The procedure can now be repeated for the main bearing caps, again making sure that all the components are marked, and that the bearing shells are kept in order.

The crankshaft can now be removed, followed by the piston/connecting rod assemblies which are removed by pushing them up through the bores. Again note which way round the various parts go (pistons are usually marked, and any marks on the piston crown normally point towards the front of the engine) and keep them in order. Piston rings can be removed by carefully slipping a feeler gauge blade under one end, and gradually working it round to release the ring from its groove in the piston.

Each piston is secured to the connecting rod by a gudgeon pin, which may have a circlip locating it in the piston, or some other locking device inside the piston itself, which must be undone before the piston can be removed. Modern engines often have gudgeon pins which are an 'interference-fit' in the piston. This means that the pin itself is very slightly larger than the hole for it in the piston. This type of pin is removed by being heated to a certain temperature and then

Fig. 8.16. The valve timing marks on this engine consist of two dots, one on the crankshaft sprocket in line with one of the teeth, and one on the camshaft sprocket in the space between two teeth.

pressed out – or in, and therefore needs to be taken to the agents or a specialist engine restorer who has the right equipment for the job.

Clean the block very thoroughly and check it for cracks which, if they exist, are most likely to be in the water jacket and the result of frost damage. Take out all the core plugs by drilling a hole in them and prising them out with a small chisel or an old screwdriver.

Cracks in cast-iron blocks cannot usually be repaired by welding, because the heat created is likely to warp the block, so other methods have to be used. There are a few specialist firms which are able to repair cracks by means of a 'metalock' process, which consists of drilling, tapping and fitting small, overlapping studs. This is an expensive but effective way of dealing with the problem, but you can repair small cracks in accessible positions yourself by patching.

To patch a crack, first drill a small hole at each end of the crack to stop it spreading, then cut a piece of brass or sheet steel about 16swg thick and shape it according to the shape and size of the crack. Allow a good overlap, but keep to normal geometric shapes such as squares, circles or rectangles, as strange banana shapes look odd. Drill holes in the patch to take, say, 3⁄16in (5mm) screws close enough together so that the heads are spaced about the diameter of a screw head apart. Position the patch over the crack, and use it as a template to drill into the block with the appropriate size of drill, then tap for the appropriate thread. Smear silicone sealant (gasket substitute) liberally on the patch, and press into the crack before screwing the patch firmly down. If you are dealing with an alloy block or head, patching should be done with aluminium or brass plate, and brass screws used, in order to avoid the risk of electrolytic action taking place causing corrosion between ferrous and non-ferrous metals. However, welding – by specialists – is also sometimes possible, and there is a method of reclaiming alloy castings by filling with a chemical compound. The small ads in the motoring press or *Yellow Pages* should be consulted.

Fig. 8.17. Two core plugs (arrowed), one in the head and one in the block.

With the block bare and the core plugs out, this is the time to ensure that the waterways and jackets are completely clear of scale or any other impurities or obstructions. You may find great gooey lumps of emulsified anti-freeze which float about in the system and cause periodic overheating. If you are having work done by the engine specialist, he will soak the block in an unpleasant but effective bath, which will remove everything, including old paint and also any swarf produced by his machining operations.

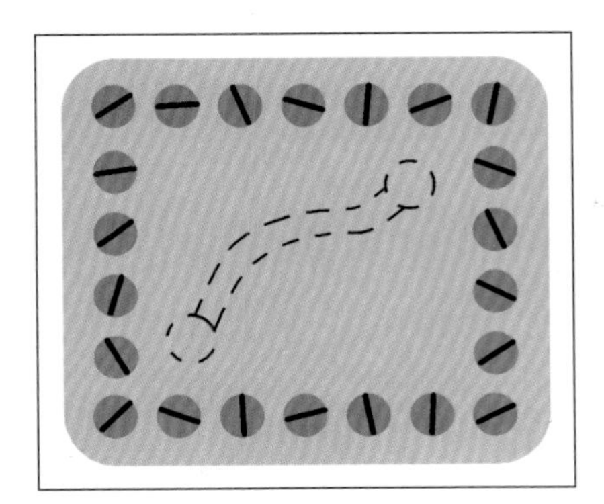

Fig. 8.18. Patching over a crack.

Fit new core plugs, first smearing the machined surface of the hole with silicone sealant, and put in the core plug with the domed side outwards. Tap the top of the dome with a hammer until it

Fig. 8.19. A selection of different types and sizes of core plugs. Those on the left are domed and are fitted with the dome outwards – the dome is then tapped which flattens the plug and pushes it into its circular housing. The other type, cup-shaped, are slightly tapered and merely tapped gently into their housing.

flattens and fits snugly into the machined recess, thus making a watertight seal.

CRANKSHAFT

The crankshaft has an oilway running through it that allows oil under pressure to be supplied to the main bearings and big-end bearings. As the crankshaft revolves at speed it acts as a centrifuge, and carbon and other impurities tend to separate out and attach themselves to the walls of the oilway, thus reducing its bore and its ability to pass oil to the bearings. It is therefore essential to clean the oilway.

Loosen the deposits by soaking the crankshaft in paraffin, then poke out the dirt and debris, if necessary using a drill of the correct size turned by hand, and finish off with a blast of compressed air.

Next fit the main-bearing shell halves into their housings in the crankcase and bearing caps, ensuring that they are a snug fit (and, therefore, the right way round) and that any oil holes coincide.

Fit the crankshaft, making sure that it is the right way round. The thrust-bearing halves need fitting (if they are not incorporated in the main bearing shell halves), and also the rear (and front, where applicable) main-bearing oil seal retainer or ring, all well lubricated. Fit the bearing caps, again checking that they are the right way round, and torque them up to their correct value, using new bolts if specified. On completion, turn the crankshaft to ensure that all is well and, where applicable, lock the bearing cap nuts or bolts with the tab washers.

PISTONS AND CONNECTING RODS

Fit the piston rings. Piston rings are made of cast iron and are very brittle, so need careful handling. New rings should come with instructions as to which ring goes into which piston groove. Check the rings to ensure that you get them the right way up. If this is important the word 'top' etched into the top of the ring will show you. Liberally lubricate the grooves in the piston and, using three thin strips of metal (such as old feeler gauge blades) equally spaced around the piston, slide the rings into place from the top. The instructions will tell you whether the rings need 'gapping' or not. The ring gap is the clearance between the ends of the rings when they are compressed in the bore of the cylinder. As a guide, the usual value is 0.001in (one thousandth of an inch) or 0.025mm for each 1in (25mm) of diameter. To measure this, the piston is placed in the bore and a ring is slid down on top of it to ensure that it is at right-angles to the cylinder wall. The gap is measured with feeler gauges and adjusted by filing the end of the ring with a fine file.

Fig. 8.20. A piston/connecting rod assembly with the three rings removed. Note that the bottom (oil control) ring is thicker and is slotted.

Some pistons have pegs in the grooves to position the rings; if not locate the gaps at equal distances round the circumference.

Lubricate the gudgeon pin bushes and the small-end of the connecting rod, and fit the pin together with its locking device, often a circlip. Connecting rods sometimes have the word 'front' stamped on them, and pistons usually have an arrow or some other indication pointing towards the front of the engine – the front of the engine is the timing cover end – so ensure that the piston is fitted the correct way round on the connecting rod.

Lubricate the pistons and bores and, using a ring-compressor tool or a large worm-drive clip lightly tightened over the rings, tap the assembly very gently into the bore from the top, using the wooden handle of a hammer on the top of the piston. If you are using the original pistons, ensure that they go back into their original cylinders and are fitted to their original connecting rods.

Next fit the main-bearing shell halves into their housings in the connecting rods and bearing caps, ensuring that they are a snug fit (and, therefore, the right way round) and that any oil holes coincide.

Pull each connecting rod down onto its crankshaft journal, then refit the bearing cap, again checking that it is the correct way round, and torque it up to the correct value, using new bolts if specified. Turn the crankshaft after fitting each piston/connecting rod assembly to ensure that all is well.

CAMSHAFT (OHV ENGINES)

If the camshaft lives in the block, now is the time to refit it, ensuring that the timing marks coincide – you did carefully note these when you stripped the engine, of course, as if they are not in their right places the engine will not run and may suffer considerable damage if the valves touch the pistons. A new timing chain or belt, properly tensioned, should be fitted, and where applicable the cam followers should be replaced in their original bores. The timing cover, if there is one, should be refitted using a new gasket and also a new oil seal for the nose of the crankshaft.

OIL PUMP

The oil pump probably lives in the sump, although on some modern engines the pump fits over the crankshaft nose at the front of the engine and is driven by flats on the crankshaft. In either case, the pump deserves some attention. If you have done major work to the engine it would be a false economy not to fit a replacement, but it is sometimes possible to buy replacement moving parts and rebuild the oil pump yourself. There are various checks that you can make to assess condition, depending on type, but on all of them endfloat of the moving parts is important. Remove the pump cover and, with a straight-edge across the housing, measure the clearance of the rotors with a feeler gauge. In general, if the clearance is more than about 0.005in (0.127mm), a new pump should be fitted, or new internals if they are available. Check that the oil pick-up pipe is sound and securely connected to the pump.

Clean out the 'gunge' from the sump and the gauze, and fit new gaskets or a smear of silicone sealant (as applicable), being

Fig. 8.21. An improvised piston ring compressor, a worm-drive clip and three short pieces of metal do all that is necessary, but should be well lubricated.

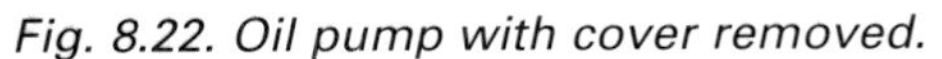

Fig. 8.22. Oil pump with cover removed.

Fig. 8.23. Testing the endfloat of the oil pump rotors with a feeler gauge and a straight edge.

especially careful of any joints over the front and rear of the crankshaft. Bolt the sump down, working from side to side to ensure that the gasket or sealant is evenly compressed.

WATER PUMP

The water pump cannot usually be serviced. If it appears to be sound and not leaking, and if it turns freely without grating and has no undue end-play, it is probably usable and needs no further attention. It is always sensible to fit new hoses to the cooling system.

DISTRIBUTOR

The various ancillaries can now be refitted, renewing or refurbishing as necessary, and using new gaskets throughout. Be particularly careful with the distributor on older engines. On many cars the drive to the distributor has an offset slot in it so that the distributor can only be refitted in one position, but if you have had the engine completely stripped, or the distributor has a gear drive, you will have to re-time it.

To ensure that a distributor is refitted in the correct position, turn the engine until the piston on No 1 cylinder (normally the one nearest the timing belt/chain end of the engine) is at 'top dead centre' (TDC). At TDC, the piston will be at the very top of its stroke with both of the valves closed. Normally there is a TDC mark on the engine casting near the rim of the crankshaft pulley, which also has a mark on its edge, or a small nick in it. The marks should coincide when No 1 piston is at TDC. Alternatively, there may be a TDC mark on the flywheel which can be seen through a 'window' in the surrounding casting.

Refit the distributor, and engage the drive so that with the distributor in position the rotor arm is pointing to the contact in the cap that will be connected to No 1 sparking plug. Final precise adjustment can be made later.

Fig. 8.24. An offset drive dog on the distributor drive ensures that the distributor cannot be refitted the wrong way round.

TIMING BELT

If the camshaft is driven by means of a toothed belt, it is wise to renew it while it is easy to get to. The manufacturers state that these belts should be changed at certain intervals varying between about 35,000 and 65,000 miles (56,000 and 104,000km). Since you are unlikely to know when the belt was fitted, renewal is a wise precaution, as on many engines a failed belt can mean that the tops of the pistons will come into violent and expensive contact with the valves.

It is essential that the timing marks on the belt pulleys are correctly aligned with the marks on the appropriate castings or covers, and that the crankshaft and camshaft(s) are not allowed to move while the belt is being fitted. The slack in the belt is taken up by a tensioner which will have to be released before the belt can be removed. When fitting the new belt, always follow the belt tensioning procedure given in the workshop manual.

FLYWHEEL AND CLUTCH

The flywheel and clutch can now be dealt with. The clutch is removed by undoing the bolts securing the cover plate to the flywheel, slackening each a little at a time. The face of the flywheel should be smooth and not scored. If it is scored, it can be skimmed in a lathe. Examine the starter ring gear for wear. An engine tends always to stop in the same position, which means that the starter pinion, which engages the ring rather brutally on many engines, does so at the same place each time. If the ring gear is not too badly worn, refit the flywheel at 180 degrees from its original position if this is possible. If

Fig. 8.25. Flywheel ring gear removed by drilling hole.

the ring gear is unserviceable, on many engines it can be renewed, but on some modern engines the ring gear is integral with the flywheel and so the complete flywheel must be renewed.

If a ring gear is to be renewed, remove it from the flywheel by drilling between two of the teeth and splitting it with a cold chisel. Polish four opposing parts of the new ring and heat it evenly by means of an oxy-acetylene flame until it reaches a temperature of about 315°C, when the polished portions will turn a dark blue colour. The ring should be held at this temperature for a few minutes to give it time to expand. It is then slipped over the flywheel, tapped gently on to its register, and left to cool.

Inspect the clutch cover plate and driven plate, and renew if necessary. (If in any doubt about clutch components, it is always best to renew them when the engine is out, as it tends to be a big job when all is assembled in the car). Refit the clutch, but do the bolts up finger-tight only at this stage, as it is necessary to centralise the driven plate. This is done by using a plug with two diameters, one to fit into the end of the crankshaft where there is a bush (the spigot bush), and the other with the same diameter as the splined hub of the driven plate. If you have access to a lathe you can quickly make a suitable tool, or you can borrow one from your local garage, although universal tools are now cheap, so it may be worth buying one from an accessory shop. The tool is engaged with the spigot bush in the crankshaft, and then the driven plate is moved until the alignment is correct, when the tool can be fully engaged with both the spigot bearing and the driven plate. The bolts in the clutch cover are then tightened progressively and the tool can be withdrawn.

STORING THE REBUILT ENGINE

The engine is now complete and ready for installation. If it is not to be used for some time, pour about an egg-cup-full of oil into each cylinder, loosely fit the spark plugs and, to exclude dirt, cover any apertures with masking tape. Put oil in the sump and occasionally turn the engine over to circulate the oil. In my experience, the reason why unused engines are often difficult to start is that they become dry as oil drains away from the piston rings, which will then not hold compression. When the engine is churned over by the starter in a dry state it does it no good at all, until oil circulates and spreads to the rings, which often takes a long time and causes unnecessary wear. I once rebuilt an engine and kept it for three years before installing it and attempting to start it. It fired at the second attempt and started at the third, which I felt was not too bad, but it was only because this procedure had been followed.

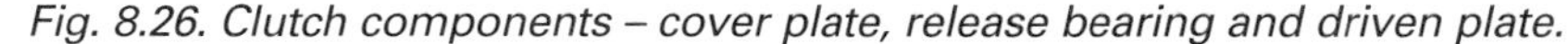

Fig. 8.26. Clutch components – cover plate, release bearing and driven plate.

Chapter 9

Drive train

GEARBOXES

The drive train consists of the gearbox, differential and the components that transmit power and motion from the engine to the driving wheels.

Gearboxes are enclosed, and with the exception of those which share their oil with the engine (such as that fitted to the Mini), are not subject to contamination from combustion and its by-products. Therefore, if they have not been physically abused by constant misuse in service, gearboxes are extremely reliable and usually outlive the car and engine. If the car is front-wheel-drive, the gearbox may either be a separate unit, or may share the engine sump, as on the Mini. If the car is rear-wheel-drive, the gearbox will in all probability be a separate unit, bolted to the engine – except in the case of some Morgans where it is bolted to the chassis and driven by a short shaft from the clutch. A very few cars, like some Alfa Romeos, have the gearbox mounted at the rear as part of the final-drive unit.

Most cars with mid- or rear-mounted engines, like many of their front-wheel-drive counterparts, have gearboxes which are part of a 'transaxle' which includes the differential and the complete drive train.

If you are using a second-hand gearbox, and you drove the donor car, you would have noted whether the gears were unduly noisy, difficult to select, and whether the lever jumped out of gear on the overrun (this was common with 2nd gear on some BMC boxes). If you know of any problems, they will need to be rectified, or it may be wiser to seek a different gearbox, but if there are no problems the box is best left alone apart from draining the oil and refilling with the correct grade.

Should work be necessary, and if you are not able to use an alternative box, you can either have a go at overhauling the box yourself or send it to the specialists. If you decide to do it yourself, you will need the appropriate workshop manual to show you step-by-step what is involved with that particular gearbox and what specialist tools are needed. The manual may also tell you the likely causes of any problems and their cure. If you have experienced difficulty in changing gear, the first suspect is likely to be the clutch. If this does not disengage properly, engaging gear to start, and subsequent changes, can often be noisy and awkward.

Automatic gearboxes are not really a do-it-yourself job as, in addition to being complex, they need special equipment for testing and setting-up. If the control linkage is in order, fill the box to the specified level with the correct fluid. If it still does not work satisfactorily, you will have to consult the experts or change the box for a better one.

Fitting a non-standard gearbox

It is sometimes desirable to mate the engine to a non-standard gearbox if you need different ratios, or if you want a five-speed box instead of a four.

If the two units are from the same manufacturer, and were used

Fig. 9.1. Gearbox bellhousing and adaptor plate.

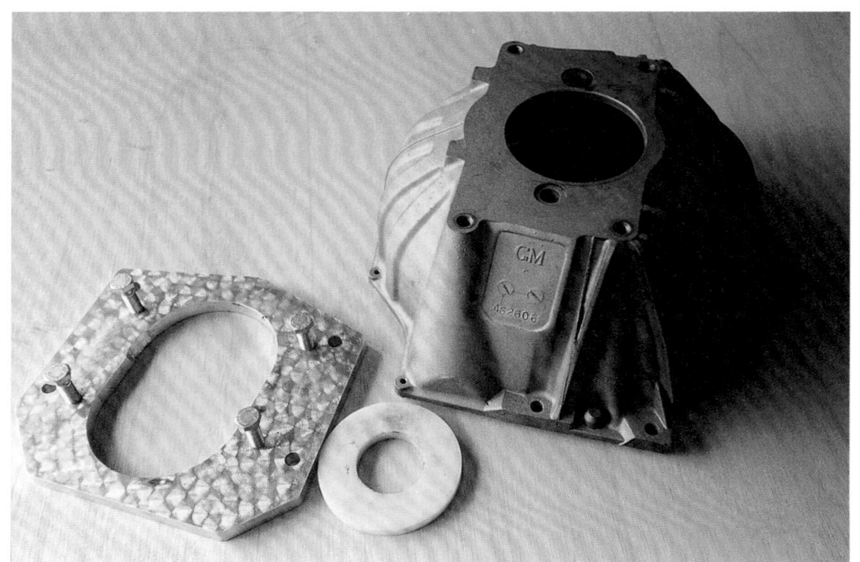

together in one of the vehicles in the manufacturer's range, there should be little difficulty, as the various fittings and dimensions are probably compatible. The trouble arises when you want to fit units from two manufacturers together, such as a Chevrolet bellhousing and a Jaguar gearbox.

The first thing to establish is whether the gearbox input shaft spigot is long enough to fit into the spigot bearing in the end of the crankshaft. If it is, then the bush in the crankshaft will need to be of a suitable diameter to accept the gearbox input shaft spigot. If necessary, a bronze bush can be turned up to suit.

Once the gearbox input shaft fits into the crankshaft spigot bearing, the thickness of the adaptor plate can then be established. The dimensions and layout of the bellhousing fixings on the engine unit shown are quite different from those of the gearbox, so an adaptor plate had to be made to enable the two units to be connected. An adaptor plate has to be of adequate strength for the power to be transmitted. In this case, as the 'Chevy' produces some 500 brake horsepower, the plate is of substantial thickness. The white plastic ring is necessary not for structural reasons, but to centre the gearbox, and as it has to remain in situ while the two units are bolted together, it cannot subsequently be removed. The most precise workmanship is required in order to ensure exact alignment of the gearbox input shaft and engine crankshaft, since there is no form of universal joint to compensate for inaccuracies.

Gearchange mechanism

The gearchange mechanism may need alteration before fitting into a special. Front-wheel-drive gear linkages that depend on levers and cables are sometimes slow and can often be improved by the fitting of new bushes and, where applicable, careful adjustment of cable length. If you are using a front-wheel-drive

Fig. 9.2. Bellhousing and adaptor plate bolted into position between engine and gearbox casing.

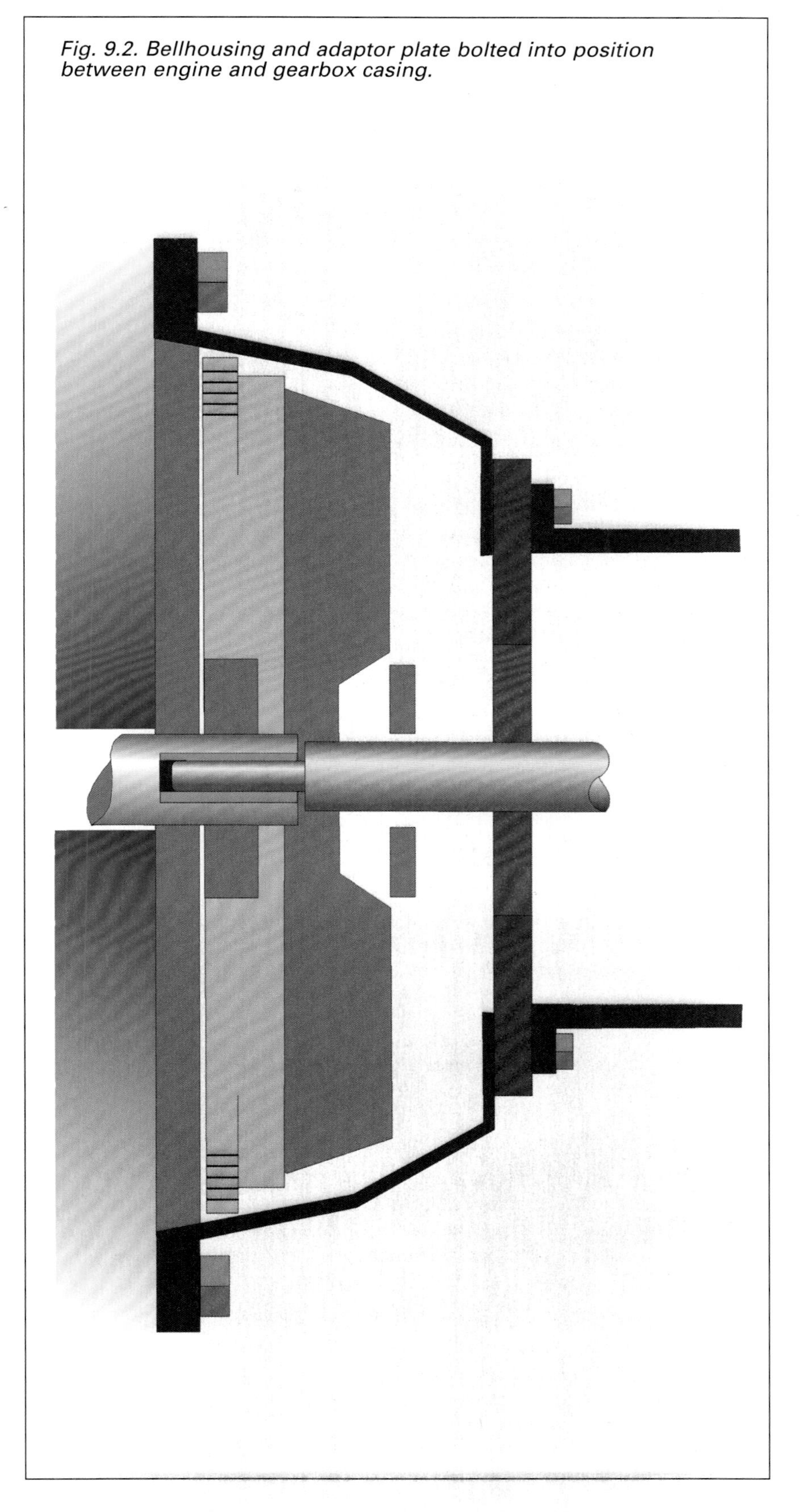

set-up for a mid-engined special, you will need to redesign the linkage anyway.

Remote-control gearchange systems, such as those found on some BMC cars, are sometimes too long to be comfortable in a small special, as they bring the lever too far back. These can be altered by cutting a piece out of the outer aluminium casting, and a piece of exactly the same length out of the internal actuating rod, and welding them together again.

On the other hand, the Ford mechanism on the crossflow engine gearboxes used by so many special builders is not 'remote' enough. Although the gear lever on these gearboxes can be bent to bring it into a better position, this makes selecting reverse a two-handed job, or at least a very awkward one, as it is necessary to depress the lever to engage reverse.

A very satisfactory remote change can be easily made for the

Fig. 9.3. Reverse locking catch. If you have a Ford Escort gearbox and want to make a remote gear change, this is the part you need to remove (see text).

crossflow engine gearbox and others of similar construction, based on an old track-rod end, with the added advantage that a Ferrari-type gate can be incorporated! It is first necessary to remove the hardened steel reverse catch plate that protects reverse from accidental engagement on the standard mechanism. This plate fits inside the gear lever housing, so the existing lever has to be removed by unscrewing the large plastic domed nut that surrounds it, and then lifting it out. The circular plate that blanks off the very end of the tube must be tapped out from inside the housing, which will allow the reverse catch (a small hardened-steel plate in the right-hand side of the housing) to be tapped out backwards through the blanking-plate hole. Replace the circular plate, and cut down the original gear lever before refitting it. Reverse gear can now be selected without the need to depress the lever.

The mechanism for the extension is easy to construct, and a mock-up is shown in *Figs.9.4 and 9.5*. Also illustrated is the open gate, made in this case from a piece of hard aluminium plate. This should have a catch to blank-off reverse gear, thereby preventing accidental engagement (the locking catch on the gearbox-mounted gearchange mechanism

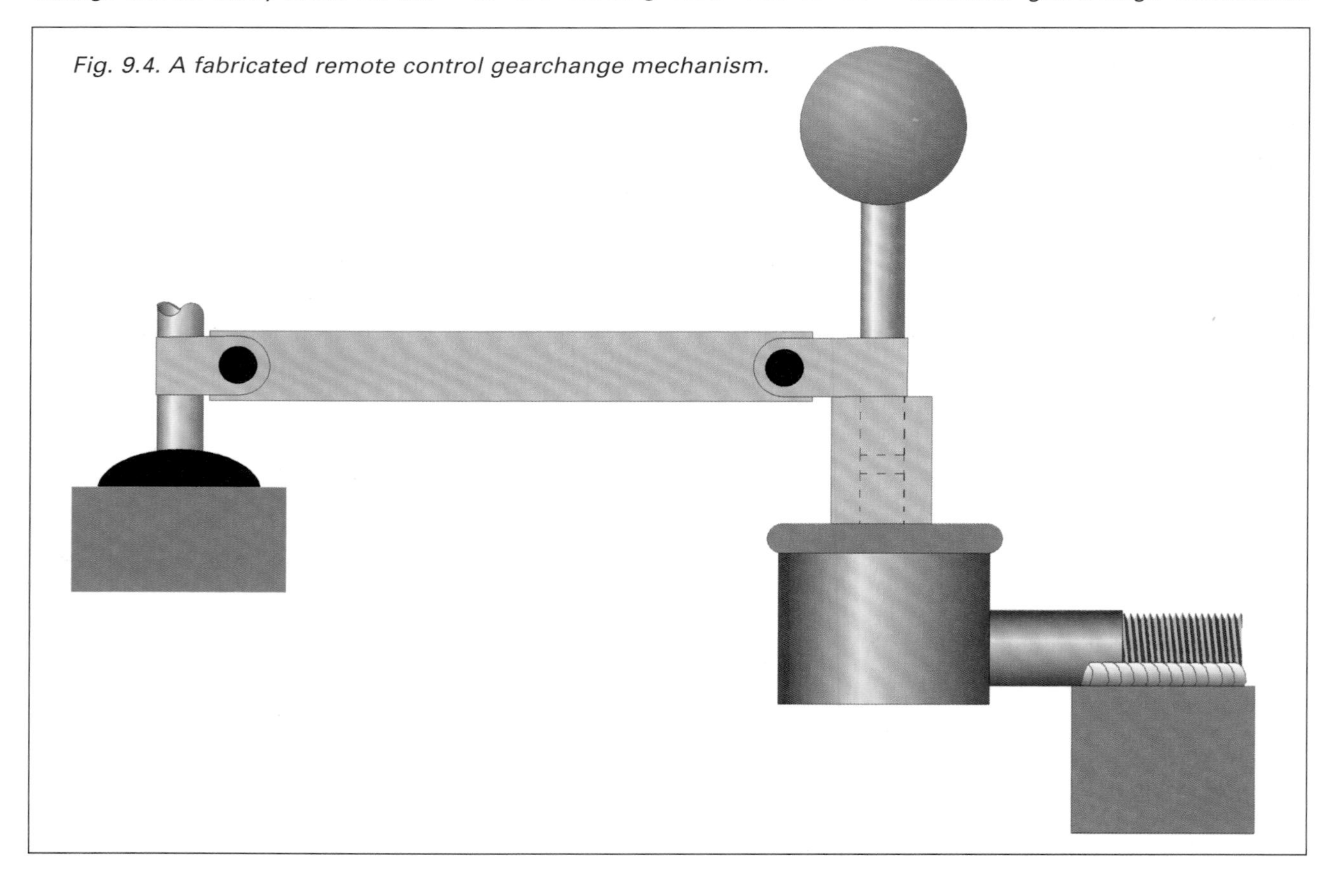

Fig. 9.4. A fabricated remote control gearchange mechanism.

Fig. 9.5. The fabricated mechanism fitted to a chassis.

Fig. 9.6. Open 'Ferrari-style' gearchange gate. Reverse should have a protective catch, similar to that shown in Fig. 13.7.

has been removed in order to allow the remote-control mechanism to operate). A gear-lever knob of your choice or manufacture will add to the individuality of your creation.

DRIVE SHAFTS

On front-wheel-drive cars, and rear-engined ones, motion is transmitted from the engine/gearbox assembly to the wheels by two drive shafts. On rear-wheel-drive cars, drive is taken from the gearbox via a single propeller shaft to the back axle (or to the differential on a car with independent rear suspension), and then by half-shafts to the wheels.

With a front-wheel-drive set-up or a transaxle, the drive shafts are an integral part of the system and cannot be easily altered, especially if you are using the subframe and suspension, so maintenance and renewal of parts is all that is practicable. The most common problem is wear in the constant velocity (CV) joints, which permit the drive shafts to move with the suspension and steering. Worn CV joints usually make themselves heard in no uncertain manner by very audible clicks or knocks, especially when cornering, and the only cure is renewal. Even if the CV joints are in good condition, check the condition of the rubber boots, because a split will allow the grease to escape which will cause the joint to wear. A split drive shaft boot will also mean an automatic MoT failure.

PROPELLER SHAFT

On a front-engined, rear-wheel-drive car with a solid rear axle, the drive to the rear axle consists of a tube (propeller shaft) with a universal joint at each end. The universal joint at the gearbox end is attached to a splined shaft which slides in the gearbox output shaft, and the universal joint at the other end is secured to the differential. If the propeller shaft is long, it is often split into two and supported at its centre by a bearing attached to the chassis, with an additional universal joint in the centre.

It is unlikely that you will need a split propeller shaft on a special, unless it is very big, in which case you will need to make adequate provision on a chassis cross-member to mount the bearing. If your special is a compact sports car, you may have to shorten a single shaft in order to make it fit. This can be done as follows.

Keep intact the splined end of the shaft that fits into the gearbox, and cut the other end, having first marked the position of the universal-joint 'yokes', as it is essential that you refit the rear joint in the same position relative to the front one, with the yokes lying in the same plane.

If the car is still in bare chassis form, load the rear so that it takes up the approximate stance of the finished car. Slide the splined end of the shaft fully into the gearbox, and mark the shaft at the point where it emerges from the end of the gearbox (you are effectively marking the depth the shaft engages with the gearbox). Withdraw the shaft from the end of the gearbox, then measure the

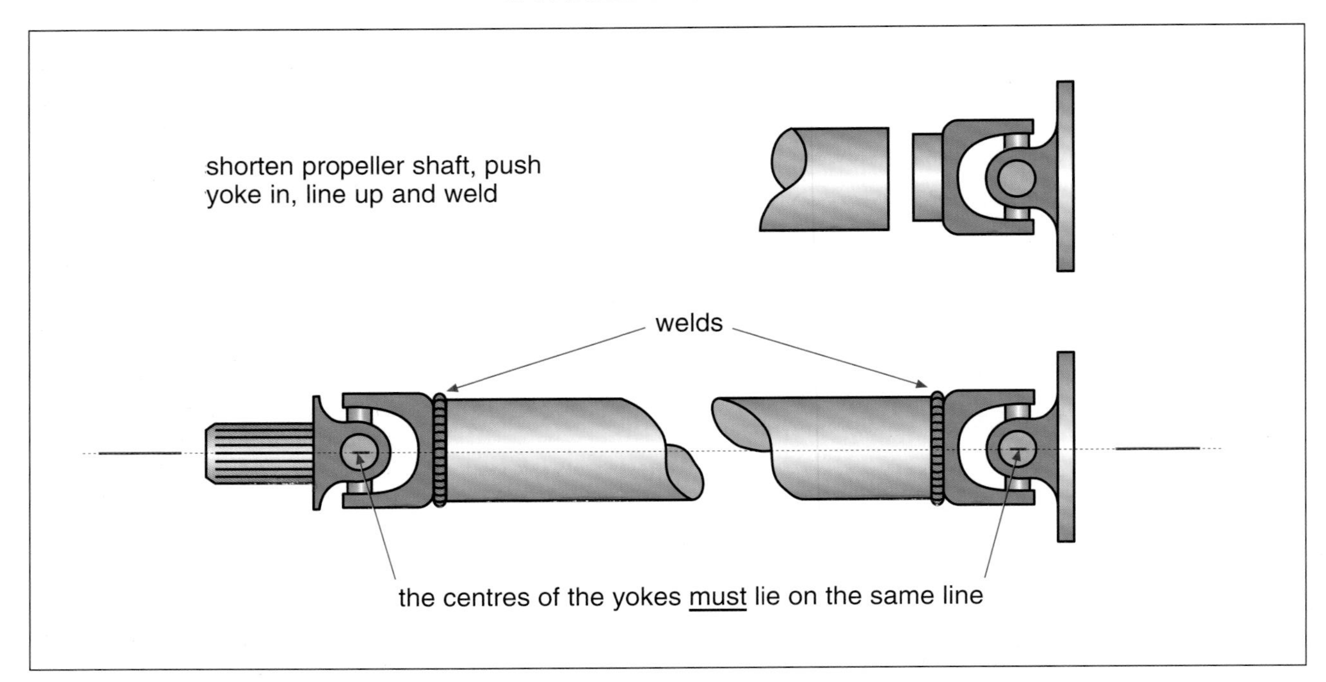

Fig. 9.7. Shortening a propeller shaft.

total length of engagement. Now measure halfway along the total length of engagement, add about ½in (13mm) for safety's sake, and make a second mark on the splined end of the shaft. Position the propeller shaft so that this second mark is aligned with the end of the gearbox, and hold the other end of the shaft against the flange of the differential. Make a mark at the differential end of the shaft, in line with the end of the differential flange. You will now be able to work out the correct length to which the shaft should be cut. Make sure that the shaft is cut accurately at right-angles to its length, and make sure that you mark the position of the universal joint yokes, as it is essential to refit the joint in the same position relative to the front one, with the yoke lying in the same plane.

You now need to prepare the universal joint you have just cut off so that it can be welded back to the shaft. This means removing the remains of the tube still attached to the joint. If you have a lathe this is relatively easy, otherwise it is a bit of a pain, as you have to part the weld. However, a hacksaw-cut all round, and a hammer and cold chisel will remove the remains of the tube, and then some filing will make it a snug fit in the end of the cut-down tube, to which it now has to be welded. When welding on the joint, ensure that the front and rear universal joints are aligned as noted before the rear joint was removed.

Should you need a longer propeller shaft rather than a shorter one, you will need mild steel tubing of about 16swg (1.5mm) for the main body of the shaft, and you will obviously have to remove the front universal joint with its splined shaft, as well as the rear universal joint, and refit both to the new length of tube.

Commercially made propeller shafts are balanced. You can have yours balanced by a specialist, but this is rarely necessary. It is worthwhile trying the car out first to see whether there is any unacceptable vibration.

If the car you are building has independent rear suspension then, as the differential is fixed (and does not move with the suspension), you will need a universal joint only at the front of the propeller shaft to allow for misalignment or flexing of the chassis/body.

Universal joints can wear and should be checked before being used. Some, like those used by Ford, are not repairable and if they are worn or damaged, a reconditioned shaft must be obtained. Repair kits are available for other types of joint, and the kits contain the necessary rollers, bushes and circlips. Pack the components well with molybdenum grease when refitting.

FINAL DRIVE

Cars with live rear axle

Rear-wheel-drive may be either by means of a 'live' axle, with the differential and half-shafts enclosed in a casing, or of the independent variety. Live axles give very little trouble in service, and if yours does you will be unlucky. The differential provides the means of transferring the drive from the propeller shaft to the rear wheels, and also automatically adjusts the speed of each of the wheels when cornering, since the outer wheel has to move faster

Fig. 9.8. Crown wheel and pinion, and differential carrier.

than the inner one to make up for the increased distance it is required to travel.

With one wheel jacked up and the car in gear, or the differential input shaft locked, try turning the raised wheel. If you get less than, say, 2in (50mm) of movement you may assume all is well, and all you need to do is to change the oil. If there is more movement than this, you should be looking for a replacement differential.

If the car is rare and a replacement is not available, drain the oil and remove the rear differential cover. This will lay bare the crown and sun wheels. Rotate them slowly and look for broken teeth and wear, which is usually very obvious from the polish on the teeth where they mate. If the wear is considerable, the teeth may be recessed. The pinion on the input shaft meshes with the crown wheel and is adjustable for mesh, but do not make the mistake of trying to adjust it. Provision is made to enable the mesh to be adjusted when the differential is assembled initially, and if you alter the setting after wear has taken place, you will finish up with a very unpleasant and audible whine. Better to stick with excessive play and to try to source a new crown-wheel-and-pinion set, which you can renew as a paired assembly.

On cars with a live axle, the inner ends of the half-shafts are splined into gears which are called 'sun wheels' and these in turn are connected together by small pinions, called 'planet wheels' or 'star wheels', the whole making up the differential assembly. Some differentials have two, some four, star wheels. Those with two have probably had to work very hard, and will be showing signs of wear in their bearings. These are usually plain bearings, the star wheels being fixed to short axles which run directly in the cast iron carrier. If the bearings have been short of clean lubricant, the female bearing has probably suffered, with consequent 'slop' in the sun wheel, which allows excessive free-play in the transmission. A partial, but effective, cure for this is to line the female bearing surface with a piece of shim steel sheet (obtainable in various thicknesses) cut carefully to size, using the sun wheel's axle as a pattern. Experiment with different thicknesses of shim until the right one has been found that will just allow the axle to enter. As a better long-term cure, it is preferable to bore and ream out the bearing, if there is enough metal, and fit a bush.

There are bearings at each end of the half-shafts. Those in the differential run constantly in oil and rarely give trouble. The ones at the outer ends are often lubricated by the oil in the differential, but are sometimes dependent on being greased, in which case there will be a grease nipple in the hub.

The appearance of oil or grease in the brake drum indicates that the oil seals need to be renewed. The hub on which the wheel is mounted is fitted to splines on the half-shaft, and is secured by a large nut. There should be no movement whatsoever between hub and splines. If you remove the hubs from the half-shafts, you will sometimes see signs of the splines twisting at the root, which suggests constant fierce acceleration, particularly from rest. If the splines have twisted, new half-shafts should be fitted. At one time, broken half-shafts were very common, but over the years the improvement in materials used now makes this a rare complaint.

Cars with independent rear suspension

Cars with independent rear suspension have the final-drive unit attached to the chassis, or body (sometimes on a subframe) and receive the drive from the engine by means of a propeller shaft in the same way as cars with a live axle. Since the differential unit is fixed, the drive shafts must have universal joints, and two are normally fitted to each shaft, the inner joints being splined into the differential sunwheels, or bolted to flanges attached to the sunwheels.

The drive to the wheels on an independent suspension system is by short shafts with universal joints which are usually lubricated 'for life' – or you may have rubber 'doughnuts', in which case 'life' is likely to be short, and if a conversion is offered to metal universal joints it is worth considering.

Many of the principles explained for the differentials fitted to cars with live rear axles apply equally to the differentials fitted to cars with independent rear suspension.

Cars with front-wheel-drive

On front-wheel-drive vehicles the differential and final-drive mechanism is usually integral with the gearbox casing, with the crown wheel driven directly from a pinion in the gearbox, and with the inboard constant velocity joints splined into the differential sunwheels, or bolted to flanges attached to the sunwheels. In most cases it will be necessary to remove the gearbox in order to work on the differential.

Many of the principles explained for the differentials fitted to cars with live rear axles apply equally to the differentials fitted to cars with front-wheel-drive.

Chapter 10

Cooling system

THE EVOLUTION OF COOLING SYSTEMS

Adequate cooling of car engines seems to have caused designers a lot of grief over the years. In the early days, before there had been much development, radiators themselves were not very efficient and were very vulnerable to damage by debris from the roads of the day and from the twisting of frail and flexible chassis. The cooling system was very elementary and described as 'thermo-syphonic'. Fans and water pumps were not fitted. Consequently, hot weather, hills or other circumstances where the car could not travel quickly enough to get sufficient air through the radiator to cool it adequately, meant that the water boiled away merrily. This necessitated long waits by the roadside for the system to cool down enough for more water to be added. (Handbooks contained dire warnings of the danger of undoing the filler cap too soon, and of cracking the engine block by adding cold water to an overheated engine.)

The engine has a 'water jacket' around it, which picks up heat from the cylinders, and cylinder head(s) in particular. As warm water is less dense than cold, it moves upwards through the hose connecting it to the top of the radiator. There the cooling begins, and the water descends through the radiator passages, where it is cooled by the air flowing through the radiator. The water then continues upwards through the engine's water jacket in a continuous cycle.

The addition of a fan helps the flow of air through the radiator when the car is not moving quickly, and a water pump circulates the coolant more quickly so that, when all is working well, coolant temperature remains within reasonable limits.

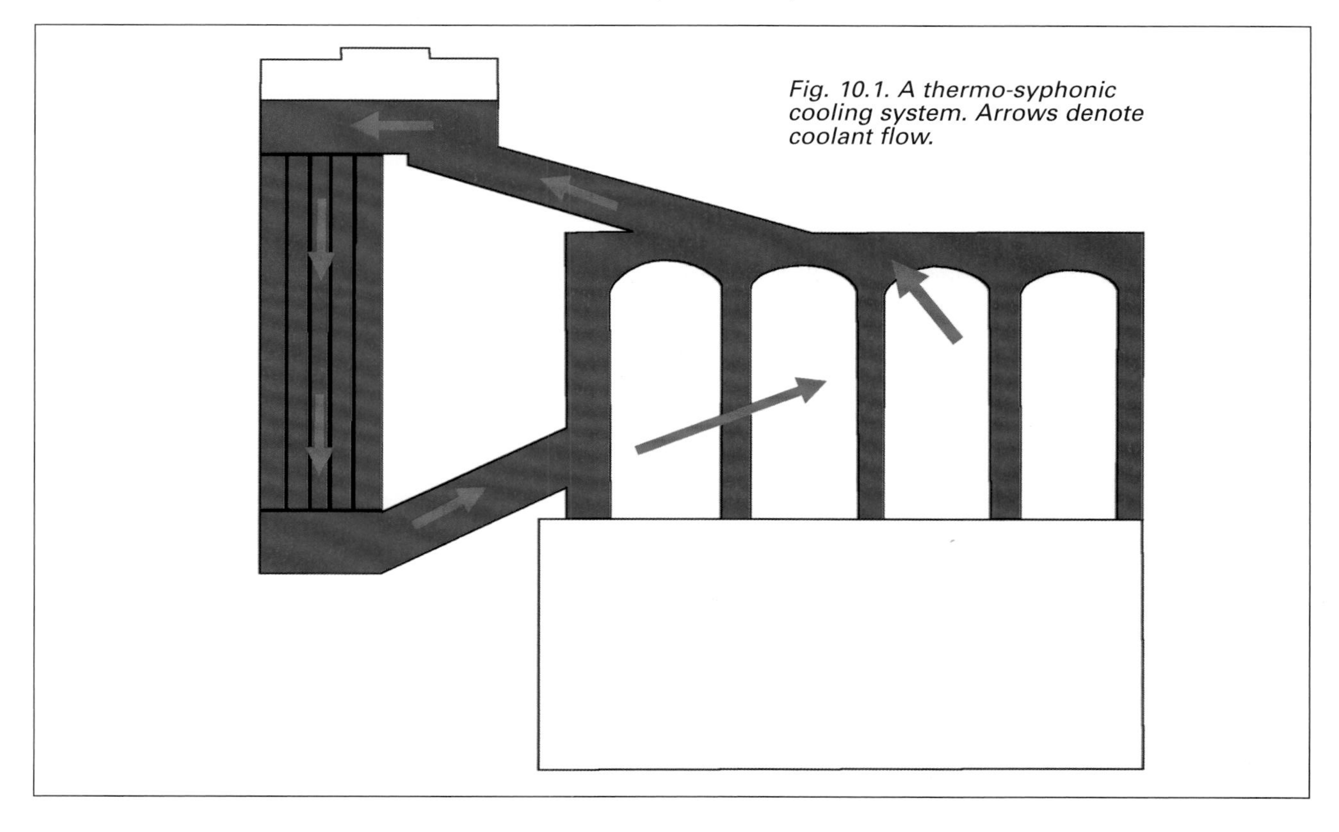

Fig. 10.1. A thermo-syphonic cooling system. Arrows denote coolant flow.

Fig. 10.2. An electric fan and radiator for a small car.

Overheating, or a tendency towards it, can be caused by factors other than the actual cooling system itself. Large engines in small spaces with no proper arrangements for removing the hot air from under the bonnet are likely to suffer. The Alvis TD 21 I once owned, a very fine car, was marginal in this respect, even when I cut louvres in the bonnet to help air to escape. Triumph Stags, for different reasons, are greatly improved by the fitting of radiators with more 'cores' (water passages) and, like most other examples, my Stag now has an additional (electric) fan.

It is significant that, to this day, cars fitted with equipment that will make additional demands on the engine, such as air-conditioning or towing gear, are usually fitted with a second fan. It follows, therefore, that the cooling system of your car needs to be in good order, if you are carrying out a rebuild, and well-designed if you are building a special.

COOLING FANS

Belt-driven fans, common to all vehicles for so many years, were modified in the search for greater efficiency, and the ever-increasing cost of petrol has made designers pay real attention to improved economy. It was eventually realised that for much of the time a belt-driven fan was unnecessary, as the air flow through the radiator was adequate for normal running, coupled with the fact that the fan absorbed about four horsepower (which had to be paid for in petrol) and when the car was travelling at speed could actually reduce air flow through the radiator. So, part-time fans came into being, often driven through a viscous coupling that 'declutched' the fan when it was not needed. Later, with alternators replacing dynamos, a more generous supply of electricity was available, and electric fans became common. Electric fans are switched in and out by a thermostatic switch and are often 'hot wired' (not wired through the ignition switch), which is why they sometimes continue to operate after you have parked the car and switched off the ignition.

Restorers will naturally want to keep their original equipment, but for builders of specials, an electric fan is the only type of fan worth considering. There are two basic types of electric fan, the type with a cylindrical motor found on most modern cars as standard equipment, and the 'pancake' type, with a very slim motor, originally designed as a replacement for the belt-driven version, where often there is very little room between radiator and engine block. Either will do, but the former are far more common.

The fan should be arranged either to blow through the radiator, if in front of it, or to suck air through it if behind. Do make sure that the fan rotates the correct way round. If it does not, reversing the electrical connections will normally alter the direction of rotation. The thermostatic switch that operates the fan should be positioned in the coolant flow, normally in the top hose, header tank, or in the top of the thermostat housing.

RADIATORS

Use either the radiator from the donor car or one of greater capacity, and remember that it is no use expecting a Mini radiator to cool a Jaguar engine. If, however, cooling turns out to be marginal, or you cannot accommodate a radiator with a built-in header tank, you can increase the capacity of the system by fitting a separate header tank.

Before installing the radiator, clean out all the sediment that may have settled in it over the years, by 'back flushing'. Back flushing is carried out by inserting a hosepipe in the bottom radiator outlet, to provide a surge of water in the opposite direction to the normal flow of water through the radiator. This should dislodge and flush away any deposits.

When installing the radiator in the car, it should be positioned in an unobstructed air flow, making sure that there is room to fit the fan.

Make sure that the radiator mountings are not subject to twisting and are sufficiently robust to carry the weight of the radiator when filled with coolant. Rubber mounting blocks or grommets help to prevent vibration and minor shocks being transmitted to the radiator core, which is made of very thin, and consequently quite delicate, material.

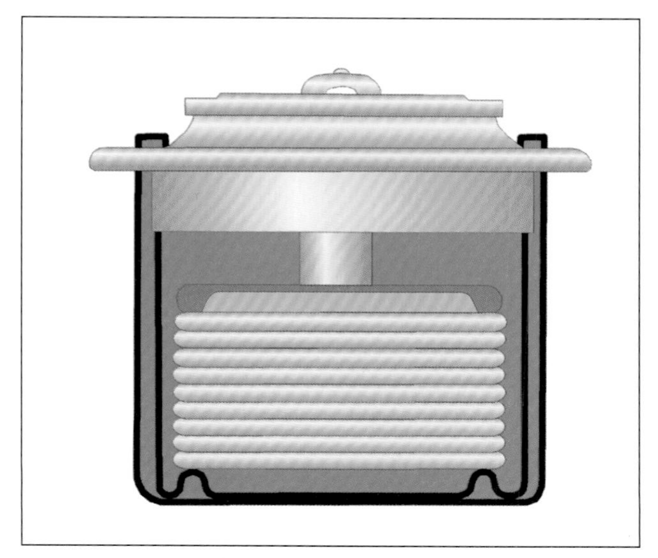

Fig. 10.3. A liquid-filled bellows-type thermostat.

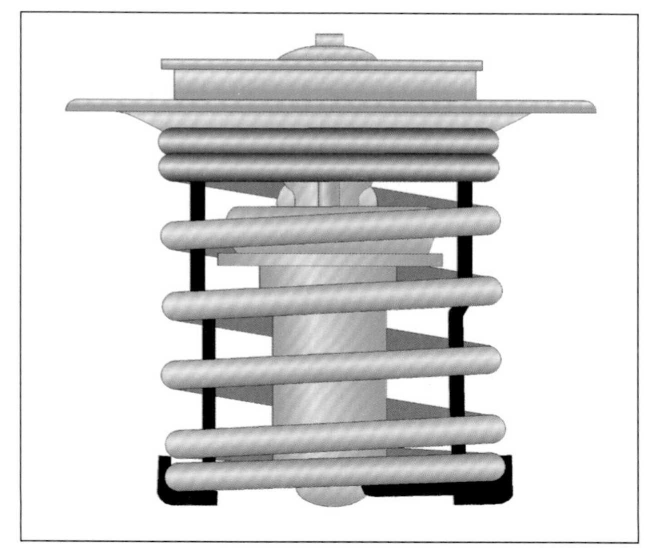

Fig. 10.4. A wax-filled bulb-type thermostat.

THERMOSTATS

The purpose of the thermostat is to keep the engine temperature within the range required for efficient running, and to allow rapid warming-up of the engine by confining the coolant flow to the water jacket until the engine has reached operating temperature. It is worth remembering that if you have a car that consistently overheats, the probability is that the thermostat is faulty (provided you actually have water in the system).

The thermostat, which is normally positioned in a housing at the engine end of the radiator top hose, consists of either a liquid-filled brass bellows, or a wax-filled bulb. The brass bellows type is designed to expand as the coolant warms up, opening a valve at a predetermined temperature, which allows the coolant to flow through the radiator. The wax-filled bulb thermostat is designed so that as the coolant warms up, the wax melts and a piston pushes the valve open against the pressure exerted by a spring.

The liquid-filled type of thermostat is pressure-sensitive (as well as heat-sensitive) and is not recommended for systems working pressures of more than 7psi (0.5 kg/sq cm), whereas the wax type can be used for systems operating up to 15psi (1.05 kg/sq cm). Note that thermostats are available with different opening temperatures, and the opening temperature is normally marked on the body of the thermostat.

If in doubt about which type of thermostat to fit, keep to the original pattern if you are using the original engine/radiator combination.

PRESSURE CAPS

Modern cooling systems work under pressure so that the engine can run at a higher (and more efficient) temperature than can be achieved by a non-pressurised system, and the system cap is really a safety valve that allows pressure to escape at a predetermined figure. The pressure varies, but is often between 13psi to 15psi (0.9 to 1.05kg/sq cm) and should be indicated on the cap.

The pressure cap may be fitted to the radiator or the expansion tank, depending on the age of car and the cooling system layout.

EXPANSION TANK

Modern systems often have an expansion tank, which allows for

Fig. 10.5. An expansion tank.

the fact that the coolant expands as it warms up. As the system cools down, some of the coolant in the expansion tank is drawn back into the radiator to which it is connected by a tube. This type of system rarely needs filling, but should always be checked. Topping up takes place in the expansion tank and should not exceed the level indicated.

PLUMBING

If connecting hoses of the right shape are not available, use convoluted hose which bends easily to almost any shape, and always use new hose clips. Coloured hoses and special fittings to cover the clips are available from specialist suppliers. These look very smart if you are making a feature of the engine, but are expensive.

COOLANT

Antifreeze solution not only lowers the freezing point of the coolant to a level likely to cope with most climates, if used in the correct quantity, but also inhibits corrosion. It is essential to use antifreeze in engines with alloy cylinder heads. It is also very insidious, and will search out any cracks or poor joints in the system, which will then need attending to.

AIR-COOLED ENGINES

Air-cooled car engines are not common, except for those used in the VW 'Beetle', the Citroën 2CV and Fiat 126. Like motorcycle engines, they rely for cooling on air passing over 'fins' on the cylinders and cylinder heads, which increase the surface area and so help the cooling process. Instead of relying on the forward motion of the car to provide the requisite air flow, which would be difficult with a rear-engined car such as the Beetle and 126, a fan is provided to circulate air through ducts that surround the cylinders, and channel it to where it is most needed.

Fig. 10.6. Convoluted hose, worm-drive clips, and cooling system pressure cap. The pressure cap is marked '15psi', the maximum working pressure of the system.

Fig. 10.7. Convoluted hose used as radiator top hose.

The system should be checked to ensure that the fan is working properly, that bearings and drive belts are in good condition, and that there is no damage to the fan blades themselves. Although protected by a grille or mesh, they sometimes come into contact with hard objects, and the resultant damage not only affects the air flow but can cause unwelcome noise, so, check the grilles also. Clean out any debris that may have collected in the system, and ensure that the fins are clean and that the air passages between them are unobstructed. Check the ducting to ensure that it is secure and that none of its fixings are missing, as loose ducting, apart from affecting cooling, can cause a terrible noise, and it is often difficult to get at when the engine is installed in the car.

Chapter 11

Fuel system

THE EVOLUTION OF FUEL SYSTEMS

A petrol engine is fuelled by a mixture of petrol and air in a ratio of about 16 parts of air to one of petrol. Until the early 1990s, every petrol-engined car had a device called a carburettor which measured and mixed the two ingredients, supplying the correct quantities to the engine. In recent years fuel injection systems have replaced carburettors. Early fuel injection systems were operated mechanically but now, much more efficient electronic fuel injection systems are used. Early fuel injection systems had a reputation for being troublesome, such as those fitted to the Triumph 2000 and the TR6, and many proud owners rapidly became less proud and swapped their injection system for carburettors.

CARBURETTORS

Principles of operation

As many of the engines likely to be used by builders of specials and kit cars are fitted with carburettors, we shall consider them first.

The principle of the carburettor is simple. As the engine turns, the descending pistons, with inlet valves open, create a vacuum in the inlet manifold to which the carburettor is attached. Air rushes through the carburettor 'choke' tube into the cylinders to fill the vacuum, and in so doing pulls a small flow of petrol up from a reservoir through a tiny hole called a 'jet'. The airflow is such that it separates the liquid petrol into very fine droplets as it mixes with it. A valve (the 'throttle' or 'accelerator') in the choke tube can be opened or closed progressively to control the flow of the mixture; the more mixture, the more power can be produced by the engine.

Four-cylinder engines that are designed to produce considerable power for their size are often equipped with two carburettors – three for a six-cylinder engine, four for a V8 and some specials in the past have had one carburettor per cylinder, which undoubtedly improved the 'filling' of the cylinders, even if it did not do much for fuel economy.

Many early cars had carburettors mounted low down on the side of the engine to enable them to be gravity-fed from a scuttle-mounted petrol tank (petrol pumps were a long time coming), and the long inlet tract was often of surprisingly narrow bore considering the size of the engine. The superb Rolls-Royce Silver Ghost had its single carburettor on the side of the engine opposite to the inlet manifold, the induction pipe running up and over the cylinder heads. This meant that the mixture from the carburettor had to travel upwards against the force of gravity and against the friction of the narrow tube walls. Air has weight and, as even a small engine can easily consume about 300lb to 400lb (135kg to 180kg) of air per hour, the engine was working unnecessarily hard just to feed itself and, especially when cold, there was a tendency for the petrol

Fig. 11.1. Triple SU carburettors fitted to a Jaguar six-cylinder engine. Air is supplied through a collector box.

Fig. 11.2. Rolls-Royce Silver Ghost. The carburettor is on opposite side of the engine to the inlet valves.

to fall out of the petrol/air mixture suspension.

As gravity feed was replaced by pressure-fed systems, horizontal carburettors with short induction tracts came into use, and eventually some manufacturers began to use vertically-mounted 'downdraught' carburettors, where the force of gravity actually helped the flow of the mixture. The original 328 BMW had three Solex carburettors mounted directly on top of the cylinder heads, which made the engine very tall, but very efficient.

In addition to mixing air and petrol in controllable quantities, carburettors must maintain a supply of petrol at the main jet, make provision for cold starting when a richer mixture (a higher proportion of fuel) is required, and must also provide a richer mixture for acceleration.

Petrol is pumped to a reservoir in the carburettor in which there is a float (the 'float chamber') to maintain the petrol level at a height suitable for the jet to operate satisfactorily. As petrol flows into the float chamber, the float rises and presses against a valve, eventually cutting off the flow. Twin-choke carburettors are actually two separate instruments with a shared float chamber.

On most carburettors there is a valve ('the choke') which cuts down the supply of air to the engine, thus increasing the amount of petrol, or enriching the mixture, to make starting easier. Some carburettors have a small pump that is used to increase the supply of petrol to improve acceleration when the throttle pedal is pressed.

While all carburettors perform the same functions, there are two basic types; the constant-vacuum (or constant depression) type, and the constant-choke type. SU and Stromberg CD carburettors (both of which look like the top of a beer bottle) are examples of the constant-vacuum type, and most Zenith, Ford and Weber carburettors are of the constant-choke variety.

The constant-vacuum type carburettors have pistons or diaphragms (in the 'beer bottle'

Fig. 11.3. An SU constant-vacuum carburettor.

Fig. 11.4. A Stromberg constant-vacuum carburettor.

top) that rise or fall according to the requirements of the engine in response to the driver's demands. These pistons or diaphragms in turn carry a piston that is a close fit in the choke tube, and regulates the airflow through it, and also a tapered needle which fits in the jet to regulate the flow of petrol. As the piston rises to admit more air, so the needle rises to admit more petrol. A constant air velocity and, therefore vacuum, is created over the jet.

The constant-choke type of carburettor has a choke tube which does not vary in size and, therefore, the petrol/air mixture varies with the velocity of the air rushing over the jet orifice, which is not controlled by a needle. Consequently, the more air, the weaker the mixture, and this is compensated for by additional jets and devices which adjust the mixture more closely to the requirements of the engine.

Both types of carburettor rely on a butterfly valve activated by the throttle pedal to vary the quantity of air entering the carburettor, therefore varying the quantity of mixture entering the cylinders in order to produce the required power from the engine. In older, worn carburettors this butterfly valve can produce problems, and this is dealt with later.

For a long time after its introduction in the 1920s, the constant-vacuum carburettor was preferred by the majority of manufacturers for use on their sports cars, although the Weber twin-choke type superseded it in popularity in later years.

Since carburettor manufacturers offer such a wide range of models, mostly to suit the needs of specific engines, you will need to refer to the relevant workshop manual, or owners' club, for details of your particular carburettor. However, some procedures are common, including the need to note carefully where everything fits when dismantling, so that you can reassemble it correctly, especially as in some cases jets can be interchanged by mistake, with disastrous effects on petrol consumption.

Fig. 11.5. A downdraught Weber constant-choke carburettor.

A word of comfort. A very wide range of spares is available from the specialists for Zenith, Stromberg and SU carburettors. Weber spares are also obtainable for many models of carburettor, and Weber can also supply replacement carburettors for a wide range of vehicles that were not originally fitted with Weber units. Some addresses are given at the back of the book.

Servicing carburettors

To service a carburettor, remove it from the manifold and disconnect

Fig. 11.6. A Weber twin-choke constant-choke carburettor.

the various controls and pipes, noting their locations. Clean it thoroughly, preferably with special cleaning fluid which will remove the gummy deposits inside, and dry it carefully. The flange that mounts the carburettor to the manifold is sometimes bowed and should be checked with a straight-edge. If the flange is bowed, the bow can usually be corrected by careful filing. Air entering around this mounting flange upsets the carburation by weakening the mixture, and can cause difficult starting. It can also cause a loud 'raspberry' noise if the gasket is free to vibrate.

Check the throttle-spindle bushes for wear and renew them if badly worn, as air entering at this point will also upset the mixture. The jets should be unscrewed and cleaned with compressed air – not a piece of wire, which can enlarge the orifice – and all internal passages should also be blown clean. Jets are made of brass and are, therefore, relatively soft. Some are very fine, and even a small scratch can increase their effective diameter quite considerably.

Clean out the float chamber, and empty it of any deposits that may have collected in the bottom of the bowl. Remove the float and valve, then examine the needle for wear, and make sure that the float is not punctured. If the needle is worn, it will have a visible ring round the tapered part and should be renewed. If renewal is not possible, lap the needle into its seat using metal polish (make sure that all traces of polish are cleaned off afterwards).

If the float is punctured, it is likely to be made of brass, as plastic floats give little trouble. To repair the float, pop it into boiling water to suck out the petrol that is inside it, and then solder the hole. Be very economical with the solder, so that you do not unduly increase the weight of the float. Also, be careful not to alter the float level, as this can be critical. If you have a manual, it will tell you how to check the float level and reset it if necessary.

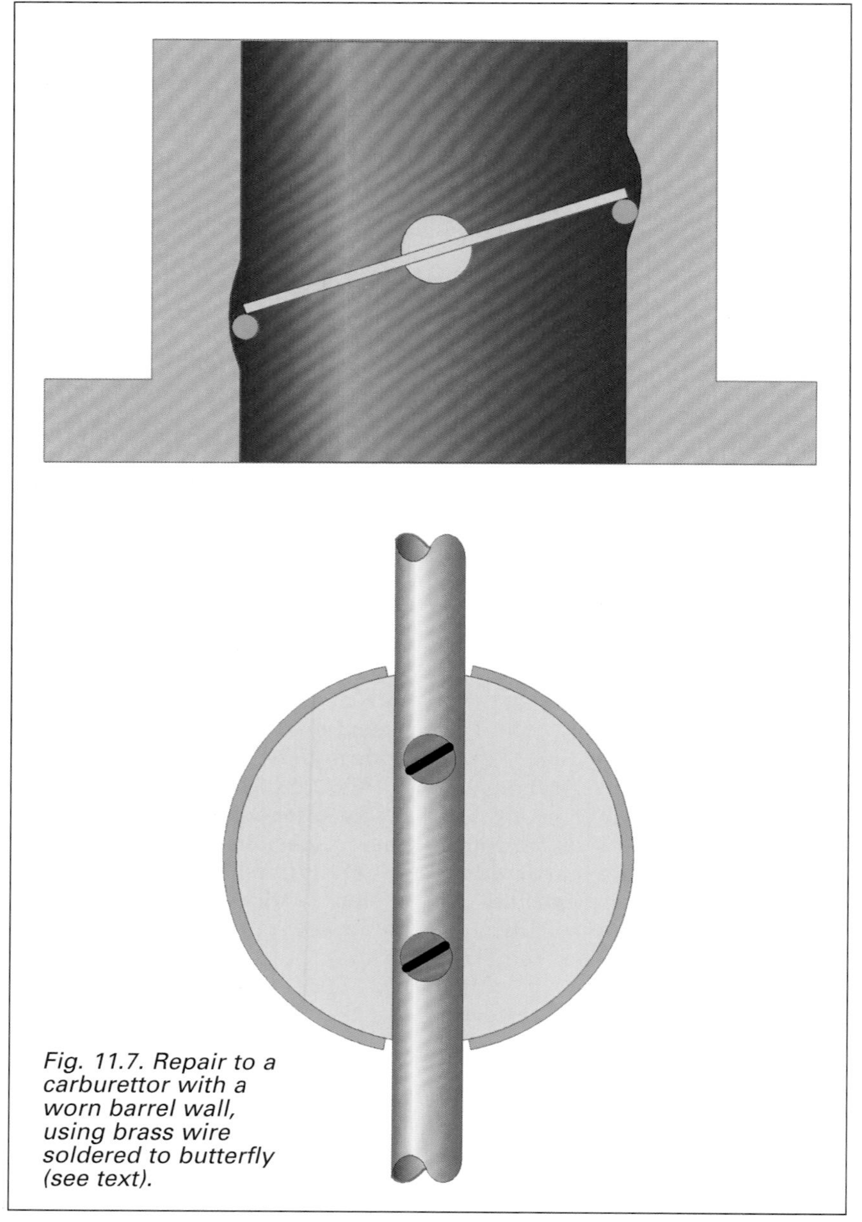

Fig. 11.7. Repair to a carburettor with a worn barrel wall, using brass wire soldered to butterfly (see text).

Some fuels leave a gummy deposit or a shiny varnish finish on the carburettor components, and this should be removed, as it can partially dissolve and cause the float needle to stick. Use an aerosol carburettor cleaner such as Wynn's 'Air Intake and Carburettor Cleaner'.

Refit all the parts carefully, keeping them clean and free from screwdriver damage. If you are not using a part immediately, store it in a polythene bag out of harm's way.

Examine the carburettor for wear in the choke tube where the butterfly fits, as this is sometimes enlarged and makes slow running impossible.

The screw on the spindle that controls the slow running should be adjusted so that the throttle butterfly does not quite make contact with the inside of the barrel. But, over the years, the slow running may have been hard to achieve, resulting in successive owners allowing the butterfly to close completely and thereby hit the wall of the barrel when the foot is taken off the throttle pedal. The effect of this is an indentation on the inside of the tube, making it impossible to obtain the proper slow running speeds as too much air is allowed through.

A Singer Sports Nine which I once rebuilt suffered from this in both carburettors, and the minimum slow running speed was so excessive that it was responsible for breaking a half-shaft, and I had to do something about it. Serviceable replacements were not then available, and I needed to find a cure. Having tried several ideas, I eventually thought of one that was easy to carry out and proved most effective.

A piece of brass wire, of about ⅛in diameter (3.2mm), was shaped into a ring inside the choke tube, and a piece was cut out of the middle to give two arcs that fitted neatly, one on either side of the butterfly spindle. With the butterfly closed, these were then soldered to the periphery of the butterfly itself, using moderate heat from a small blowlamp and allowing the solder to flow to the walls of the barrel. This allowed the butterfly to close completely, and a slow tickover became possible again. In use, the cool air being drawn into the carburettor kept the solder from being affected by engine heat, and no problems were ever experienced.

SU and Stromberg CD carburettors, in addition to needing the same general treatment outlined above, call for attention to the suction disc/diaphragm/needle assembly. Before taking the top off this assembly, mark the two parts so that you can refit them in the same relative position. The SU piston should be free from scores or marks, and the needle should be straight so that it is a free fit in the jet. Clean the inside of the suction chamber, piston and rod, and put a smear of thin oil on the piston rod only, leaving the walls of the chamber and the piston clean and dry. The needle is clamped with its shoulder in line with the base of the piston. When assembled, the whole should fall freely on to the carburettor bridge with a distinct 'clunk', with or without the spring, and with the jet raised as far as it will go. If it does not, the jet needs centring.

To centre the jet, with the control linkage disconnected from the jet, mark it so that it can be correctly repositioned, remove the jet locking spring and, refitting the adjusting nut, screw it up as far as possible. Refit the jet, then slacken the large jet-locking nut so that the assembly can be rotated. Remove the piston damper, and hold down the top of the piston rod firmly while tightening the jet locking nut with the jet pushed upwards; the piston should now fall freely, the locking nut can be re-tightened, and the spring and controls can be refitted. Top up the damper with thin engine oil (SAE 20 preferred) and refit. The damper is designed to delay the opening of the piston momentarily when the throttle is opened, in order to enrich the mixture to improve acceleration.

Stromberg CD units have a diaphragm instead of a piston, and the tapered needle is not centred in the jet, which is fixed, but offset. There are several models, some having top needle adjustments, some bottom, and special tools are required for this purpose. Without the tools, some limited maintenance is possible, including cleaning of the float chamber and renewal of the diaphragm, which is recommended every 24,000 miles (38,400km) or every two years. Access to the diaphragm is gained by removing the four screws in the cover, withdrawing the assembly, and then removing the four screws in the diaphragm retaining ring. There is a small tag on the underside of the diaphragm that engages with a recess in the body of the air valve, and another on the main diameter that locates with a recess in the body.

Fig. 11.8. Stromberg carburettor diaphragm, needle and piston assembly. Unlike the SU, the Stromberg metering needle is offset.

Examine the components for wear, especially the needle valve in the float chamber, and renew as necessary.

The metering needle should be straight, undamaged and unworn. You will have to replace it if it is not up to standard, but if there has been wear in the jet itself a new body will be required, as the jet itself cannot be renewed.

Tuning carburettors

Tuning carburettors and balancing them, if twin or multiple carburettors are fitted, should be carried out after the accurate adjustment of the tappets and ignition timing, but the procedure is included here since we are dealing with carburation.

Tuning consists of making those fine adjustments required to meet the fuel and air requirements of the engine at all speeds. Remove the air cleaner and run the engine until it reaches normal operating temperature. Mixture adjustment is carried out by means of the mixture control screw on a constant-choke carburettor, and by adjusting the relationship between needle and jet on constant-vacuum types. On an SU carburettor, adjustment is carried out by raising or lowering the jet, and on a Stromberg unit by adjusting the needle using the special tool.

The most accurate way of achieving the correct mixture is by using an exhaust gas analyser. This equipment is now available to the amateur, but whether it is worth the cost only you can decide. It may be better to have the final adjustment made at the local garage/MoT testing station, which uses an exhaust gas analyser for MoT tests. Alternatively, if you have a vacuum gauge, connect this to the inlet manifold by means of a flexible tube and an adaptor tapped into the manifold. By turning the slow-running screw, adjust the engine speed to about 1,200–1,400rpm, and then slowly turn the mixture screw (which should be unscrewed about two complete turns to start with) in and out by very small amounts while observing the vacuum gauge. The aim is to get the highest possible vacuum reading, while slowly reducing the engine speed to normal tickover. Check that the engine responds cleanly to both progressive and sudden opening of the throttle.

On an SU carburettor, enrich the mixture by one sixth of a turn (one 'flat') of the jet adjusting nut. Once the vacuum gauge has been disconnected, do not forget to blank off the hole in the manifold with a screw, unless you intend to fit the gauge to the dashboard.

If you do not possess a vacuum gauge, you will have to make the adjustments by observing the exhaust and listening to it. A mixture that is too RICH gives a regular misfire and emits blackish smoke, and one that is too WEAK gives an irregular note at the exhaust with a splashy misfire, and is colourless. The CORRECT mixture gives a regular even exhaust beat.

On constant-vacuum carburettors the pistons should be lifted slightly (there is a pin for this purpose underneath the body of the SU) at tickover speed. If the mixture is too rich, the revs will increase appreciably, and if too weak the revs will decrease and may stall the engine. A small increase in speed denotes that the mixture is correct. A very slight weakening of the mixture may be desirable to compensate for the reduced airflow when the air filter is refitted.

Balancing carburettors

If your engine has two or more carburettors you will need to 'balance' them to ensure that they are all doing the same thing at the same time, in fact, that they are synchronised. With the air cleaners removed, first ensure that the linkage to the throttle butterflies is correctly set. To do this, slacken the clamps on the connecting rods or cable, and unscrew the slow-running screws so that the butterflies are just closed, then readjust the screws so that they just make contact with their stops. Hold the screws in this position while you retighten the clamps on the linkage, having adjusted it as necessary. Inspect the choke control mechanism and make sure that this does not interfere with the throttles; many chokes open the throttles a little as well as operating their own mechanism.

Now start the engine and, with one end of a length of tubing placed at the mouth of one of the carburettor barrels and the other to your ear, listen to the hiss of the air being drawn into the choke tube. Repeat this procedure at the other carburettor barrel(s) and adjust the slow-running screws as necessary to obtain the same note for each carburettor.

Air filters must be clean. There are two types, one a cartridge type which is made of paper and is renewable, the other being a fine gauze which is impregnated with oil. To service the gauze type, wash the gauze in petrol, blow it dry, and soak it in thin oil. Filters can often be improved upon, and the specialist suppliers have a wide range for different types of carburettors.

FUEL PUMP

There are two distinct types of fuel pump, mechanical and electrical. Mechanical pumps are normally mounted on the crankcase or camshaft cover, in such a way that

Fig. 11.9. Mechanical fuel pump, mounted on cam cover.

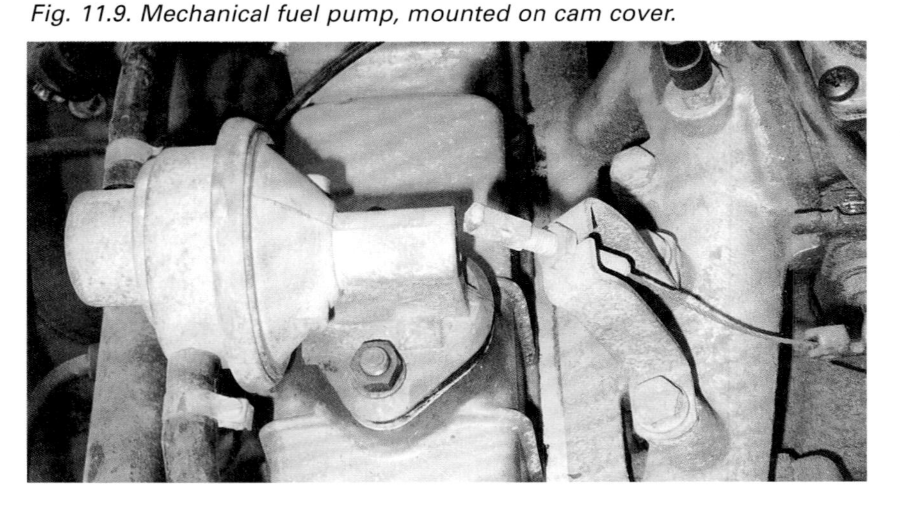

Fig. 11.10. Electric petrol pump, showing inlet and outlet ports.

they can be driven by an extra cam on the camshaft. Electric pumps are normally situated either close to the petrol tank if of the high pressure type, or on the bulkhead in the engine compartment if of the suction type – or, on the Mk V1 Bentley, most inconveniently half-way along the outer chassis rail.

If you are using a pump taken from the donor car, you will have to mount it in the same relative position. Most pump types use a diaphragm to suck petrol into the pump and then, by means of valves, to transfer it to the pressure side and pump it to the carburettor float chamber. The pressure is provided by means of a spring, the strength of which is carefully calculated to suit the needs of the carburettor and which is itself compressed either electro-mechanically or by a lever operated by the cam on mechanical types. Some electric pumps are of the roller-cell type, and do not have a diaphragm.

Some types can be dismantled and serviced, usually by cleaning the filters, renewing the diaphragm and valves, plus, in the case of the electric variety, paying attention to the contact points. When older electric pumps give trouble, the problem is usually caused by the contact points which corrode, or get burnt, and so are unable to pass the necessary current to operate the solenoid that, in turn, operates the diaphragm. The contacts should be cleaned with very fine emery, or renewed if too far gone. These older types of electric pumps can now be replaced by small, solid-state electronic devices, which are compact and quiet. These solid-state units are a very worthwhile improvement over the older types of electric pump.

PETROL TANK

Petrol tanks may be made of aluminium, mild steel or stainless steel. They used to be made of tinplate, and if you are going to use one from a donor car, some are made of plastic. Plastic tanks are light and, of course, do not rust. If you are rebuilding, or using a tank from a donor that requires repair, much the best course is to send the tank to the specialists. Used tanks, even with holes in them and which may not have been used for many years, can still act like bombs, and specialists take very great care in dealing with them. If you insist on repairing a tank yourself, you must **on no account**, use a naked flame anywhere near it, and **must not** attempt to solder it with a blow lamp.

Soldering of seams and patches is possible using a large soldering iron heated well away from the tank. (This, of course, rules out stainless steel and aluminium tanks, but you are unlikely to come across these second-hand, anyway.)

Like all soldering, success depends on preparation and having the iron at the right temperature. The area to be soldered must be clean, bright and free from grease. Coat the area with flux and 'tin' it well by melting solder on to the area, with the

Fig. 11.11. This tank is cleverly designed to need just two parts. It is made of stainless steel which is protected by plastic sheeting, hence the colour.

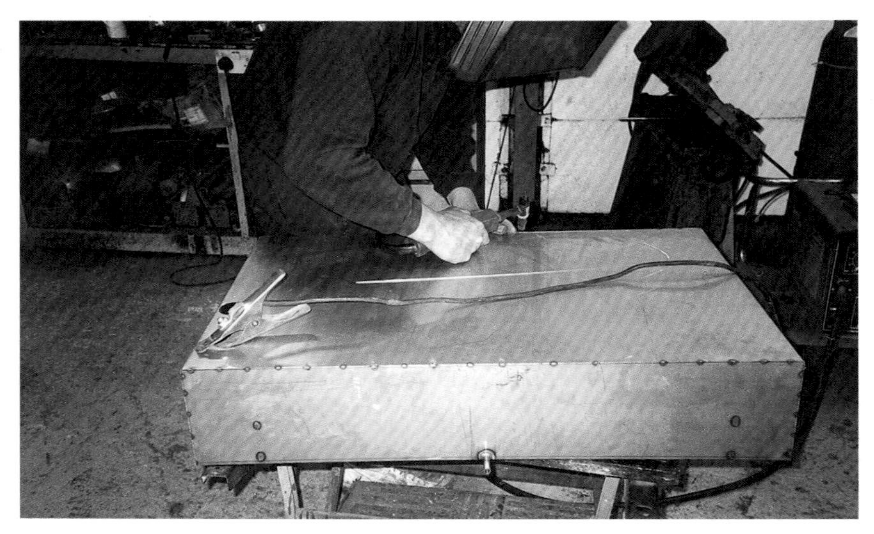

Fig. 11.12. Tack welding the two halves of the tank together.

Fig. 11.13. Fuel tank brackets, filler pipe and breather pipe connection in place.

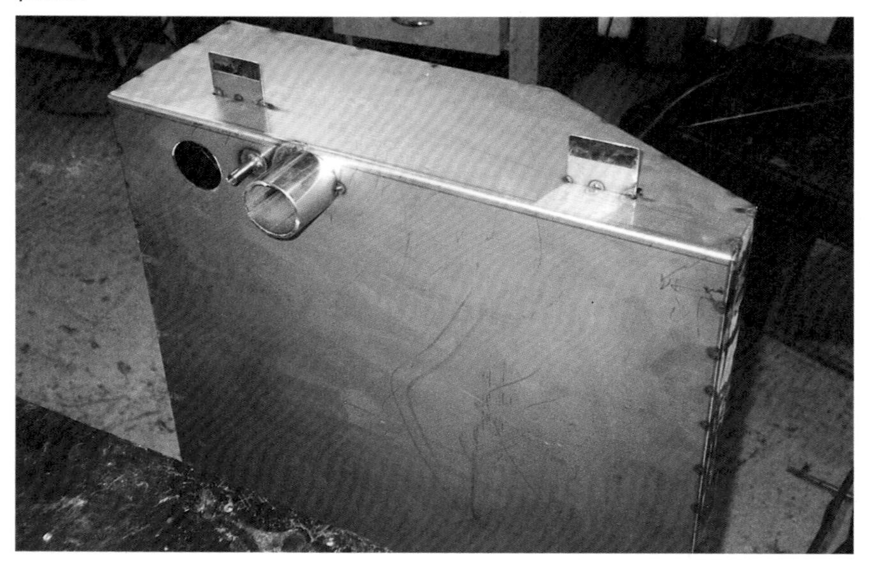

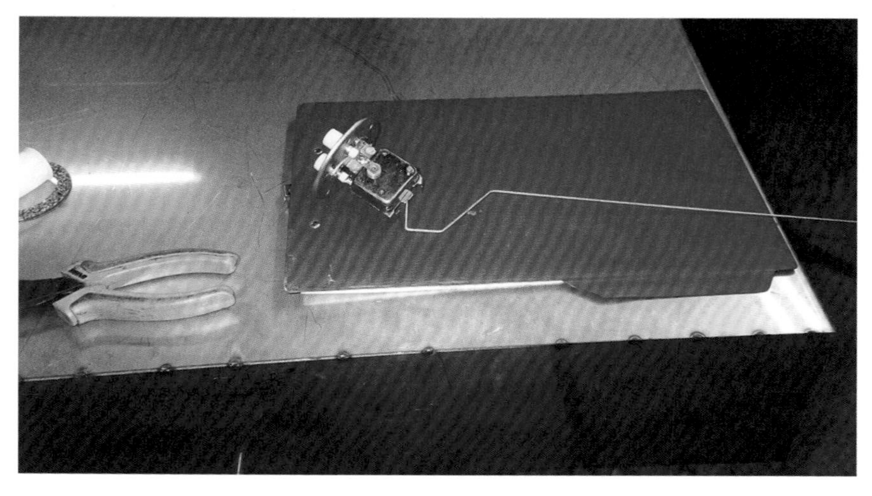

soldering iron at the correct temperature, heating the metal as well as the solder. Unless you have a very large electric soldering iron, you will need a large old-fashioned iron that can be heated with a gas blow lamp – away from the tank!

You can tell at a glance when the soldering iron reaches the correct temperature. The 'bit' of a soldering iron is made of copper. When the correct temperature is reached, the flame in which the bit is being heated becomes bright green.

Tin the patch in the same way previously described, lay the patch on the tank, and feed some more solder to the edges as the iron melts the tinning. Clean the repaired area thoroughly afterwards, and scrub well with water to neutralise the flux, as some types are corrosive.

If you make a tank from scratch, use aluminium of 16swg thickness, or mild or stainless steel of 20swg. Any of these materials can be welded, aluminium and stainless usually by a specialist, or you can solder mild steel, using a gas blow lamp instead of an iron since there will be no petrol in the tank. Do not forget to put at least one baffle in the tank (a plate similar to one of the end-plates, but with holes in it) to prevent petrol surging from one side of the tank to another when cornering, or you may have problems with fuel starvation, and you may get some unwelcome oversteer when cornering energetically!

You will need to reinforce one area of the tank where you can mount the sender for the petrol gauge (new units are available from the spares specialists) and a tube for the filler, as well as possibly a drain plug. A small diameter breather pipe from the top of the tank is necessary, as well as the fuel delivery pipe. The delivery pipe can be positioned in the top or bottom of the tank, but

Fig. 11.14. Fuel gauge sender before arm is shortened.

Fig. 11.15. Fuel gauge sender with arm shortened and float fitted.

Fig. 11.16. Finished fuel tank with provision for twin fillers.

ensure that it cannot draw from say the bottom ½in (13mm), as this is where water and sediment can collect.

When mounting the tank, consider its weight when full. A gallon of petrol (4.5 litres) weighs approximately 10lb (5kg), so a tank of six gallons will weigh about 60lb (30kg) when full, plus its own weight. Mount the tank on the chassis if you can, or sit it on a substantial framework, well strapped in at least two places and insulated with thin rubber strip against chafing.

Where you mount the tank may depend on safety legislation, which may require that it is not mounted in the 'crumple zone' at the very rear of the car.

The fuel line connecting the tank to the pump and the pump to the carburettor should include an in-line filter, and can be made from special flexible tubing, or from rigid copper pipe with flexible tubing making the final connections. Run the fuel line inside the chassis rails, where it is protected from damage, and support it using clips at intervals of not more than 300mm. Keep fuel lines away from the exhaust system as, apart from danger of fire, heat from the exhaust can cause vaporisation and consequent problems with carburation. With some fuel systems, it is necessary to include a fuel return line to return excess fuel from the pump, or sometimes from a pressure regulator, to the fuel tank. If a fuel return line is required, bear in mind the same points mentioned for the fuel feed line.

The petrol filler cap must be made of metal, with a positive closing action (screw or clamp type) – rubber filler caps are no longer legal.

FUEL INJECTION

When fuel injection was first fitted to British cars, Alex Issigonis, the famous designer of the Mini and builder of a superb special in the

1930s, was interviewed on the subject and said something like: 'If we had started with fuel injection and then developed the carburettor we would have said how marvellously simple it was.' Despite this, fuel injection is fitted to a large proportion of modern cars as it is able to assess the engine's needs and can meter fuel much more precisely than can a carburettor. On the whole, fuel injection systems are more economical and much 'greener' than carburettors. Modern cars have to use fuel injection systems in order to meet current exhaust emissions regulations.

There are many different types of systems that differ in detail, but typically, fuel is circulated by a pump to either a single injector in the manifold (single-point) or to a series of injectors (multi-point, one for each cylinder), surplus petrol being returned to the tank. Injectors are operated electrically (though early ones were mechanically operated), and are either fully closed or fully open, the amount of petrol supplied being governed by the time for which the injector remains open. Despite the fact that many systems use multi-point injection, with an injector for each cylinder situated near the inlet valve, the operation of the injectors is not always related to valve opening. The system takes into account ambient and engine temperature, airflow into the engine, and engine speed and throttle position, and the fuel is metered accordingly by means of an electronic control unit (ECU) which attempts to match the requirements of the engine as closely as possible with those of the driver.

Fuel injection systems vary enormously, but most should require very little work in terms of servicing. The air filter can be renewed, and engine idle speed and mixture strength may be adjustable, a tachometer being necessary for the former and an exhaust gas analyser for the latter – provided you know where to look for the adjustment points. The workshop manual for the donor car is very helpful at this stage.

If you are using an engine equipped with fuel injection from a donor car, the advice must be to make sure that you remove every part of the system including, of course, the ECU that may be hidden away under a seat or behind a trim panel, as well as all the electrical equipment such as relays (also probably hidden away), and if applicable the fuel cut-off switch which is likely to be in the engine compartment or passenger compartment.

You may need to depressurise the fuel system before you can dismantle it safely. This is, therefore, one aspect of special building where you really do need access to the manual for the donor car, and where you must be sure to label the wiring loom connectors if you ever hope to get the system running again.

There are specialists offering units designed to uprate the performance of fuel-injected engines by 're-mapping' the ECU to provide the extra power and acceleration that the manufacturers were too cautious to exploit.

Chapter 12

Exhaust system

When the petrol/air mixture which feeds the engine has been ignited by the spark plug in the cylinder, the rapid expansion of the gas forces the piston to the bottom of its stroke. The burnt mixture has then expended most of its energy and is useless for any other purpose. So, as the piston rises, the exhaust gas is pushed out of the cylinder, through the now open exhaust valve, with any remaining energy helping its movement.

The exhaust gas, still very hot, passes through the exhaust manifold and into the exhaust pipe. As the gas passes through the system, it travels through an expansion box (often more than one) and/or a silencer, where it is allowed to expand in order to reduce noise and slow the gas down. The exhaust gas then passes through the tail pipe into the atmosphere. Rolls-Royce, and other manufacturers of luxury vehicles, may have several silencers to allow the gas to expand fully before reaching the atmosphere and so reduce noise even more, whereas sports car enthusiasts often like to hear the exhaust note, equating (wrongly) noise with power.

Some cars have a characteristic exhaust note. The vintage Bentley, with a low compression ratio and long stroke had a note that was once described as being 'like a bloodhound lapping soup', a sort of slurp, slurp, noise, whereas a vintage Bugatti's exhaust note was said to be like 'tearing calico'. Racing cars with open, or 'straight-through', exhausts without silencers are

Fig. 12.1. Full length exhaust pipe in position with two silencers. They are rarely straight and generally look like an afterthought.

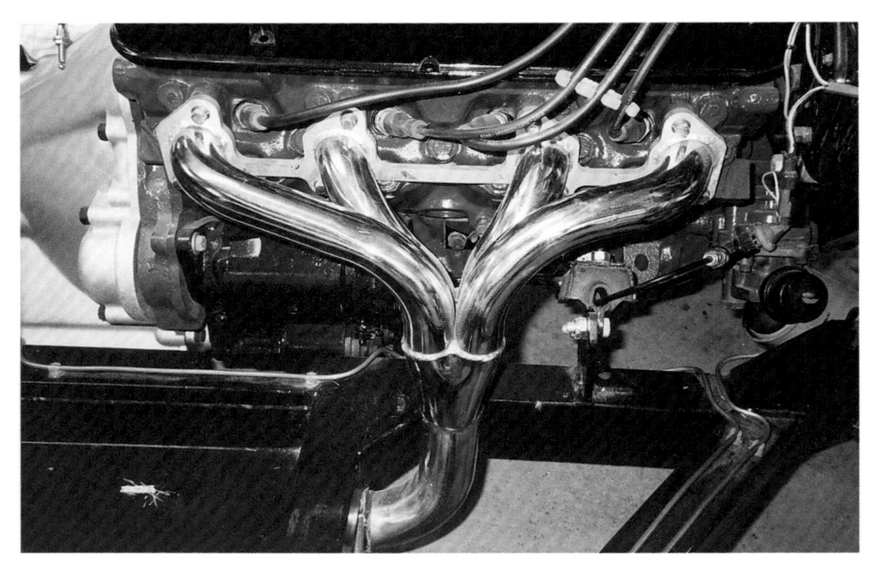

Fig. 12.2. Four-into-one Cobra exhaust manifold.

Fig. 12.3. Racing free-flow exhaust system.

exciting to the enthusiast, none more so than the truly fantastic 'scream' of the supercharged 1500cc V16 BRM, and V8 engines make their own rather 'woofly' sound which is music to the ears of their owners.

For road use we are limited by law to a maximum noise level of 101 decibels, but the aim should be to remove the exhaust gases from the engine with the minimum loss of power due to 'back pressure'. Back pressure is caused by narrow pipes and obstructive silencers. Excessive noise, apart from being environmentally unfriendly, is very tiring on a long journey.

For an ordinary road car, a system similar to that of the donor car should be quite adequate. If you are building a sports car, you can aim for something that passes the gas more freely, but the limiting factor will be the manifold. If this is the standard one from the donor car, it may be restrictive to gas flow.

An engine fitted with twin carburettors (or a twin-choke set-up) is likely to have an efficient free-flow exhaust manifold fitted by the manufacturer, since there is no point in getting more gas into the cylinders to produce more power if it cannot be removed efficiently when burnt.

Under-sized pipes will create back pressure, and over large ones will look amateurish. Depending on engine size and the number of cylinders your engine has, something between 1½in (38mm) and 2½in (63mm) bore should be appropriate. A well-designed exhaust system should be of similar effective length for each cylinder, from the piston crown at top dead centre to the end of the tail pipe, which accounts for the rather tortuous systems used on some cars and especially on multi-cylinder motorcycles. A really well-designed system will be harmonically tuned so that it not only allows a smooth passage for the exhaust gases, but it actually helps to extract them, and, by doing so, improves the efficiency of the engine. With both inlet and exhaust valves open during the period known as 'valve overlap', a harmonically tuned exhaust system helps to suck fresh petrol/air mixture into the cylinder.

As engines are flexibly mounted, provision must be made for the exhaust system to move. All modern designs seem to have opted for the easy way out and the whole exhaust system is usually rubber mounted to allow it to rock with the engine. A better engineering solution, especially where a side exhaust system is used, is to mount the system rigidly, but to connect it to the 'headers' or downpipes with special flexible tubing.

Tyre and exhaust fitting establishments stock, or can obtain, lengths of exhaust pipe, bends, fittings and clamps for you to make up your own system by welding or brazing the various parts together. This is much easier if you fit everything into position first on the car and tack weld it, and then finish welding it off the car.

Most exhaust components will be made from mild steel, and if the system is going to be conspicuous, you will need to finish it in some way to protect it and make it look attractive. There are several makes of VHT (very high temperature) paints available from accessory shops, in a rather limited range of colours. Alternatively, you could have a system specially made from stainless steel, or you could have the system chromium plated.

Silencers come in all shapes and sizes, designed not only to keep noise in check, but also to fit into some convenient area underneath the car where they are unlikely to be damaged by road debris. If you have no space for a single silencer of adequate size, you may have to find room for a second smaller one.

Side-mounted systems are well catered for, with a wide choice of silencers in chrome or stainless steel from your accessory shop. Specialists will sell you everything you need to make up a complete system, including manifold plates and even the parts to make your own silencer.

Ensure that the system has sufficient clearance above the ground to prevent damage from road bumps, and ensure that the clearance allows for the suspension travel and axle movement. If the system is not mounted under the car, you need to ensure that neither you nor inquisitive admirers can be injured by accidental contact with the system. A heat shield over the silencer (or any other part of the system) is a good idea, and special heat-insulating tape is available for the pipe itself. Also make sure that the exhaust gas (containing lethal carbon monoxide) is expelled from the tailpipe well clear of the car, and does not get sucked back into it.

Cars such as Cobra look-alikes, and others with vee engines where the exhaust systems are visible, require two matching systems. Alternatively, twin systems can be run independently, or can be joined at the silencer and then given one or more tail pipes.

Fig. 12.4. A simple exhaust system, incorporating a flexible section to allow for flexing of the pipe.

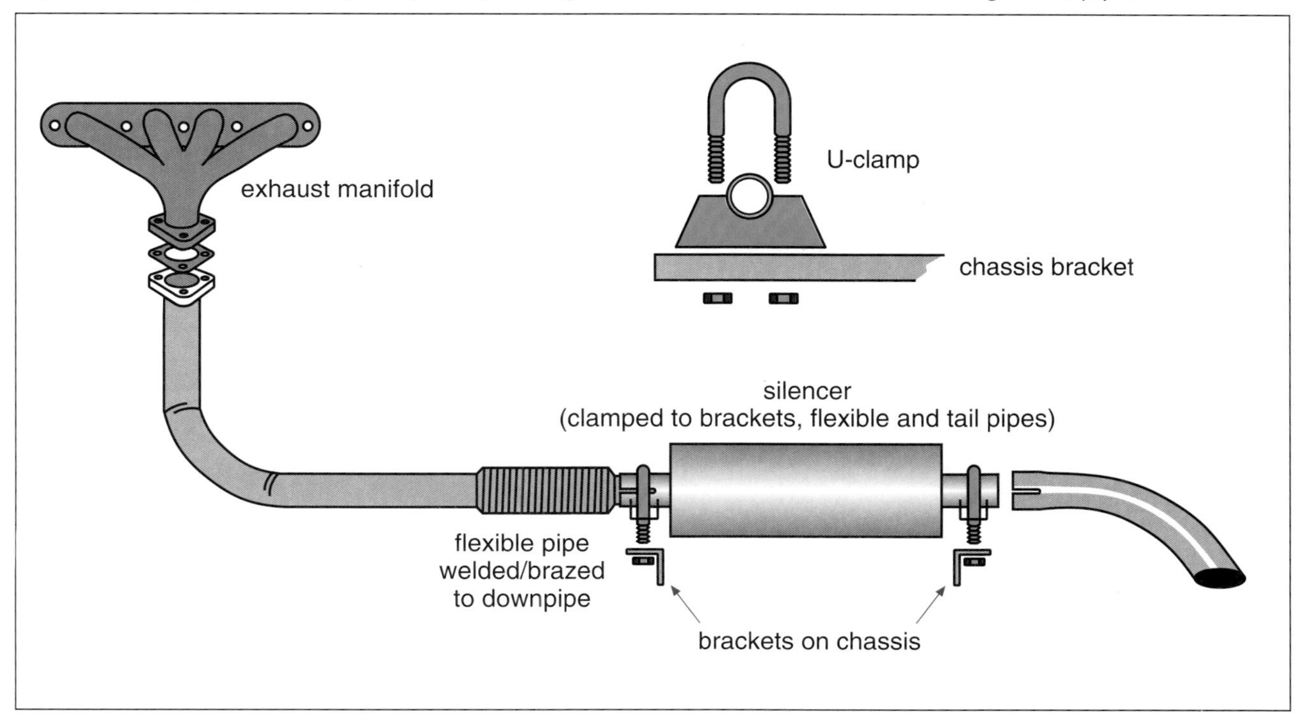

Chapter 13

Dashboard

DASHBOARD DESIGN AND RESTORATION

The purpose of the dashboard is to provide a convenient location for the minor controls and the instrument display. It is in some respects the most important part of the car, and it is the part that everyone looks at first. If the dashboard is not well finished, you will find it a permanent source of dissatisfaction and, if the layout of switches and instruments is not right, it will be a constant source of irritation.

When I am restoring a car with a detachable dashboard, I usually deal with this part first. Complete, shiny and with reconditioned dials, it hangs in my workshop, carefully protected, and is shown off to visitors as the standard that I hope to achieve with the rest of the car. In moments of low-motivation, such as chassis de-rusting or de-gunging filthy components, I look at it and think how pleasant it is going to be when I am sitting behind it driving!

For those rebuilding a car, originality will be important, so it is essential to sketch or photograph the dash complete before removing the instruments and fittings. If you have been able to drive the car, you will know which instruments work and which need attention. If the instruments are

Fig. 13.1. Design for a basic dashboard with glove box.

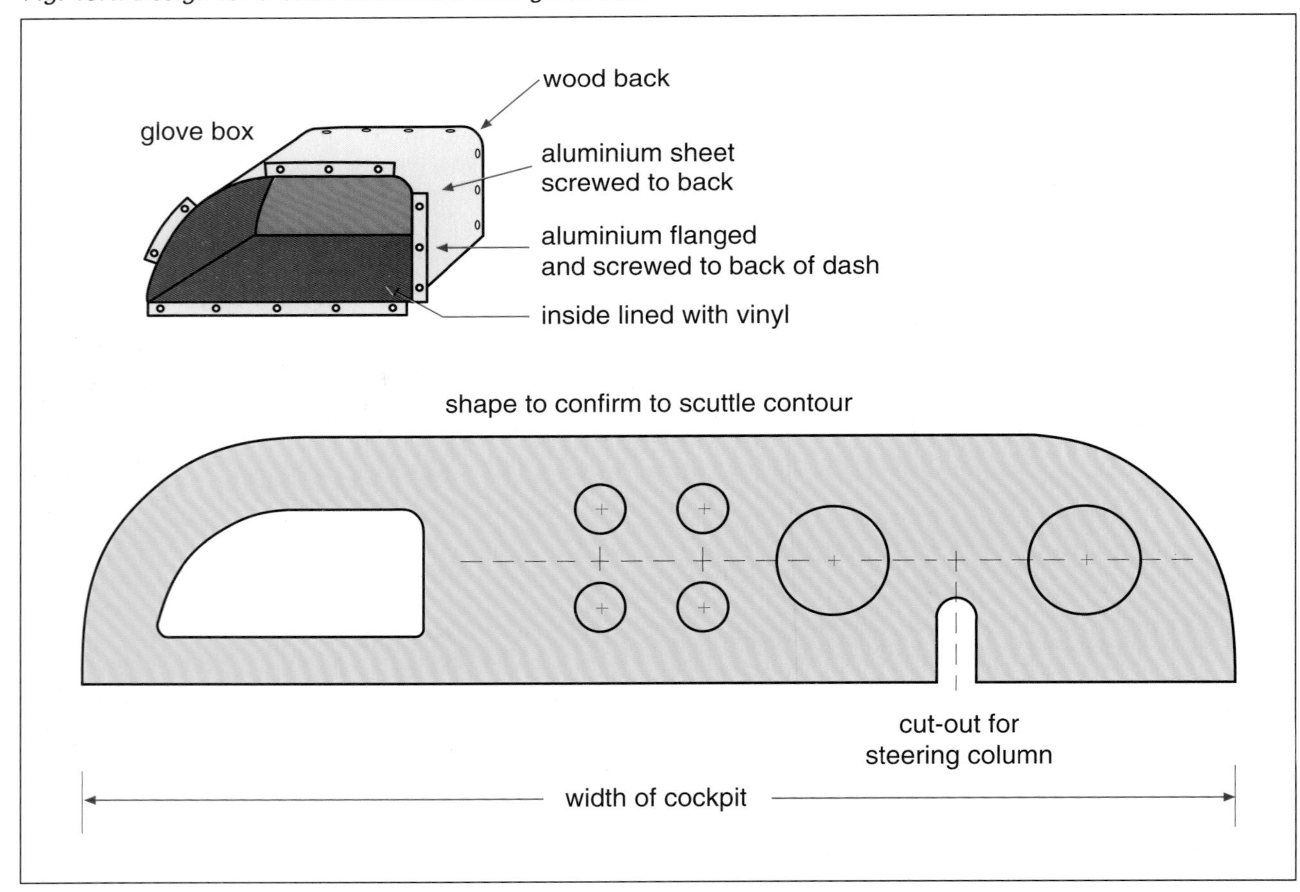

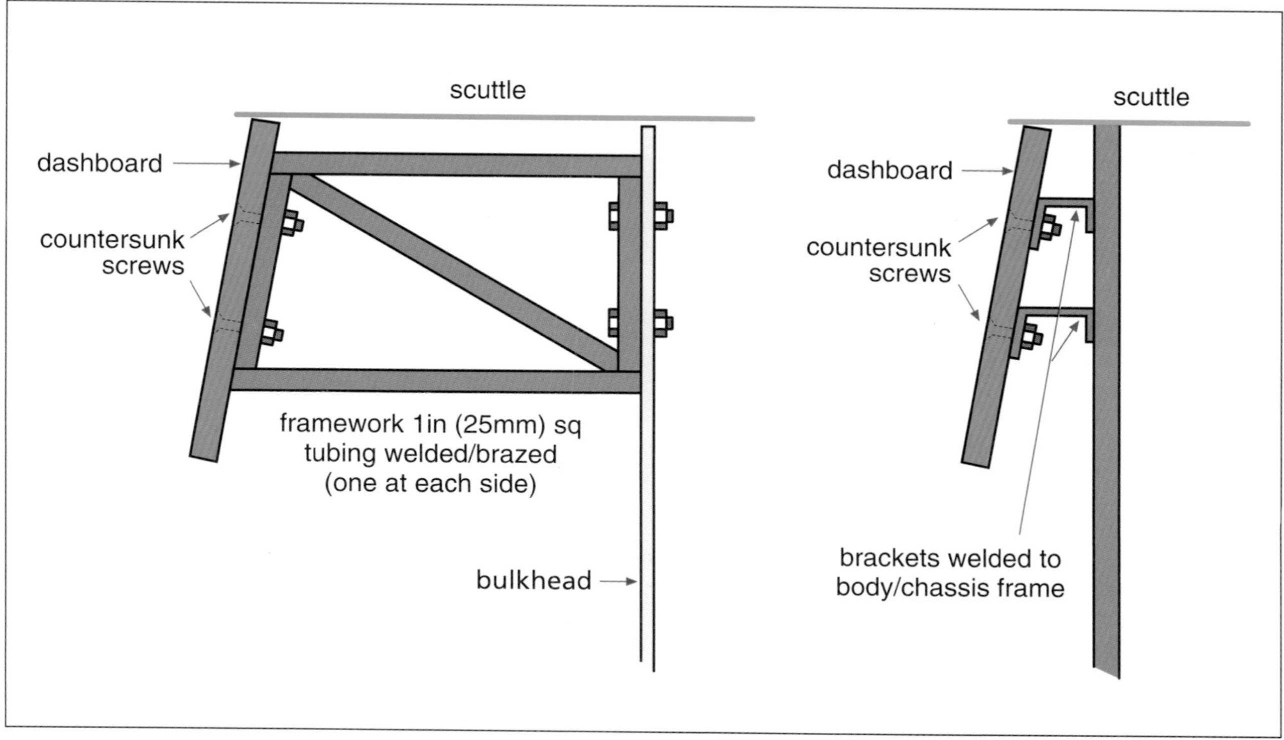

Fig. 13.2. Two methods of mounting a dashboard.

grouped in a pod or nacelle, and are without separate rims ('bezels'), the likelihood is that they are all part of a single assembly on a printed circuit board. In this case, if any of the instruments do not work, you will probably find that repair is difficult and that a complete replacement pod is required, but before condemning an instrument, first check that whatever drives it – cable, wire or sender – is in order.

Single instruments that are complete in themselves and have a circular bezel can usually be taken apart. Often all that is required to refurbish the instrument is attention to the dial, and perhaps a re-plated bezel to make it look like new. Bezels are often designed

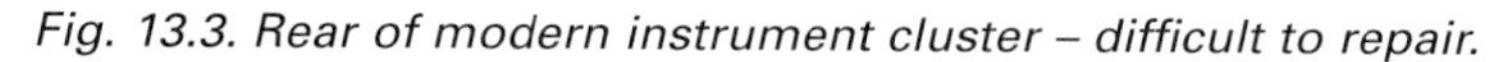

Fig. 13.3. Rear of modern instrument cluster – difficult to repair.

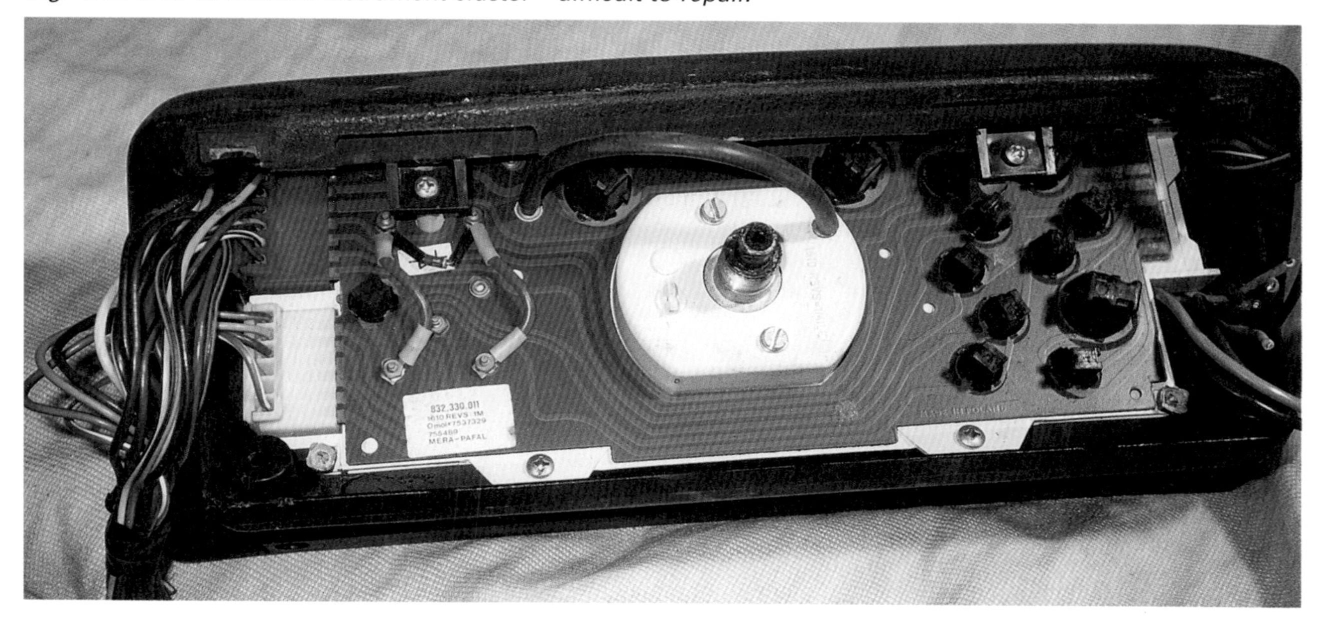

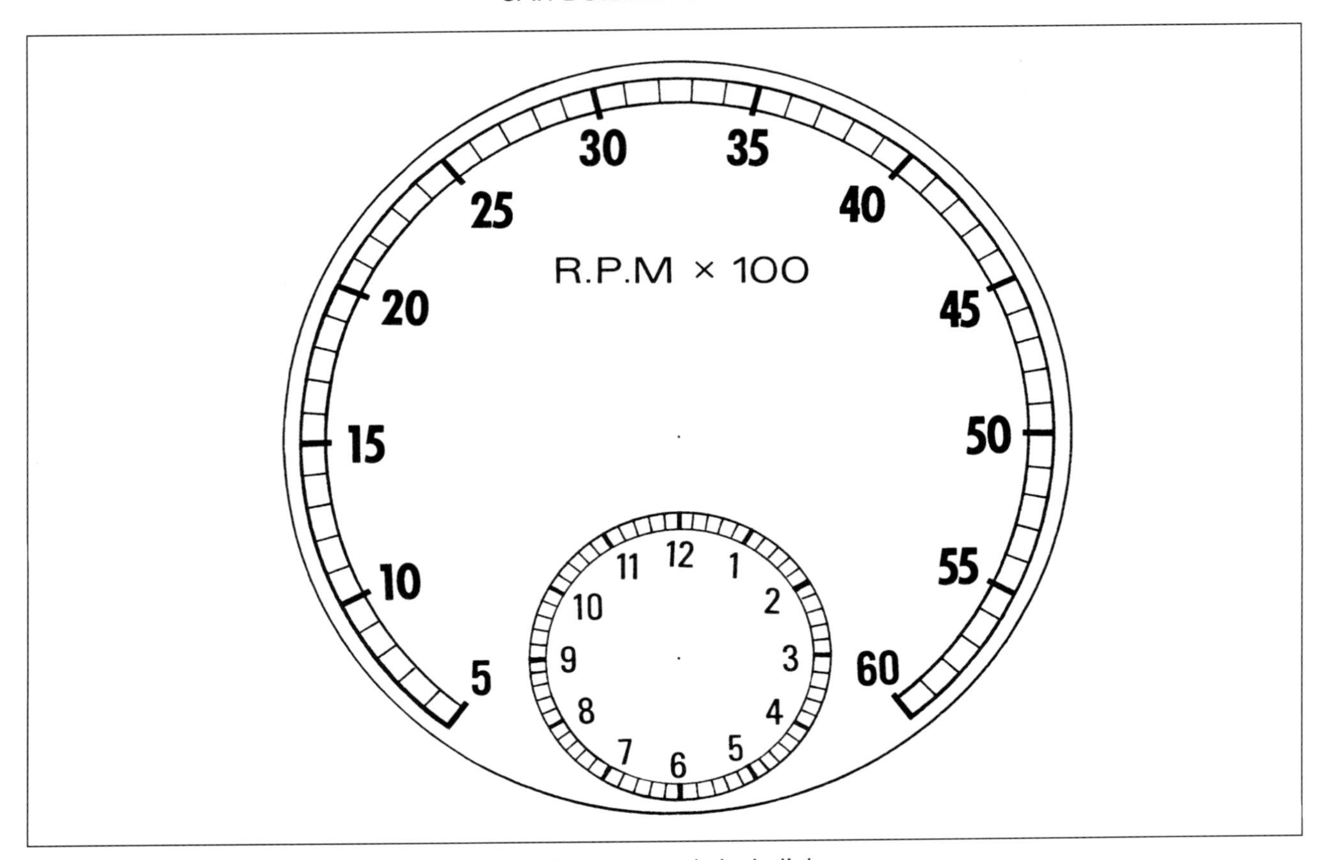

Fig. 13.4. A home-made rev-counter dial with incorporated clock dial.

with bayonet-type fittings so that a half or quarter turn will detach them from the case. Even if it has been crimped all the way round, the bezel can usually be levered up by careful use of a screwdriver with the body of the instrument held firmly face down on the bench. Small file cuts at intervals around the circumference help.

The seal between glass and bezel is usually rubber and is frequently perished. I discovered years ago that a good substitute is available from bicycle shops in the form of the small-diameter rubber tubing that is used on old-pattern bicycle inner tube valves, known as 'Woods' valves.

Dials are usually made of metal or plastic with the figures printed on, but these have often suffered over the years and are grimy or illegible. The dials can be renewed by specialists, who will also rebuild and recalibrate the instrument for you, although you can make a new dial yourself from a drawing of the original face, using small transfers of the 'Edding' or 'Letraset' variety. (You could also do this on a computer with drawing software.) The original dial can be reproduced as is, or in reversed out form to obtain white on black. A sample of a home-made dial is reproduced in *Fig. 13.4*. The smaller dials in *Fig. 13.5* were photographed from the originals.

Switches are often made of hard dark plastic, and may have lost their original shine. This is easily remedied by polishing, using metal polish if you do not have access to a polishing mop on the end of a grinder. Some switches have lettering on them; this is normally engraved and can be filled carefully with white paint, any surplus being wiped off while still wet.

The dashboard itself may need attention. If it is made of wood it can be repaired if necessary and any unwanted holes filled before sanding and polishing, or it can be re-veneered. A new wooden dash can be made easily either from genuine 'tree wood' or from a piece of plywood with veneer stuck on. Cover the whole dash first, and cut the holes out very carefully after the covering has stuck.

If they are painted, metal dashboards can be refinished by flatting and spraying. Some dashboards had an instrument panel with a black-crackle or wrinkle-finish let in. This type of paint is available in spray cans, and does an excellent job if the instructions are carefully followed.

Leather or plastic covering is much used and very attractive, especially if padded with thin foam between dash and covering. As with veneer, cover the dash first and then cut the holes using a sharp knife.

Kit car and special builders can keep the original GRP finish (where

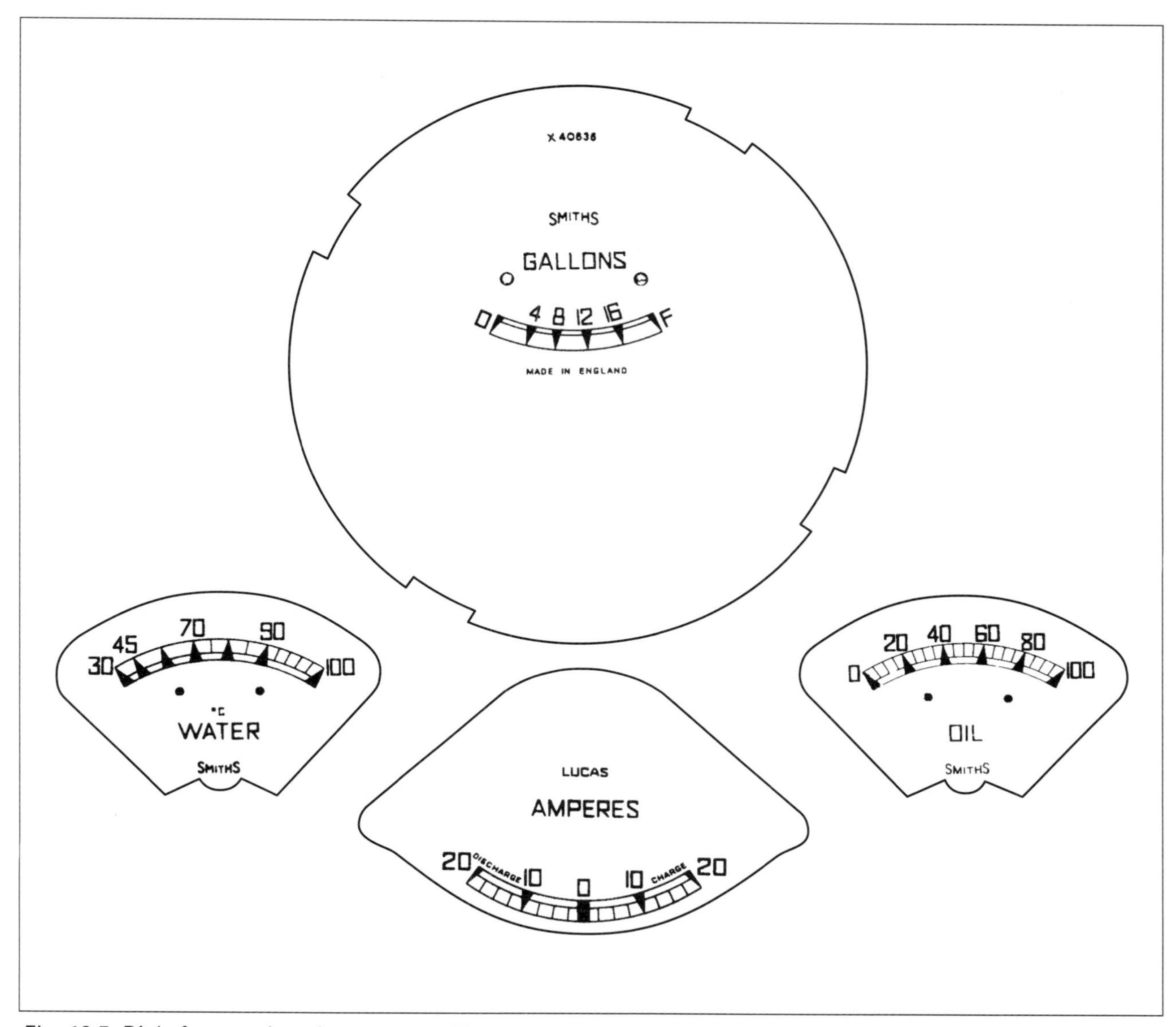

Fig. 13.5. Dials from various instruments. These were photographed from the originals.

Fig. 13.6. A polished wood version on a Triumph Roadster.

Fig. 13.7. Engine-turned metal finish on the author's Locost.

applicable), or cover it in leather, vinyl or veneer. Alternatively, builders may opt for a more modern finish like carbon fibre or Kevlar if the curvature is not too extreme, or an aluminium dash can be made and finished by engine-turning (mottling) like the author's car.

This type of finish was much used on aluminium engines like the Bugatti, and on the cast aluminium bulkheads of good quality sports cars. The effect is easy to achieve, but needs care. Aluminium sheet, photo-etched with a suitable pattern, is available for the lazy, though to my mind the scrolls are rather large and a bit lifeless, as they are too perfect.

A piece of aluminium of 16swg or 18swg is used, and the job is easier if you leave the metal sheet as a rectangle slightly larger than the finished size, rather than cut it to shape at this stage. All that is needed is a piece of felt in a circular holder of about ¾in (18mm) diameter, and a small quantity of fine grinding paste. The holder is rotated at slow speed in a pillar drill, and the paste-impregnated felt is lightly touched on the face of the aluminium.

The panel is then moved on by half a diameter of the felt holder, and the next circle is made. The second row of circles overlaps the first by half a diameter, and it is all made much easier if lines are pencilled in for guidance. When finished, the panel is stuck to a shaped plywood backing, cut to the same shape as the backing, and then the holes for the instruments are cut out. After the remains of the paste have been gently wiped off with a paraffin-soaked cloth, a coat of transparent lacquer is sprayed on to protect the finish.

An easier and less messy way of doing the job is to buy from your local motorcycle dealer a block of rubber-like substance that contains a fine abrasive, and is used by keen bikers to polish aluminium castings.

Sheet metal can be stuck very easily by roughening the surface with emery cloth or wet-or-dry paper, and then using an impact-adhesive such as 'Evostik', but you have to get it right first time as no adjustment is possible.

INSTRUMENTS

Builders, unlike restorers, are free to choose both the instruments and the layout, and so do not have to add rather unsightly supplementary instruments, attached to the top or bottom of the dashboard, if they want to add to the instruments the manufacturer provided in the first place.

All too many modern cars have warning lights rather than instruments, presumably to save on cost, and because the average driver prefers very simple instrumentation. Warning lights only tell you what has happened when disaster has already struck, whereas suitable auxiliary instruments can give warning of a possible problem by some abnormality of reading. An instrument, in fact, measures a parameter and indicates the result – speed, temperature, pressure or whatever – and it is up to you to decide what you want to know.

A speedometer is essential, and a tachometer (rev counter) helps you to get the best out your engine without over-stretching it. Correct oil pressure is essential to prolong the life of the engine, so a pressure gauge will assure you that all is well or, conversely, warn you of impending trouble. Similarly, a water temperature gauge will allow you to keep an eye on the engine temperature. A battery condition indicator, or an ammeter is useful for keeping a check on the electrical system. An external air temperature indicator can be useful if you use the car in the winter, as it gives you warning of black ice – some instruments draw your attention to freezing temperatures by means of a warning light. Vacuum gauges (connected to the inlet manifold) are useful test and diagnostic instruments, which can be fitted permanently and may help the driver to achieve good fuel economy. A fuel gauge is a necessity and a clock is obviously useful.

What you include in your dashboard is up to you, but some restraint is necessary. It is easy to have too many instruments and switches, making the dash look like a jet fighter and an object of ridicule rather than a thing to be admired.

The layout of the various items on the dash is important and should be carefully considered

Fig. 13.8. All these instruments, and more, are available from accessory specialists. (Demon Tweeks)

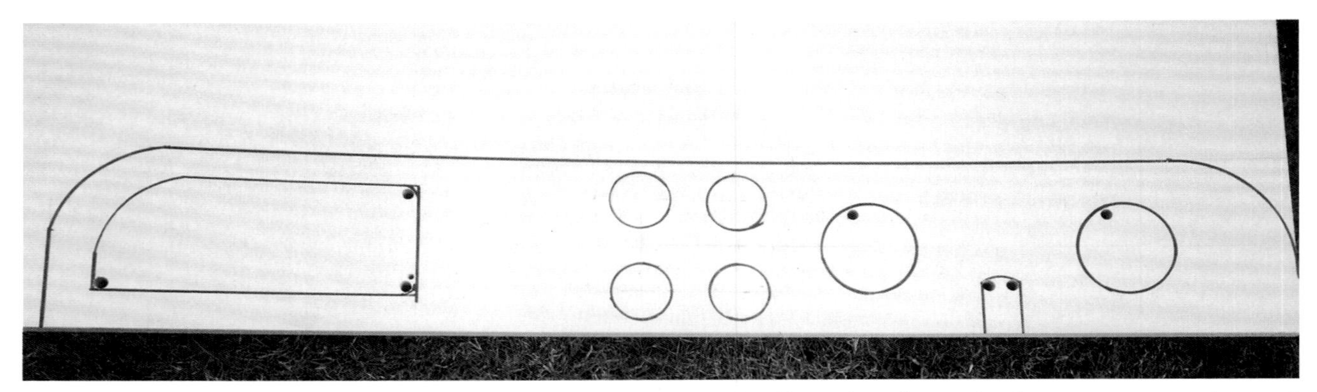

Fig. 13.9. Dashboard drawn out on a piece of plastic-covered blockboard which will be covered in vinyl when finished.

Fig. 13.10. Cutting out the holes. The dashboard and larger holes were cut with the jig saw. The smaller holes could be cut with the saw, or a circular cutter of the correct size.

from both an ergonomic and aesthetic point of view. The steering wheel may mask a part of the dash from the driver's view, consequently the most used instruments, speedometer, rev counter and oil pressure gauge, should be carefully sited where they can always be seen. If in doubt, cut card circles to represent each instrument and pin them to the dash to see if they will be visible when you are driving. Similarly, important and much-used controls must fall easily to hand, for instance the flasher switch must be easily accessible even if the choke is not.

Kit cars often use the donor car's instrument cluster and switch gear complete. This will probably be steering-column-mounted and easier to work on when it comes to

Fig. 13.11. Completed dashboard ready for mounting to the brackets/framework.

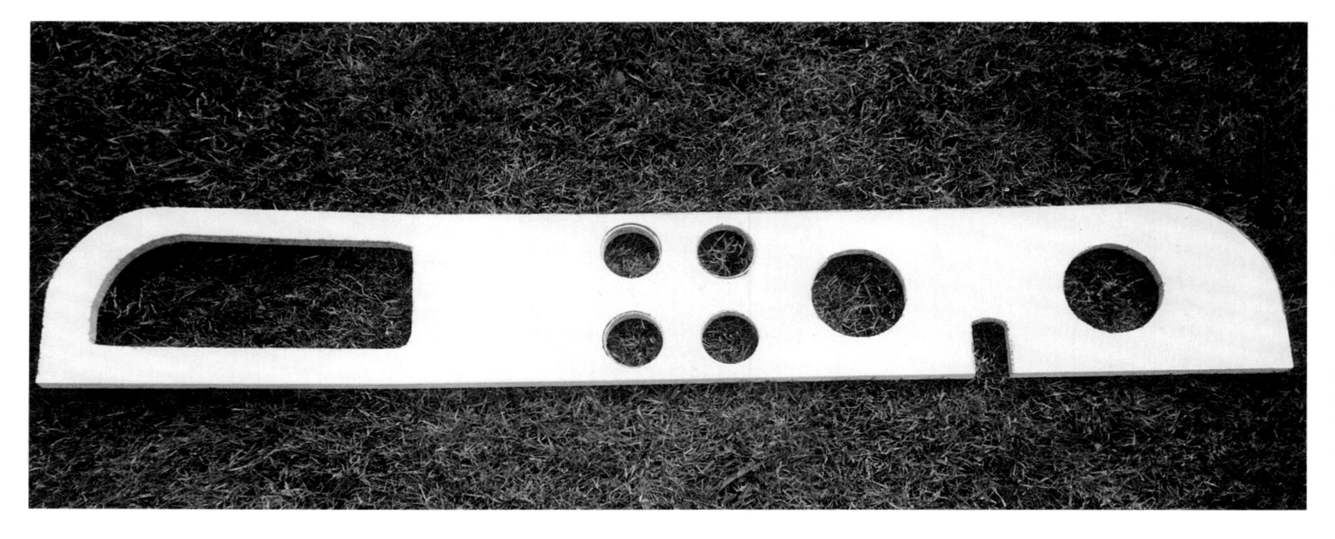

Fig. 13.12. 'Stirrups' holding instruments in place.

wiring, as the original loom can be used.

The bodies of metal-cased instruments are normally earthed, so if you have a metal dashboard you can be economical with wiring. Such instruments are usually held in place by a metal stirrup or two small L-shaped brackets. The fixings are easily made from steel strip if missing. Alternatively, a worm-drive clip pushed hard against the back of the dash and encircling the instrument case makes a good substitute.

Consider fitting a lockable glove box on the passenger's side, as secure storage for small items, especially on open cars, is often difficult. A map-reading light is also very useful.

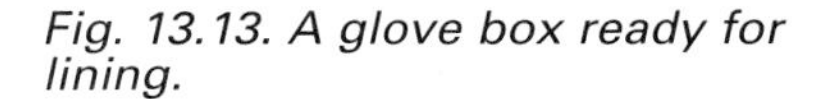

Fig. 13.13. A glove box ready for lining.

Chapter 14

Electrics

WIRING

This is the part of a project that most builders and restorers find difficult. It is certainly easy to be put off by the complexities of a wiring diagram, particularly that of a modern car loaded with electrical equipment, or by the sight of a mass of wiring behind the dashboard. In fact, wiring or re-wiring is both easy and enjoyable, giving a real sense of satisfaction as each unit comes to life when it is switched on. The secret to success is in taking a methodical approach, dealing with each individual circuit in turn.

On a new build, wiring is often left until the end, but it is preferable to install the wiring at an earlier stage when you have easy access and can route the wires where you want them. The best time to install the wiring is after installing the engine and before the bodywork is fitted.

Ideally, the dashboard should be complete, so that the switches, instruments and panel and warning lights are available, but you can leave the fitting of other electrical components, such as lamps, windscreen wipers and so on, until later. If wiring is being installed for components that have not yet been fitted, all that is necessary is to label the end(s) of the wire after you have tested the circuit, so that you can easily identify the appropriate wire later when you need to connect it. I use a Dymo label to identify wiring, for instance 'O/S FL' (off-side flasher) and 'N/S DIP' (near-side dipped headlamp), but masking tape will serve just as well. The wire colour coding, as explained later, also helps. Be generous with the wire and leave a little more length than actually necessary.

Fig. 14.1. Multi-purpose crimping pliers, with terminals, cable ties and sheathing.

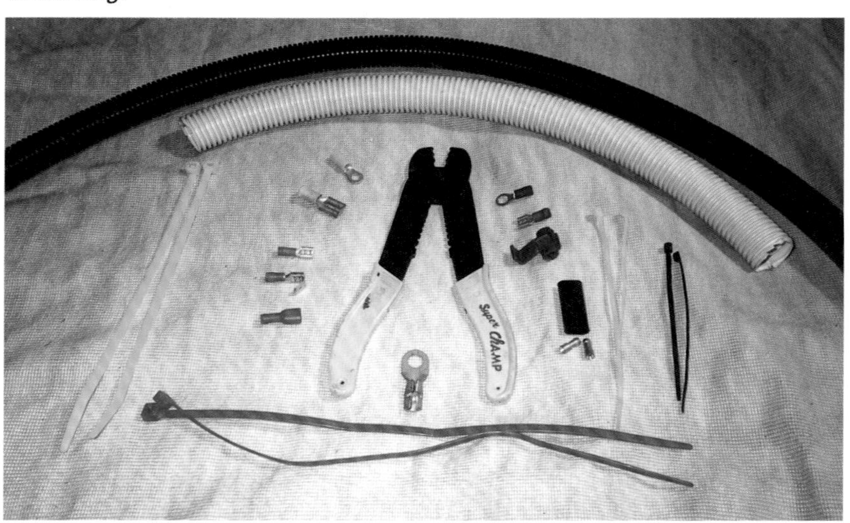

You will finish up with a good number of wires that will later be bound together to form a wiring loom or harness. This keeps them neat and, when well supported, provides the strength necessary to protect them from any damage due to vibration.

When a circuit is in use, electricity flows through a wire and energises the unit to which the wire is attached (and nothing else). To prevent the possibility of a wire touching surrounding components, the metal wire itself is covered with insulating material, usually PVC, which is coloured to assist identification. A small portion of this insulation has to be stripped away to expose the end of the wire, and often a fitting is attached to the end of a wire so that the wire can be screwed or plugged to the appropriate terminal on the unit. Fittings always used to be soldered to the wire but are now often, much more conveniently, crimped (squeezed) on to the wire by means of crimping pliers (see *Fig. 14.1*).

Wire, technically known as 'cable' when insulated, is available in many different sizes depending on the electrical load it has to carry. To provide flexibility, cable is made up of a number of strands of wire, and is identified by the number of strands it contains and the cross-sectional diameter of each strand. For example, metric 14/0.30 cable means that the cable has 14 strands, each strand having a diameter of 0.30mm. You will need a supply of this cable, in different colours, and a smaller supply of cable of twice the capacity (28/0.30) will also be required. These cables will carry a current of 7 amps and 14 amps respectively. A small supply of heavier cable will also be needed to connect the starter motor, solenoid, battery and alternator (generator).

Many colours of cable are available, both solid colours and those with a 'tracer' in a different colour. Although there is a British Standard for colour coding, and some other countries have developed their own, specifying wiring colours for each circuit, there is no international agreement, and most manufacturers choose their own colours. Lucas, one of the largest suppliers of electrical units in the UK, use the following main colours:

Black	earth ('ground')
Brown	main battery feed
Green	feed to units controlled by the ignition switch
Purple	feeds to units not controlled by the ignition switch
White	ignition circuits
Red	side and rear lights
Blue	headlamps

Whatever colours you decide to use, it makes good sense to stick to one basic colour for each type of circuit, and to make a note of it for future reference. One alternative, used by a well-known restoration company, is to use one cable colour throughout and to label the cable ends. This is certainly easier to do but makes trouble-shooting more difficult.

If you are building a kit car designed to accept the donor car's wiring loom, or if you are using a replacement ready-made loom for a rebuild, you will not need to concern yourself with colours or fittings, as they will have been provided. It is unwise to try to adapt an existing loom to your own needs, as the individual cables will almost certainly be too long or too short, or emerge in the wrong place, or have the wrong fittings. If you are building from scratch, it is much easier to do your own thing, but by all means use the cables from an existing loom, taking it to pieces carefully and checking that the insulation is intact.

When a circuit is activated, electricity flows from the positive (+) side of the battery though the unit and back to the negative (–) side of the battery. In theory, two cables are necessary, one connecting the positive side of the battery to the unit, the 'feed', and another one connecting the unit to the negative side of the battery, the 'return'. However, if you have a car with a metal chassis and/or body, only the feed wire from the battery to the unit is necessary, since if the unit is attached to, or can be connected to, the chassis, the negative side of the battery can also be connected to the chassis to provide an 'earth return'. Units not so attached are wired to a suitable point to provide the return, as is the negative side of the battery. This results in far less wiring and consequently less complication, but ensure that you make an effective connection, as a bad earth is one of the most common faults in an electrical system.

If your car is made of glassfibre (GRP) you will need to provide return wiring of a size not less than that of the feed, either to the metal chassis, or back to the battery. Similarly, if you have a car with a metal body, but with lights that are set into GRP wings, you will have to provide return wiring.

Whatever type of chassis you have, you must remember to earth the engine to the chassis (or battery) by means of a flexible earth strap, as the engine is usually insulated from the chassis by means of the rubber engine mounts. Also, if the metal body is insulated from the chassis, ensure that an adequate earthing wire connects the two. On cars with metal dashboards, if the engine is not earthed or the strap has broken, the choke cable is sometimes the only earth that the engine's electrics have. As this cable is not adequate for the load, it will get hot and may even glow quite brightly. Since the choke cable is usually hidden under the dashboard, it is not until the smell of scorching trousers is noticed, or a merry little fire starts amongst the wiring, that you realise that the engine is not properly earthed.

As with house wiring, fuses are

Fig. 14.2. Fuses and relays on a racing Locost.

usually incorporated into at least some of the circuits to act as a 'weak link', in case a fault develops in the wiring or unit that could cause damage to other units or the battery, or even start a fire. Modern cars have many fuses protecting individual circuits, and race and rally cars may have a fuse for every individual circuit, though older cars have far fewer and some had only two, one to protect units controlled by the ignition switch, the other for circuits energised directly by the battery. This may be perfectly satisfactory, especially on a sports car with relatively little equipment, but it is convenient to use the fuse box as a junction box as well, and it is easier to trace problems if several fuses are used.

Here in our example we shall use five fuses, two connected directly to the battery (F1 and F2) and three connected to the ignition switch (F3, F4, and F5). If you are building a large and luxurious special or kit car with a lot of electrical systems, you may wish to use more fuses.

CIRCUITS

A circuit requires a feed from the positive side of the battery to the consumer unit, and a return to the negative side of the battery, as shown in *Fig. 14.3*. In the example shown, the lamp would be permanently connected to the battery and would remain alight until the battery had discharged. A switch, therefore, needs to be added to make a circuit as shown in *Fig. 14.4*, and this is the model for each of the circuits of a car. In wiring diagram form a circuit is drawn using the earth return system, as shown in *Fig. 14.5*. The whole of a car's wiring is made up of circuits like this. There are a variety of standard symbols for circuit diagrams, but they are usually obvious or are explained in the diagram itself.

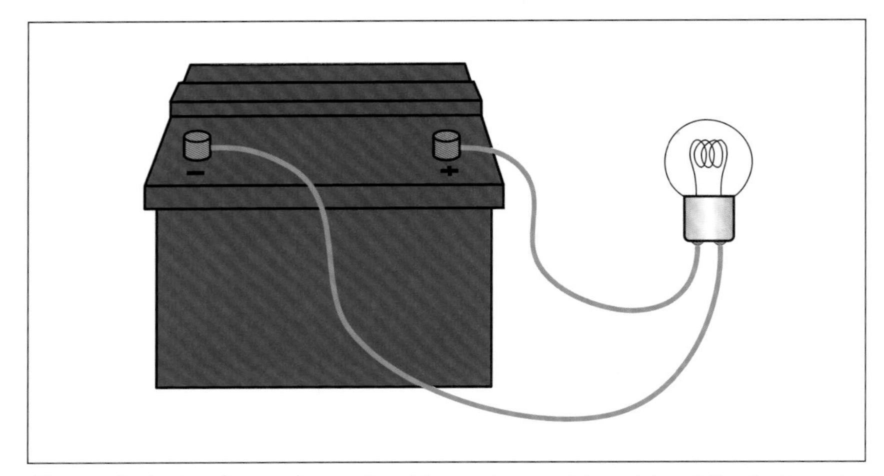

Fig. 14.3. A circuit requires a feed from the positive side of the battery to the 'consumer unit' and a return to the negative side of the battery.

Fig. 14.4. The same circuit shown in Fig. 14.3 with a switch fitted.

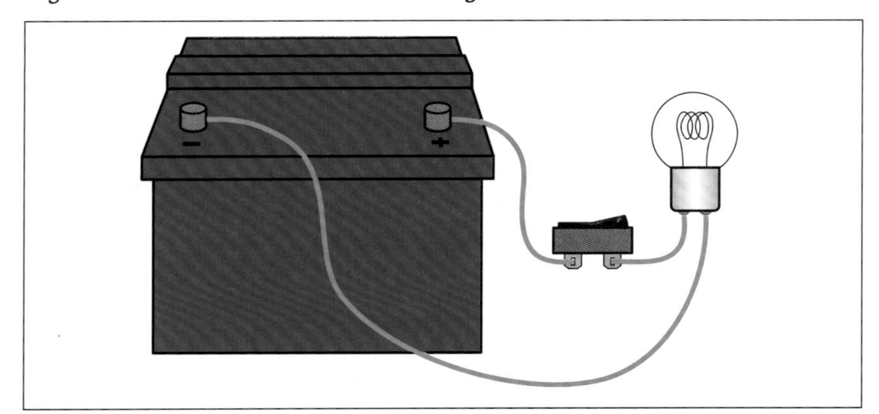

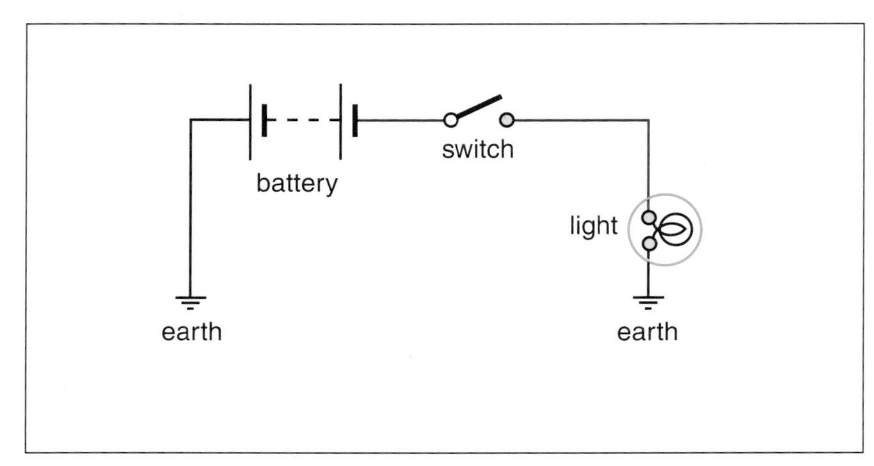

Fig. 14.5. The same circuit shown in Fig. 14.3 represented diagrammatically using the earth return system.

THE BATTERY

The battery is the heart of the electrical system, providing power for all of the units. The battery is itself kept fully charged by the generator – the alternator or dynamo. Since the 1960s, all cars have been equipped with 12-volt electrical systems and batteries, rather than the 6-volt systems much used previously and still in use on smaller motorcycles.

Batteries are available in different charge storage capacities, measured in ampere hours, which affects their physical size. A small sports car will manage very well on a battery of 35 to 40 ampere hours, unless it has a very highly tuned engine with a high compression ratio when something larger may be desirable to ensure good starting, but if you are building something larger, a saloon for example with electric windows, heated seats and so on, a battery with a bigger capacity will be necessary.

The battery is heavy and needs to be secured where it can easily be accessed and serviced; again, on the bulkhead close to the fusebox is a good place.

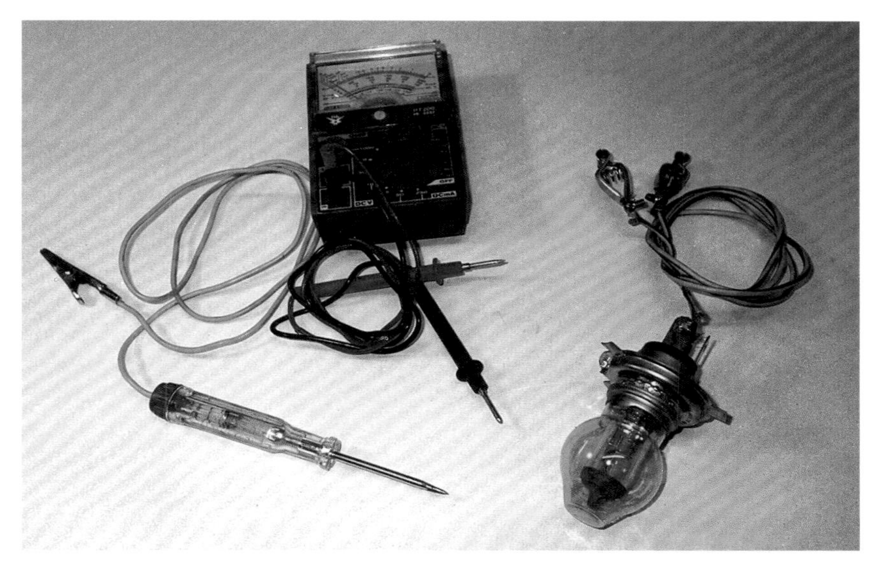

Fig. 14.6. Any of these testers will do for testing continuity.

FUSEBOX

Fuses are usually housed in a fusebox, though additional 'line' fuses in the cable itself are sometimes used for add-on accessories. There are three normal types of fuse – glass, ceramic and the more modern flat-bladed plug-in type.

Mount the fusebox in an easily accessible position; on the bulkhead in the engine bay is as good a position as any. Hella make a very neat five-fuse box, and Lucas produce separate single fuse holders which clip together to give you whatever size fusebox you need. Lucas Part No. 37552 is a particularly neat 'period' box for two or four glass fuses – ideal for restorers. Fuse boxes are also available in various sizes for ceramic fuses and flat-bladed fuses.

RELAYS

Relays are electrically controlled switches, and they are much used on modern cars to relieve the load on other switches and to allow thinner wires to be used for a part of the circuit. The relay is usually located either with the fuse box or near the unit it operates, so that the thicker wires necessary can be more conveniently routed. The 'high load' side of the relay normally has its own fuse.

If you decide to have more than one horn, or air horns, or if you fit driving or fog lights, then relays are desirable. Be careful to use the right type, although if you are buying new equipment the relay is usually included, or is specified, in the kit. The circuit will look like that shown in *Fig. 14.19.*

The wiring from the switch to the relay uses the thinner cable, but from the relay to the unit and to the battery 28/0.30 cable is used. Note that if you fit driving lights the law requires that these are usable only when the headlights are operating on main beam, whereas the fog lights may be used only in conjunction with dipped headlights.

WIRING A CAR

Now to work. First, decide on the position of the battery. Do not fit it at this stage, but fix the fusebox in place. We will proceed circuit by circuit, labelling each and testing it before moving on to the next. For circuit checking, a cheap meter is useful, or you can use a bulb attached to two wires with clips at their free ends (see *Fig. 14.6*).

You must decide whether to wire the vehicle for a positive or a negative earth. If you are rebuilding an older vehicle, especially with a dynamo, it may have a positive earth, while more modern vehicles are wired with a negative earth, the system which will be used here.

Before you make the first connection you need to know how to use the crimping pliers, though it is simple enough. These pliers are designed to cut cable, to strip it of insulation, and to crimp the fittings on to the bared wire. For each of the last two functions there are several positions on the pliers that are colour-coded red, blue and yellow; these refer to the colour of the fittings, or terminals, which are available in three sizes. Red terminals are used on cable up to 14/0.30, blue for the thicker 28/0.30 cable and yellow for terminals and cable up to 65/0.30.

Therefore, when you are stripping the 'thin' cable (14/0.30) you will use the grooves with the red dot and the jaws marked red for crimping the red fittings; similarly you use the blue fittings and blue parts of the crimping pliers for the thicker 28/0.30 cable.

The insulation should be stripped from the end of the cable for about ¼in (6mm) for the red and blue fittings, and about 5⁄16in (8mm) for the yellow, then pushed into the fitting until the insulation

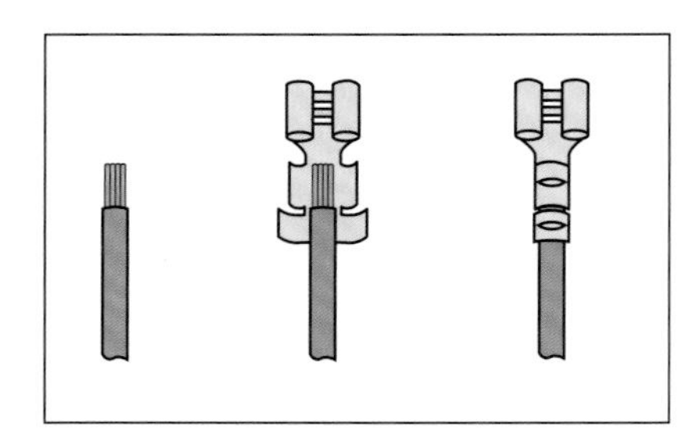

Fig. 14.7. Crimped terminal connection.

meets the barrel on the end of the fitting. Each fitting should then be crimped twice, as shown in *Fig. 14.7*, once to grip the cable and once to grip the bared wire.

Take a piece of the thicker cable (28/0.30), remove the insulation from both ends, and on one end secure the negative battery clamp, using the two screws provided if yours is like the one shown in *Fig. 14.8*. On the other end fit a ring terminal, and secure this to a convenient bolt on the chassis, keeping the cable as short as possible. Next, run a second length of the 28/0.30 wire to fuse F1 on the fusebox. The other end of this wire will eventually be connected permanently to the battery positive clamp, but a temporary fixing will do for the moment.

While the process of wiring is being undertaken, **always** leave the battery disconnected to avoid short circuits (that is a live, or feed, wire making contact with earth directly without being routed through its relevant component).

Connect fuse F1 to fuse F2, and then, still using the thicker 28/0.30 cable, connect F2 to one side of the ignition switch. The other side of the switch is connected to F3, which is then also connected to the two remaining fuses, F4 and F5. The fusebox is now 'live', with the first two fuses connected directly to the battery, the other three becoming live when the ignition switch is turned on. The circuit looks like that shown in *Fig. 14.9*.

Fig. 14.8. Battery connectors.

THE REQUIREMENTS OF THE LAW

Lighting requirements

These may vary from country to country, but in the UK, and in conformity with EC agreements, a vehicle must have a full complement of lights and they must be correctly positioned, and in the case of headlights, correctly focused.

The minimum requirements are:

2 headlamps
2 side lamps
2 rear lamps
2 stop (brake) lamps (plus one high level is optional)
1 rear fog lamp (high intensity)
Rear number plate illumination
2 front flashing direction indicators, amber
2 rear flashing direction indicators, amber
2 direction indicator side repeaters (flashing with appropriate direction indicators)
2 rear reflectors

Fig. 14.9. A circuit diagram for a 'live' fusebox. The first two fuses are connected directly to the battery, the other three becoming 'live' when the ignition switch is turned on.

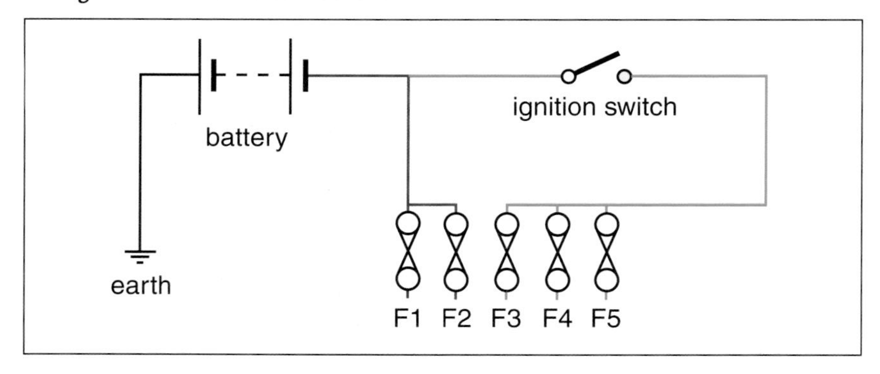

Headlamps

Must be of the same colour and power, and each must be situated at the same height and distance from the centreline of the car, and must be capable of being dipped. The distance from the ground to the lowest point of the headlights must be no lower than 500mm, and the distance from the ground to the highest point of the headlights must not be more than 1,200mm. The headlights must be a minimum of 300mm from each other and each must be not more than 400mm from the outside edge of the car.

Side lamps

Must be white and of not more than 7W (otherwise they must be capable of being dipped!).

Rear lamps

Must be red and must have a minimum rating of 5W. The distance from the ground to the lowest point of the rear lamps must be no lower than 350mm, and the distance from the ground to the highest point of the rear lamps must not be more than 1,500mm.

Stop (brake) lamps

Each stop (brake) lamp must have a rating of 21W.

Flashing indicators

Four amber lights, two at the front and two at the rear, of 21W each. They must be a maximum of 300mm from the ground and 400mm from the side of the vehicle at the front, and at the rear a minimum of 350mm from the ground and 400mm from the outer edge of the vehicle. Additionally, two direction indicator side repeater lights are required, one on each side of the vehicle, of 5W each. It must be possible to operate all the direction indicator lights at the same time, by means of a hazard warning flasher switch, in order to act as a hazard warning to other motorists.

Reversing lights (if fitted)

A maximum of two, of 21W each, which can only be operated when reverse gear is selected.

Wipers and washers

Unless you have an opening windscreen you must have at least one effective wiper and washer for the driver. Aero-screens and racing-type windscreens (really little more than wind-deflectors) are excluded from this requirement

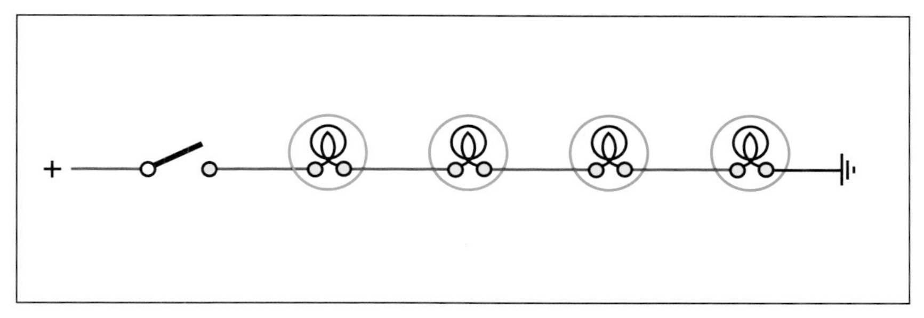

Fig. 14.10. An example of wiring lights in series.

Horn

A horn is a legal requirement. Air horns are available that play tunes, but in the UK these are illegal, as the regulations require that multiple horns must all sound at the same time.

BODY ELECTRICS

Sidelights, headlights and tail lights

Very few cars have lights controlled by the ignition switch, though FIAT have used this system for many years and it does mean that it is not possible to leave the car with the lights on – a separate switch is used to operate the parking lights when required. If you want to follow this system you will need to take a 'thick' cable from fuse F3 – if not, use fuse F1 – and connect it to the lighting switch. From the other side of the switch take a 'thin' cable to each rear light and side light, and also to the number plate lamp. You *could* wire them in series, as shown in *Fig. 14.10*, but if you did, the failure of any one bulb would break the circuit and all the lights would go out. For this reason, the lights should be wired in parallel (see *Fig. 14.11*), including any connections to the instruments or instrument panel illumination lights.

The headlights are controlled by no less than three switches – the sidelight switch (since you need the rear lights on at the same time), the headlight switch (the two are usually combined), and the dip-switch which selects dipped or full beam. If the sidelight and headlight switches are combined you will not

Fig. 14.11. An example of wiring lights in parallel, including wiring to instrument panel.

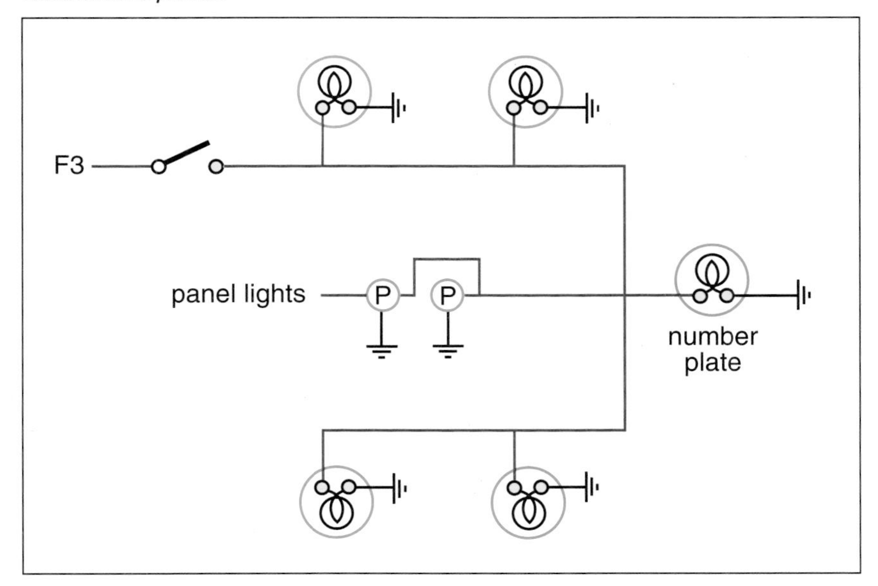

need a further connection to the fusebox, but the thicker wire is used because of the greater load. See *Fig. 14.12*. A (blue) instrument panel warning light is wired into the full-beam circuit from the relevant side of the dip-switch (see *Fig. 14.13*).

As you complete each circuit, test it with a meter or test lamp, temporarily connecting the battery. Do not forget to label the wires. You should now have all the driving lights working, and the instrument or panel illumination lights.

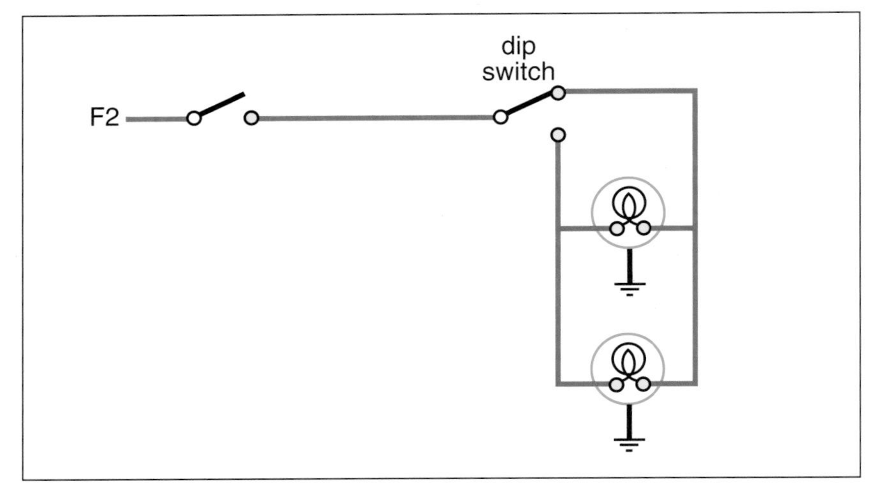

Fig. 14.12. A dip-switch circuit. Thicker cable (28/0.30) is used because of the greater load in the main beam circuit.

Fig. 14.13. A main beam warning light (blue) is wired into the main beam circuit from the relevant side of the dip switch.

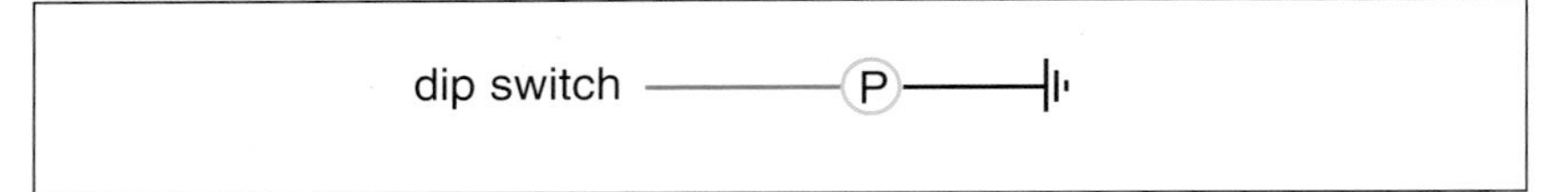

Direction indicator lights

The direction indicators are just lights that are made to flash on and off between 60 and 100 times per minute, a speed originally chosen so that if the flasher unit fails it is possible to operate them manually at the same frequency. You must have a warning lamp on the dashboard that flashes on-and-off in sympathy. If you want only one warning lamp then you need a 3-pin flasher unit; if you want two warning lights to show left and right flashers respectively, then a 2-pin unit is required. This circuit uses the 'thin' wire and is taken from one of the ignition-controlled fuses, say F4. A side repeater lamp on each side of the car is also required. See *Fig. 14.14*.

Some flasher units have their terminals numbered, which is useful.

Hazard warning lights

It is necessary to install a system whereby all the flashers can work together for use in an emergency. This circuit must have its own switch and a tell-tale light visible to the driver (the direction indicator warning light can be used for the tell-tale). Some cars use one unit for both the direction indicator lights and hazard warning lights, while others have separate flasher and hazard warning light units. If you use a unit, or units, from a donor car, take the switch as well. You will need to note the way in which the circuits are wired, or you will need to consult the wiring diagram for the donor car.

If you intend to use new direction indicator or hazard warning light units, the Lucas combined unit SFB 162, as used on many production cars, or the separate units SFB 114 and SFB 130, as used on Morgans and Rovers, will suit the purpose and will come with wiring diagrams.

Brake lights

The other main lighting circuit you require is for the brake lights. On

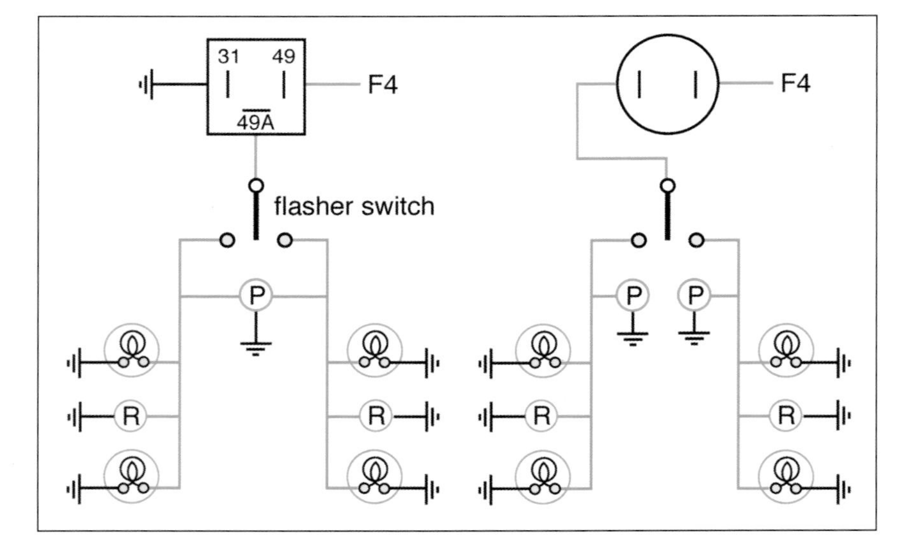

Fig. 14.14. Two direction indicator circuits. The circuit on the left has a 3-pin flasher unit for a single warning light, and that on the right has a 2-pin unit for two warning lights (left and right). Use a thin cable (14/0.30) and connect to one of the ignition-controlled fuses, say F4.

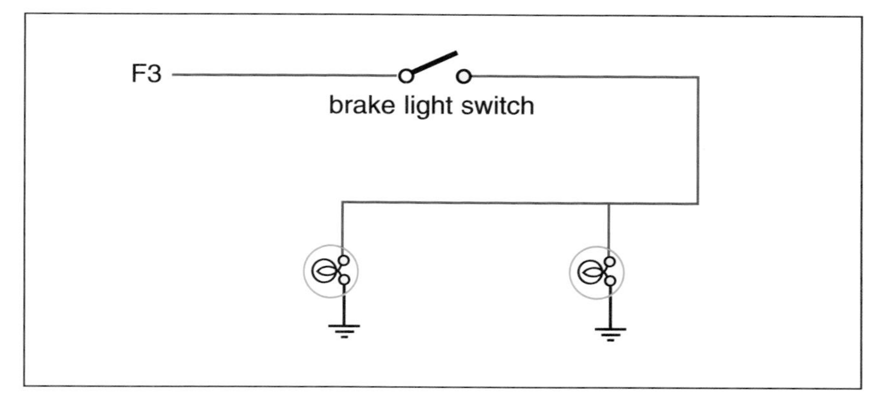

Fig. 14.15. A brake light circuit. A thin cable is taken from the F3 terminal of the fuse box to the switch, and then from the other side of the switch to the brake lights.

many older cars with hydraulic brakes, a hydraulic pressure-operated switch is built into the system, located either on the end of the master cylinder or as a separate unit in one of the brake pipe junctions. The switch is easily identified as it has two terminals sticking out of it. On more modern cars the brake-light switch is operated mechanically by the brake pedal.

A 'thin' wire from F3 should be taken to the switch, and a wire from the remaining switch terminal should be connected to the brake lights. See *Fig. 14.15.*

Rear fog light

A rear fog light, mounted on the centreline of the car or towards the offside is required. This must be separately switched and must have its own tell-tale light visible to the driver.

Reversing light

A reversing light is not essential but, if fitted, it needs to be automatic so that it only operates when the car is in reverse. On most cars, provision is made for this by the fitting of a switch which is operated by the gearchange mechanism. The circuit required is similar to that used for the brake lights.

Brake fluid level warning light

There must be a red warning lamp that illuminates when the brake fluid falls below the minimum level in the reservoir. The warning light circuit must have a 'test facility' (usually a push switch on the top of the reservoir) that enables the operation of the warning light to be checked. There is normally a float built into the reservoir cap which operates the warning light switch.

Ammeter

An ammeter shows the rate at which the battery is being charged or discharged. The ammeter is wired into the circuit through which the generator charges the battery. On cars fitted with dynamos an ammeter was very common, but since the advent of alternators, with their much higher charging rate, the ammeter has been replaced by the battery condition meter. Ammeter wiring is simple, as the unit is placed in the charging circuit, immediately before the battery. See *Fig. 14.16.*

Battery Condition Meter

This is a voltmeter which shows the state of charge of the battery, and is simply connected to F3, F4 or F5, and then to earth. See *Fig. 14.17.*

Tachometer

Early tachometers, commonly known as a revolution counters (or just 'rev counters') were mechanical, and thereafter they became electric and then electronic. There have been various types, some connected to the alternator, but more often to the coil or distributor. The most common, simple, type has two terminals, one for earth and the other for connection to the distributor. If you are using a unit from another vehicle, make sure, if you can, that it is intended for an engine with the same number of cylinders as that which you intend to use, otherwise you will get a false reading.

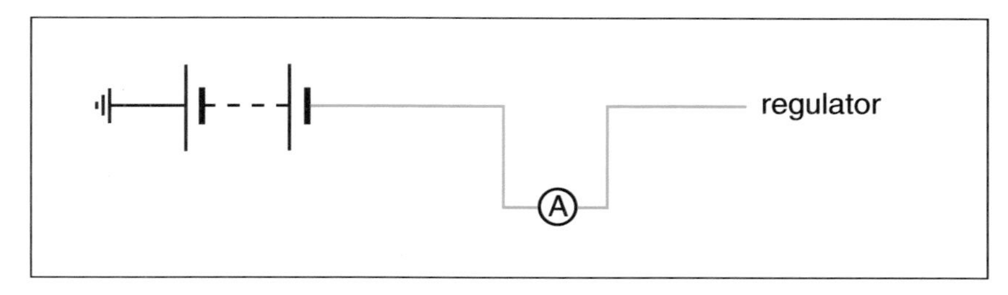

Fig. 14.16. An ammeter wired into the charging circuit between the battery and the regulator. This shows the rate at which the battery is being charged or discharged.

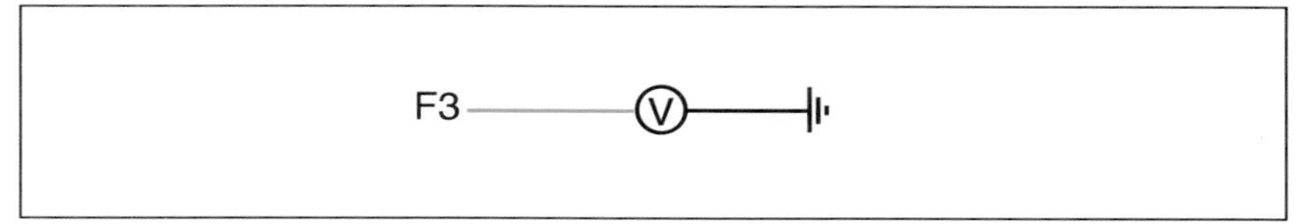

Fig. 14.17. A battery condition meter, or voltmeter (to show the battery's state of charge), can be connected to terminals F3, F4 or F5 of the fuse box and then to earth.

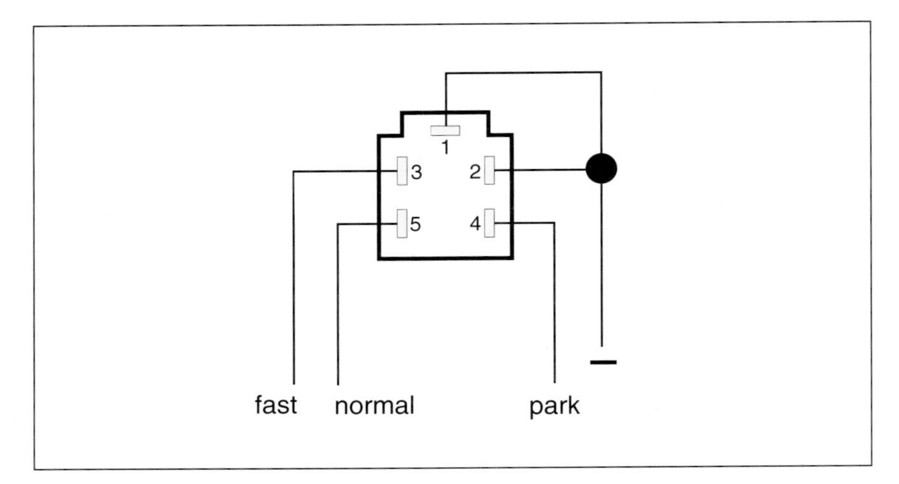

Fig. 14.18. Two-speed Lucas windscreen wiper motor connections.

Temperature and fuel gauges

Temperature gauges may be either electrically operated from strategically placed 'senders' or may be operated by a pressure system from a 'bulb' with a capillary tube routed to the instrument. Senders for water temperature gauges are often placed in the thermostat housing or upper water hose, while those for oil temperature are usually located in the sump or on the oil filter mounting. If you have the capillary tube type of gauge, handle it carefully because a broken tube cannot be mended. Electrically operated gauges should be wired with one side connected to one of the ignition-controlled fuses, and the other side to the sender, the case being earthed.

Windscreen wipers and washers

Windscreen washers were originally operated by a mechanical pump, or operated by suction from the inlet manifold, but all modern washer systems have a small electric pump unit situated either in the bottom of the washer bottle or in the pipe line. Electric wipers were originally single speed, but most modern ones are two speed, often with an intermittent-wipe facility that is sometimes adjustable for frequency. There are many variations and it is important, if you are taking the equipment from a donor, that you also take the switchgear and note the wiring connections so that you can connect the equipment correctly on your own car. If the wiper motor is a Lucas two-speed type, the wiring will be as shown in *Fig. 14.18*.

Horns

Horns usually consume quite a lot of current, and often a single horn is wired direct to fuse F1 or F2 so that it is not wired through the ignition switch, which would add to the load on the switch contacts. Using the thicker wire, this is quite in order, with one side of the horn push connected to the fuse and the other side to the horn itself, which is then earthed. If there is only a single terminal, the horn case provides the earth.

However, one drawback of this method of wiring the horn is that the horn can be sounded without the ignition being switched on. In an open car this is an invitation to small boys and other admirers to try it out, and it is also easily sounded accidentally when parked. A better system is to wire the horn through the ignition switch, using fuse F4, and to incorporate a relay.

On many cars the normal system is reversed, the feed going direct to the horn, with the switch or horn push wired into the earth return circuit. This is because horn pushes were traditionally, as some still are, placed in the centre of the steering wheel, and the wiring can be subject to chafing and consequent short circuiting if wired in the normal way. If the switch is wired into the return side of the circuit, all that happens if there is a problem is that the horn refuses to sound, which at least tells you what is wrong. I once bought a pre-war 328 BMW that sounded the horn automatically every time I was on full left lock. Needless to say I did not discover this until after I had bought it, by which time it was too late to use the fault as a means of reducing the price!

ENGINE ELECTRICS

You now have all the electrically operated equipment in place in order to make the car roadworthy, and we can now deal with the various engine and charging

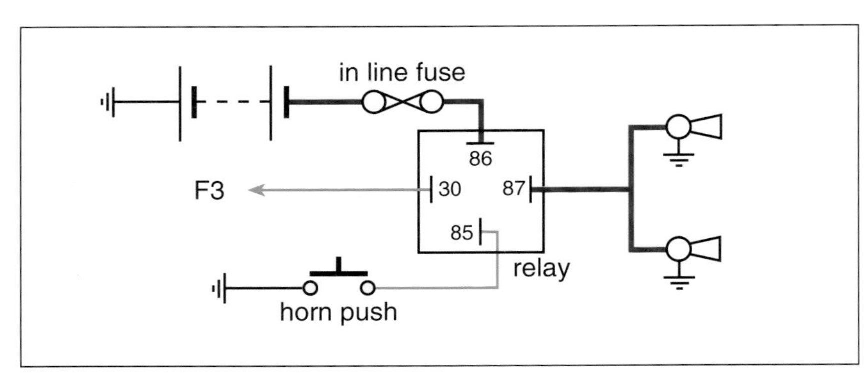

Fig. 14.19. A twin-horn circuit with a relay. Thin cable is used from the horn push to the relay, and thick cable from the relay to the horns and battery.

circuits. Of course there is no reason why you should not start with the engine electrics, as you will no doubt be anxious to get the engine running, especially if it is an unknown quantity, but I always leave it until I have finished installing the various services – exhaust, fuel supply, cooling system – since a lot of time can be wasted in rigging up temporary systems, and in any case running an engine for short periods of time is not a good idea as it leads to condensation in the cylinders, and it may harm the alternator if this is not connected to the battery. Understandably, there is a natural anxiety to hear the engine burst into life, and it is a great thrill when it does.

I have reserved fuse F5 for the engine electrics. Using a length of the thinner 14/0.30 cable, connect fuse F5 to the ignition coil, and from the other terminal of the coil take a wire to the distributor. If you have an electric fuel pump, this should have its own fuse, so if you have run out of fuses in the fuse box, fit an in-line fuse to the wire feeding the pump in an easily accessible position, and take the feed from an unprotected source. The starter motor solenoid, which is effectively a heavy-duty relay, is wired to the spring-loaded starter side of the ignition switch, if this switch combines the starter function, or to a separate starter switch, if not.

Ignition system

A conventional distributor has two functions, first to produce a spark at the correct instant and then to convey it to the relevant spark plug.

On older engines, the distributor is often driven by the camshaft, usually at right-angles to it by means of skew gears, or by an auxiliary shaft, but more modern engines with overhead camshafts often have a distributor which is driven from the end of the camshaft itself.

The contact breaker distributor consists of a shaft with a cam at one end, which has the same number of lobes as there are cylinders. The lobes of the cam open, and allow to close under spring pressure, a moveable contact which, when closed, presses against a contact fixed to the distributor base plate. These contacts are the 'contact breaker points' and are in fact merely a switch, connected between the coil and earth. Each time the points open (or 'break' the circuit) a very high voltage (high tension or HT) is induced in the coil. This voltage passes down the HT 'king' lead from the coil to the central electrode of the distributor cap and is routed by the rotor arm to the correct HT lead for the spark plug which is next in the engine cylinder firing order. The current jumps across the spark plug electrodes and goes to earth. All this takes place in a fraction of a second.

In order to ensure that the timing of the spark is exactly suited to the needs of the engine, on a conventional distributor there are two mechanisms to vary the timing, one being adjusted by engine speed, the other by the load on the engine.

The advance mechanism related to engine speed consists of a centrifugal governor in the base of the distributor housing, which is attached to the shaft, and has two bob-weights that move outwards against spring pressure and advance the ignition by turning the contact breaker operating cam.

Additional ignition advance is required when the engine is not under load, and this is achieved using a vacuum advance unit attached to the body of the distributor. The vacuum advance unit consists of a capsule with a diaphragm. The capsule is connected by a tube to the inlet manifold. As the vacuum in the manifold depends on the load on the engine, it varies, and this variation causes the diaphragm to flex. As the diaphragm is connected to the base plate, it moves the base plate and therefore the contact that is fixed to it.

Developments in electronics have made possible the alternative types of ignition systems which are used on more modern engines (modern engines no longer use conventional contact breaker distributors). Some systems use a simple distributor with an external resemblance to the traditional type distributor, and some systems do not use a mechanical distributor at all.

The contact breaker mechanism of the older type of distributor has always been potentially the most troublesome part of the ignition system since, as the points erode and the moving components wear, the gap between the points varies, which in turn alters the timing of the spark and its efficiency. Points can also stick open or closed, and they do not like damp weather or very high engine speeds. In the event of engine starting or running problems, or poor performance, the points are usually the most likely source of trouble.

Designers have therefore long been keen to find alternatives to the old-fashioned contact breaker points and to replace them with something more reliable and accurate. This has resulted in the development of magnetic and optical systems, which can be used to trigger electronic devices in order to generate HT voltage for distribution to the spark plugs through a conventional rotor arm and distributor cap.

Although the ignition coils used in electronic ignition systems may appear to be physically similar to those used in contact breaker systems, in fact they are different. The best advice that can be given regarding ignition systems is to remove from the donor the complete system and consult the relevant workshop manual about setting up and timing the system.

Many modern engines have a Distributorless Ignition System (DIS) which does not have a distributor of any kind. Such systems are triggered magnetically or electronically by a microprocessor which receives signals from various engine sensors. The microprocessor (electronic control unit) energises the relevant coil in a combined unit which is connected direct to the sparking plugs. It is important to note that such systems are designed specifically for the engine to which they are fitted, and no attempt should be made to adapt them for use on an alternative type of engine. Often, the electronic control units are matched to a specific model of car. Many aftermarket ignition and engine management systems are now available from specialist manufacturers for use on engines of all types.

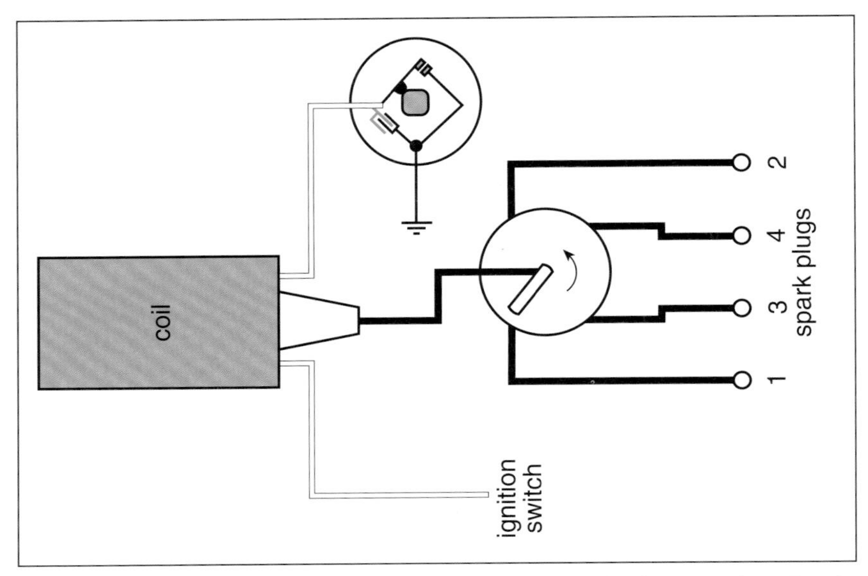

Fig. 14.20. An ignition circuit. Thin cable connects the low tension circuit of the coil to the ignition switch and the distributor. HT cable connects the coil's high tension output to the distributor's central electrode, and from the distributor to each individual spark plug.

Connecting distributor HT leads

When connecting the leads from a distributor cap to the spark plugs, the first thing to do is to check the firing order of the engine, the second is to establish which is No 1 cylinder, and the third is to establish the direction of rotation of the rotor arm in the distributor, either clockwise or anti-clockwise. The direction of rotation is easily established by removing the distributor cap and looking at the rotor arm as the engine is turned over. The other information can usually be gathered from the workshop manual. (Some manufacturers used to give the firing order on a plate on the engine, or cast it into the manifold.) It is normal to count No 1 cylinder as the one nearest to the timing belt/chain end of the engine, but some cars (including early Morgans and Lancias) are numbered from the opposite end. If you are new to engines, you might think that the HT leads are connected in sequence, 1-2-3-4, for a four-cylinder engine, but the norm is 1-3-4-2 or 1-2-4-3, and a V8 engine may have a firing order of 1-8-4-3-6-5-7-2 (Rover) or 1-2-7-8-4-5-6-3 (Triumph Stag). Other firing orders are also possible.

If the information on firing order is not available, you can work it out quite easily by looking at the valves. Remove the spark plugs and set No 1 cylinder with the piston at top dead centre (TDC), that is, at the top of its stroke. With the valves for No 1 cylinder fully closed, this is the point at which the plug fires. Turn the engine in the normal direction of rotation until the next piston is at TDC with the valves fully closed – this will be the second cylinder in the firing sequence – and so on until you have completed, and noted, the full sequence.

To determine to which terminal in the distributor cap each HT lead should be connected, with No 1 cylinder at TDC, as previously described, note the position of the rotor arm. The terminal to which the rotor arm is pointing is the terminal for the HT lead to No 1 cylinder, and the appropriate lead should be connected. The remaining leads should be connected in the correct firing order in accordance with the direction of rotation of the rotor arm. Once the leads have been connected, it is worthwhile marking them so that there is no further doubt, and you will be able to reconnect them correctly whenever you need to. (See *Fig. 14.20* for distributor circuit.)

Starting circuit

The starting circuit draws a very heavy current, and consequently needs a heavier than normal gauge of cable to connect the starter to the battery via the solenoid. Additionally, the starter circuit is not fused. Note that most solenoids are attached to the starter motor itself – taking the form of a small cylindrical device, often with a rubber button on one end – while some older types are fitted close to the starter motor, probably on the engine compartment bulkhead. The circuit is as shown in *Fig. 14.21* and uses heavy duty cables of either 37/0.71 for a current of 105 amps or 37/0.90 for up to 170 amps, though some manufacturers prefer to double up and use two thinner cables of equivalent value.

Charging circuit

The charging circuit provides the means to keep the battery fully charged, either by means of a dynamo (as on early cars) or an

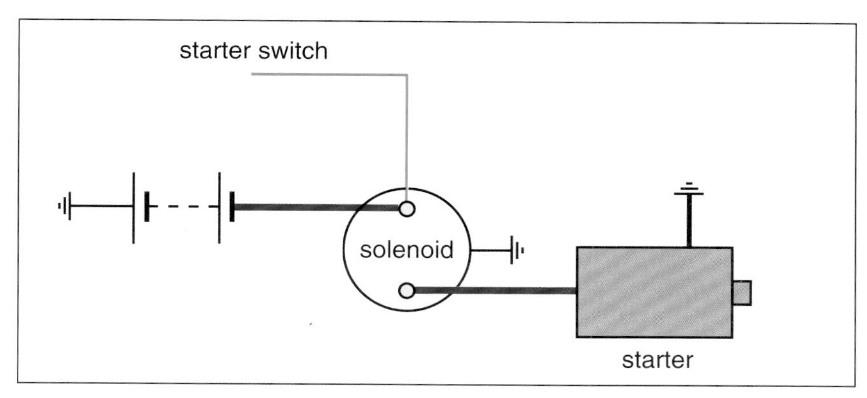

Fig. 14.21. A starting circuit. Heavy duty cable is used to connect the battery to the solenoid and then on to the starter motor.

alternator (as on later ones). Although a dynamo is more efficient as a machine, the alternator can be driven at a higher speed to produce the greater output demanded by modern cars with their many electrical units. A dynamo produces direct current (DC), which is required for battery charging, whereas an alternator produces alternating current (AC) and this has to be converted ('rectified') to DC before it can be used. On early alternators, the rectifier was a separate unit, but on more modern units the rectifier is built in to the alternator.

Dynamos have a separate unit, called a regulator, which governs the charging rate to meet the battery's requirements, and a cut-out to prevent the battery feeding back into the dynamo and treating it as a motor when it is not charging. Before wiring either dynamo or alternator, it is necessary to check the output (which, in the case of an alternator, can be considerable) to establish the correct size of cable to use. A dynamo will normally be regulated to produce no more than 30amps.

Smaller cars much used as donors, such as the Ford Escort, may have an alternator with an output as low as 28amps, but many had 35amp models and some 55amp. Larger cars may go up to between 60amp and 70amp. You may find the output marked on the unit, or in the workshop manual if you have one.

This table shows the cable sizes required for different outputs:

Amps	**Cable**
25	44/0.30
32	56/0.30
35	65/0.30
42	84/0.30
50	97/0.30
60	120/0.30

As noted previously, you can use two thinner cables instead of one thick one, provided the total cross-sectional area is maintained.

If you are rebuilding, you will have the appropriate wires and connections and need not worry about the circuit, but if you are building a kit car or special you should have kept as much of the wiring as possible from the donor car (even if you do not intend to use it). This will help in identifying the type of circuit required by the alternator, and any special fittings. This is important, as there are a number of different makes of alternator with different methods of regulation and different terminal arrangements. Two common terminal arrangements, 'Euro terminations' and 'Stud terminations' are shown in *Fig. 14.22.*

Regulators for dynamos are separate units, and are normally fitted to the engine compartment bulkhead. There are various types,

Fig. 14.22. A charging circuit with two different terminal arrangements – 'Euro terminations' and 'Stud terminations'.

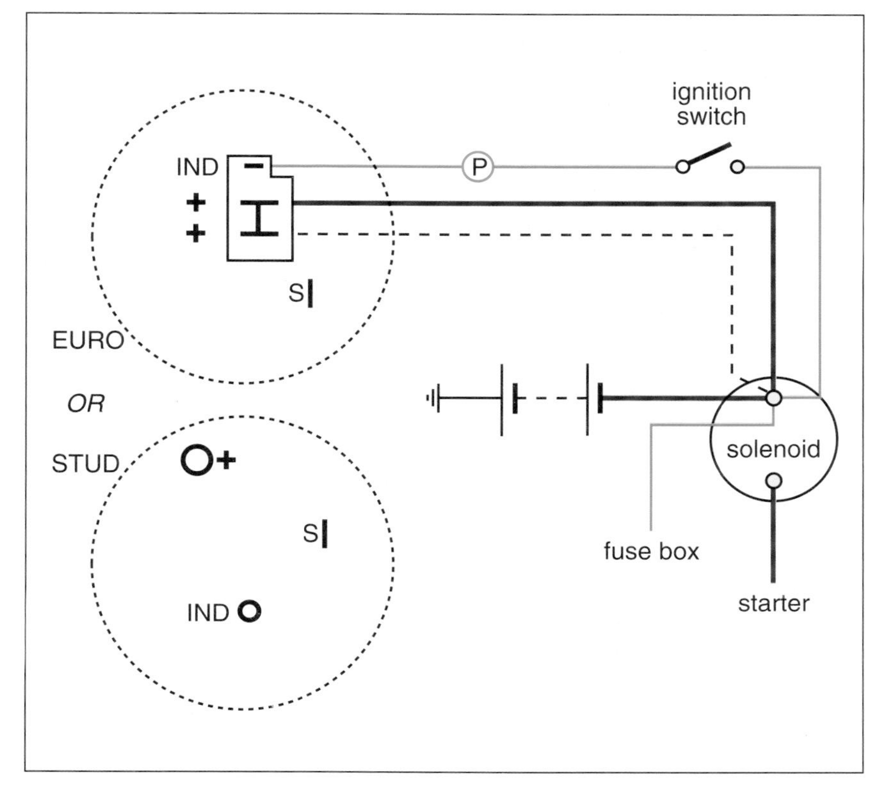

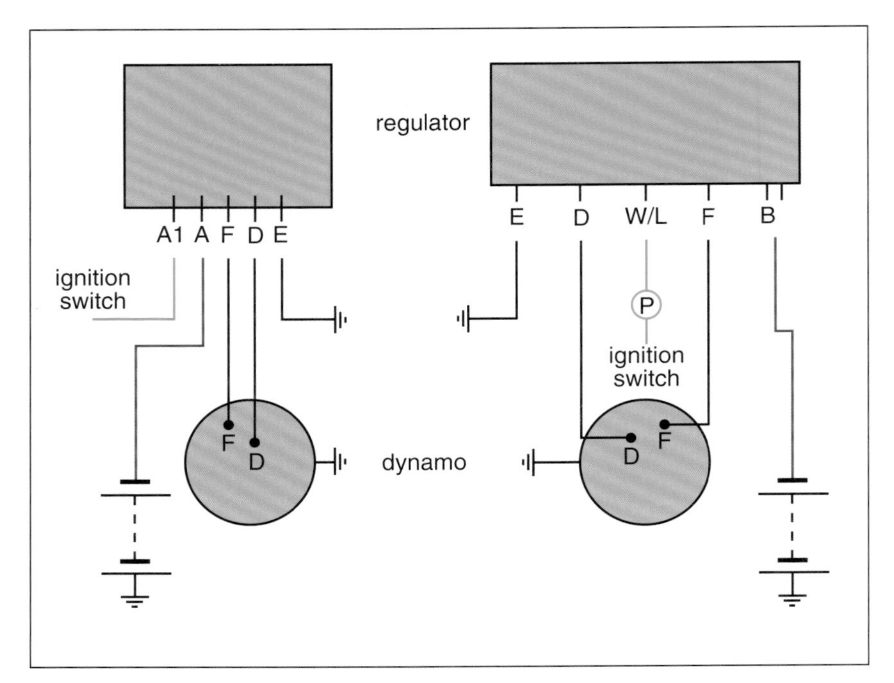

Fig. 14.23. Two typical Lucas dynamo regulator unit circuits. The one on the left is for a '2-bobbin' type dynamo and on the right for a '3-bobbin' type.

The letters on the terminals stand for:

A auxiliary; A1 auxiliary ignition; F field; D dynamo; E earth.

E earth; D dynamo; W/L warning light; F field; B battery.

but *Fig. 14.23* shows typical Lucas circuits. Delco-Remy regulators have three terminals, marked 'BAT' (battery), 'Gen' (dynamo armature windings) and 'F' (dynamo field windings). Auto-Lite units also have three terminals, the upper one for the battery, the lower-left - hand one for the dynamo armature and the central one for the dynamo field windings.

FINAL PREPARATIONS BEFORE CONNECTING THE BATTERY

Once all body and engine electrical circuits have been completed and tested, you may now make permanent the temporary battery connection. Wires can be tidied up by binding them together with harness tape, or insulating tape, or concealing them in flexible convoluted tubing which comes in different sizes and colours, and is split laterally so that you can clip it round the cables. Aim for a neat finish, and support the harness with clips or cable ties.

Where cables pass through metal or GRP panels they need to be protected against being cut or chafed. Rubber grommets can be used for this purpose, and can be pushed into the holes before the wires are led through them.

There are two other points which are worth considering. One is that, if you want to make parts of the car (or the whole body) easily removable, you can cut the cables in appropriate places and connect them to multi-plugs. These plugs fit together only one way, thereby ensuring that all wiring is correctly reconnected after any dismantling operations.

It is also worth considering the installation of a battery master switch. This is very useful when you are working on the engine or electrics, since you can isolate the battery merely by turning the switch. When hidden away it can also be a good security measure, but if you are going to compete in motorsport events you will need a master switch located in an obvious position and clearly labelled 'On-Off'. Modern isolating switches have removable handles so that they are still useful for security purposes even if they are not hidden. If you decide to fit a master switch, but you do not wish to isolate every circuit, for instance you may wish to maintain an electrical supply to the clock or alarm, you merely need to by-pass the switch when wiring those circuits.

Fig. 14.24. Cable ties, sheathing and tool for tightening cable ties.

EQUIPMENT RESTORATION

Whether building or restoring, you will need to ensure that the electrical equipment is operating satisfactorily. Most towns have an automobile electrical specialist who can offer testing facilities, and can either service your equipment for you or offer you a replacement, although there is quite a lot you can do yourself.

I suggested previously that you got rid of the battery unless it was obviously nearly new, but if you want to preserve it, top it up with distilled water to the top of the plates (unless it is of the sealed variety when there is nothing that you can do but charge it). If the battery will not charge, or will not hold a charge for very long, then there is no point in keeping it, and you should get rid of it responsibly as it is potentially dangerous in the wrong hands. When you actually need a battery, buy yourself a new one, suited to the size of your car and the electrical loads which it will have to cope with.

Dynamo

The battery is kept charged by a dynamo or an alternator. A dynamo consists of an armature, with coils of wire wound on it, which revolves inside a casing that also has coils of wire, known as 'field' coils, attached to it.

The field coils have a slight residual magnetism, and the small current produced by the rotating armature is fed into the field coils by means of 'brushes' (carbon blocks which pick up the current from contact strips, known as a 'commutator', on the armature). This causes the magnetic field to intensify rapidly, which needs to be controlled, so a 'regulator' is used to keep the current within prescribed limits, and to provide the battery with the amount of current it needs to keep it fully charged.

If the dynamo appears not to be working while on the car, first check that the wires are in their correct places. Check that the dynamo drive belt is not slipping, by trying to turn the pulley by hand. If you can turn the pulley, the belt is too loose and needs adjusting. On most dynamos, adjustment is carried out by slackening the two locking bolts on the dynamo casing, and a third one on a bracket with a slot in it, and swinging the dynamo away from the engine until the belt has only about ½in (13mm) play in its longest run.

The operation of the dynamo can be checked with the engine running and an ammeter connected in the circuit, as shown in *Fig. 14.16*.

If, after adjusting the drive belt, there is still no charge, remove the dynamo, turn the pulley and feel and listen to the bearings. If there is any sideways play, or a grating noise, the bearings need replacement. A further check can be carried out, this time on the commutator and brushes. As the brushes are in constant contact with the revolving commutator, they gradually wear away, and they are designed to be renewable. To renew the brushes, slip the brushes out of their holders, which should be cleaned before fitting the new brushes. Shape the ends of the new brushes to the curvature of the commutator by fitting a thin strip of fine sandpaper round the commutator, and pulling it backwards and forwards with the brushes pressed against it. The commutator should be cleaned with a rag soaked in petrol, or, if scored, with fine sandpaper, not emery cloth.

Earlier dynamos have a removable band giving access to the brushes, but on later ones the end of the dynamo must be removed by undoing the two long bolts that run the length of the casing. If, after carrying out these operations, there is still no charge, then a fault exists in the wiring and a new or exchange unit will be required.

Regulator

Regulators are normally adjustable, but once set very rarely need attention. Apart from carefully cleaning the contacts, they should not be interfered with unless, with the dynamo known to be working, you still have trouble. You will then need a meter, and a workshop manual which shows what the settings should be, and how to adjust them.

Alternator

Although the alternator is rather differently constructed, it is similar to the dynamo in that an armature (usually known as a rotor) revolves within a casing containing coils of wire (known as a stator), and current is picked up by brushes, not from a commutator as on a dynamo, but from two slip rings. An alternator produces alternating current that has to be converted to direct current by a rectifier before it can be used to charge the battery. In modern alternators the rectifier, a diode pack, is built into the alternator casing with the electronic regulator.

If problems occur with charging, the checks given previously for dynamos should be made on electrical connections, drive belt and brushes, as well as the slip rings. The charging, or ignition warning light is also an important factor, as if it fails it can break the charging circuit.

Alternators are more sensitive than dynamos because of their electronic controlling equipment, which is liable to fail through poor connections to battery or earth, or through temporary reversal of polarity. Alternators are also likely to be damaged if the engine is run without the battery being connected to it, and it is important to disconnect the battery before charging it. If any electric welding to the vehicle is carried out, the alternator must first be disconnected. Regulator units can usually be renewed, but it is worthwhile first consulting a specialist as to whether it is more economical to renew the complete regulator and alternator.

Starter motor

Starter motors (in fact all electric motors to be found on the car) are very similar in principle to the dynamo, though of heavier construction. Of course, electric motors work in the opposite sense to the dynamo, using rather than generating current. Servicing is, therefore, very similar to the procedure described for servicing the dynamo, but additionally the drive to the flywheel needs to be inspected.

On the end of the armature shaft is a small gear wheel, called a 'pinion', which engages with the teeth on the flywheel when the starter is operated. There are several different ways of making this happen, the most common being to slide the pinion into engagement with the flywheel by means of a solenoid, which then switches on the motor itself. This is the more civilised way of doing it, but older cars have an ingenious but rather brutal system called the Bendix, or inertia, drive.

When the starter is operated, the inertia of the pinion makes it reluctant to revolve and it consequently screws itself along the screw thread on which it is mounted until, when in mesh with the flywheel, it is forced to revolve with the motor shaft. This screw thread and pinion should not be oiled or greased, otherwise it tends to collect dirt and the pinion then sticks to the shaft instead of sliding along it. When the engine starts, the flywheel throws the pinion out of mesh and back up its screw thread, its return cushioned by a strong spring.

Pinion teeth are shaped at the side where they enter into mesh with the flywheel. The other end of the armature shaft often has a squared end, under a protective cover, which can be turned with a spanner to disengage the pinion if it becomes stuck with the engine running.

Solenoid

The solenoid is a switch that is operated by the ignition or starter switch, and handles the very considerable current needed by the starter motor when turning the engine. If, with a fully-charged battery, the engine does not turn and there is a noise like a machine gun, the solenoid is probably at fault and a new one will be required.

Distributor

When overhauling a distributor, especially if taken from a donor car, ensure that the tube connecting the vacuum unit to the inlet manifold is intact. The tube is usually narrow bore plastic, attached at each end by rubber connectors which tend to split, thus upsetting both carburation and ignition timing.

Check the distributor shaft to ensure that there is no sideways play in its bushes, as this leads to uneven wear of the contacts in the distributor cap and irregular running.

Attention can now be turned to the contact breaker points. The spark at the points gradually erodes them, despite the presence in the circuit of the condenser (which should prevent it). The points should be clean and not pitted – a small fine file can be used to clean them, unless they are so badly worn that they have to be renewed. The points then need to be set to the correct clearance using a feeler gauge. The clearance is set by moving the rotor arm, or distributor body, until the moving contact rests on the peak of the distributor shaft cam. Slacken the screw securing the fixed contact to the base plate, and insert the feeler gauge to achieve the gap specified in the manual between the contacts, usually about 0.022in to 0.028in (0.56mm to 0.71mm).

There are various methods of adjusting the points, perhaps the most common being by inserting a screwdriver into a gap in the fixed contact base, with the securing screw only partially slackened. The screwdriver can then be used to lever the fixed contact.

A more accurate measurement can be made by means of an automotive electrical meter. The meter must be able to read the 'dwell angle' of the points. This is the period that the points remain closed during the rotation of the cam. A dwell angle of about 54 degrees is common for a four-cylinder engine.

Inspect the rotor arm and distributor cap contacts, and if the contacts are at all worn replace them. Clean and dry ignition leads are essential for efficient running of the engine and easy starting in damp weather. The leads should preferably not be bunched together but held apart by an insulated separator, as in very damp weather it may be possible for the leads to spark across to each other.

The distributor shaft cam should have a light smear of grease on it, and a few drops of oil should be put on the felt lubricator at the top of the shaft under the rotor arm.

When the distributor is refitted to the engine, it should be timed as mentioned in Chapter 8, using timing marks on flywheel or fan pulley if available, the body being turned until the points are just about to open. Final tuning can take place with the engine running by turning the distributor very slightly. To advance the ignition timing, turn the distributor in the opposite direction to the direction of rotation of the rotor arm. To retard the ignition timing (this is required if the engine 'pinks', especially under load), turn the distributor body fractionally in the direction of rotation of the rotor arm.

The type of distributor described was fitted to the vast majority of cars for many years until superseded by the electronic systems mentioned previously, which are largely maintenance-free. The only renewable items in electronic distributors are those liable to wear, the rotor arm, distributor cap and the vacuum capsule. If the unit is to be removed, it should be first checked to see whether there are any timing marks on the distributor and engine. If not, alignment marks should be made before removal.

Some types of electronic distributor that resemble the traditional distributor are capable of being dismantled in much the same way as the older type. The mechanical parts should be cleaned and lubricated. If worn or damaged, a complete new unit may be required as spares for these units are often not available, though repair kits or spares such as pick-up coils, vacuum capsules, rotor arms and caps are usually available. Where applicable, care must be taken on reassembly to ensure that there is no contact between the reluctor poles attached to the distributor shaft, and the surrounding stator pack arms, and if an 'O'-ring is fitted between the distributor and its mounting, it should be renewed.

As with all electronic systems, cleanliness is essential. A Bosch magnetic-trigger type distributor is shown in *Fig. 14.25*.

Fig. 14.25. Bosch magnetic-trigger type distributor.

Chapter 15

Bodywork

GENERAL

Restoration, kit car or special? A different approach is required for each, but as some of the techniques are the same it may be worthwhile reading the whole of this section whatever type of body you are building or restoring.

THE MONOCOQUE

A monocoque consists of a structure made up of pressed steel panels of various shapes and sizes welded, or spot welded, together for strength. The pressings are in themselves light, almost flimsy, but gain enormous strength by careful design and bracing with other panels. On some cars, easily damaged parts like front wings, which do not add to the structural strength of the whole assembly, (are not 'stressed') are bolted on for ease of replacement. Some cars, like the Citroën DS range and the Rover 2000, have a monocoque structure underneath, the outside panels being merely a cosmetic covering.

Cars are used in all weathers and are subject to extreme conditions of heat and cold, salt used to melt ice in the winter, mud left on roads by inconsiderate farmers, and abrasive grit from road surfaces, as well as the possibility of accident damage.

If a monocoque has suffered major accident damage which has deformed the basic shape of the structure, it may be rectified by specialists with the appropriate jigs and hydraulic equipment for pushing and pulling it back to shape. Most damage that the amateur is likely to need to repair will be light accident damage and body rot, mainly in sills, wings and door bottoms. If you look in *Yellow Pages* you will find the address of your local supplier of body panels. Many of these are 'repair' panels; that is, not the full pressing used in the manufacture of the car, but part-panels designed specifically to repair those areas most likely to rot, which are, therefore, less expensive than the complete pressing.

One-make car clubs often commission replacement panels when the panels are no longer commercially available, as do some of the major specialist suppliers, although many such panels in the past have been a poor fit and, before ordering, it is as well to check with club members who have themselves undertaken repairs. Minor panels are simple to make, and if flat or of single curvature can be fabricated from 20swg steel sheet (also available from the panel supplier). If panels of double curvature or complex shape, like wings, are not available, you will have to find a panel beater who can make or repair them for you.

Panel beating is a considerable art that has become much rarer since the demise of coachbuilding, but fortunately there are still firms that build complete bodies. It is, however, a very time-consuming, hands-on job and, therefore, expensive. Before you buy your restoration project it is wise to check on the availability of panels if much bodywork is required.

When renewing panels, especially complete ones, it is best to remove only one at a time, or the

Fig. 15.1. A panel-beater at work making by hand an otherwise unobtainable panel.

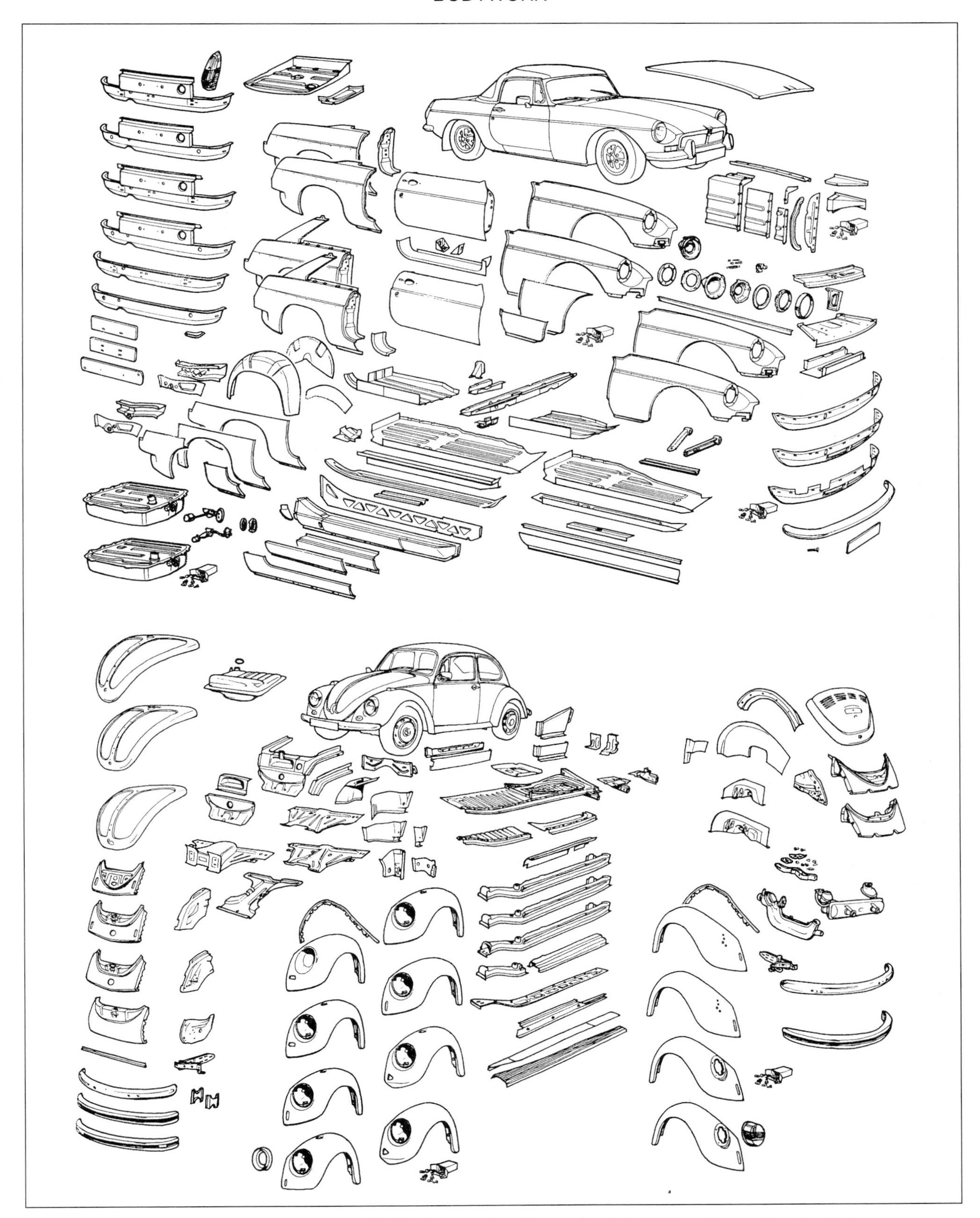

Fig. 15.2. Repair panels like these are available for nearly all cars. Look in Yellow Pages *for stockists.*

Fig. 15.3. A joggled panel, and joggling tool.

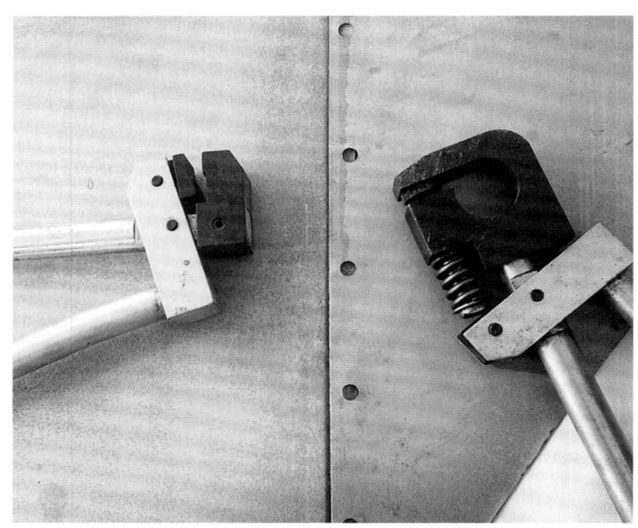

Fig. 15.4. A panel punched ready for welding to the joggled panel.

bare minimum to do the job. If you remove too many panels, especially in the central area of the car, you can very easily lose the basic geometry of the structure and finish up with ill-fitting panels, a twisted or bowed structure, and doors and bonnet that do not shut properly. If you have to cut out major structural parts, you can avoid this nightmare by temporarily bracing the monocoque using clamped wooden beams, or by tack-welding strong metal sections to relevant parts of the structure.

Rotted or damaged panels that are spot-welded can be removed by chiselling through the weld, and a compressed-air-operated chisel can be used for this very noisy operation. Alternatively, you can drill through the 'spots' using a special cutter such as a Sykes-Pickavant 'Zipcut' that cuts away only the top section, but you must have reasonable access to be able to use such a tool.

Rotten panels or sections can be cut out with snips, a power-operated nibbler, a small high-speed air-driven rotary cutter, an angle grinder or a jig saw. It is sensible to buy the replacement section first, which will allow you to see just how much of the metal you need to cut away, and then mark it carefully. Tack-weld or clamp the new section into position to ensure that everything lines up before attempting to weld. Thin panels with long joints, such as half wings or wheel arches, need careful work and 'stitch'-welding, before seam-welding, to prevent the panel from buckling through local overheating. Professionals will butt-weld these edges together, but an easier method of joining is to cut the old panel to allow an overlap that can be 'joggled' behind the replacement. The new panel can then be secured by welding through a series of punched holes in the outer section, so that the effect is like spot welding. In this way there is little risk of distortion, although the panel must be finished with filler before painting. Joggling strengthens the repair, but can cause distortion in panels with double curvatures.

In all cases where welding forms a part of an outer panel, the weld will need 'fettling' – grinding flush with an abrasive disc in an angle grinder. As it may be some time before painting takes place, the panel should be treated with a coat of primer.

As always when welding, adequate precautions should be taken against fire or explosion. A bucket of water should be to hand, and paint, underseal and filler should be removed from the area to be welded (as well as being a fire risk, fumes given off may be toxic). Plastic trim, upholstery, window glass and the fuel tank should be removed if welding is to be carried out anywhere near them.

Fettling with the angle grinder should also be carried out with care, as a stream of sparks will be produced which can easily ignite flammable material and mark finished surfaces. Goggles or protective glasses *must* be worn, as must industrial gloves – a fast revving abrasive disc is very painful if it comes into contact with your hand! Protect any polished surfaces, paint, and especially working parts, from the sparks using something which is itself non-flammable.

COACHBUILT BODIES

Coachbuilt bodies used to be constructed on a framework of wood, covered in fabric or metal panels and then mounted on a chassis frame. This method persisted for a long time for many limited production cars, especially where customers wanted a body made to their own requirements, and is still used by Morgan to this day. In a way, this method of construction is rather like building a model aeroplane, where formers give the body shape when seen from end on, and stringers, joining the formers together, give the shape when seen from the sides.

Ash is the wood most commonly used for the framework, as it is tough, but has elasticity and can be steamed to give curved shapes. If you are a keen woodworker it is well worthwhile considering building your special in this way, cladding it in aluminium, although you will have to design it without compound curves unless you are prepared to pay for professional help from a panel beater.

Repair of wooden-framed bodies is carried out by carefully removing the cladding – usually 'half-hard' aluminium or mild steel sheet – from the area affected by rot or damage, and then using the old piece of timber as a pattern for the new one. This is fine when there is an old part to copy, but the difficulty arises when the old one has completely rotted away. It is then necessary to use the panel itself as a pattern to give the correct shape and curvature.

Rot is normally limited to the bottom of wooden members and the sill boards which run along the chassis rails on which the structure is built, and it is unusual to have to make a complete new part. The rotted section should be cut off beyond the affected area, and the new part should be fitted to the sound section by means of an appropriate joint, glued and screwed together.

Curved sections can be difficult to make, as it is often necessary to use short sections joined together to avoid the weaker cross-grain of the timber. This problem can be overcome by steaming timber until it is soft and pliable so that it can be bent to the required shape, or by laminating thin sections, and gluing them together while clamped to a former of the appropriate shape.

Fig. 15.5. New wooden sections cut in ash, ready for fitting.

SPACE-FRAME

A space-frame needs only a floor, panels for the sides, and a scuttle. These panels can be made from GRP, aluminium or, most probably, a mixture of both.

Unless you want to save every bit of weight, 18swg mild steel sheet should be used for the floor (welded to the frame), the seat back and the front bulkhead, as this will add considerably to the strength of the chassis. If you need to save weight, these panels can be made from 18swg aluminium. The side and rear panels are probably best made of aluminium (18swg) in its 'half-hard' state. (Three grades of aluminium are available – soft, half-hard, and hard.) Half-hard aluminium is soft enough to be workable, but strong enough to resist minor damage. If you intend the bodywork to have a polished aluminium finish, buy metal that is polished on one side and, to prevent scratching, leave the

Fig. 15.6. Beginning aluminium panelling round a space-frame chassis.

Fig. 15.7. An easy and accurate way of cutting sheet metal.

Fig. 15.8. Aviation snips for cutting sheet metal – left, straight and right cutting. Most of us make do with just the straight pair.

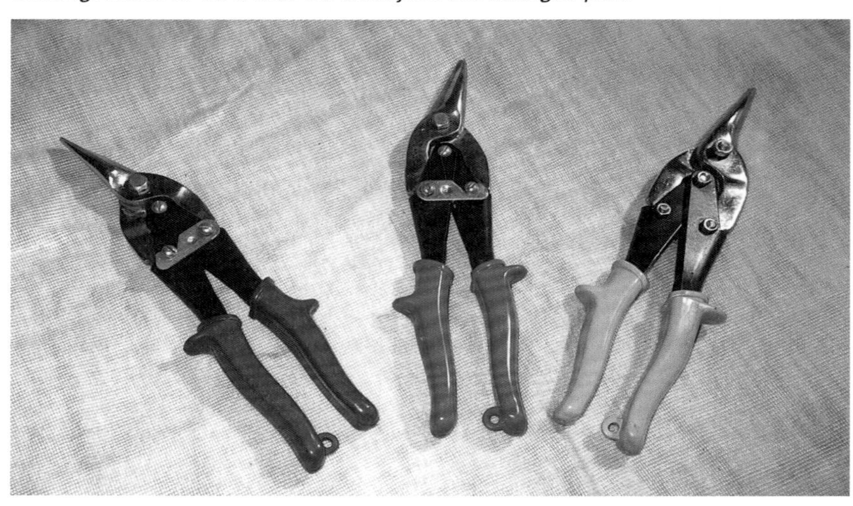

protective plastic covering on it until you have finished the build.

Simple shapes can be measured, and the measurements can be applied to the sheet direct, but for anything at all complicated it is best to make a template from card, stiff paper or thin hardboard, ensuring that the template is a good fit before transferring the shape to the aluminium.

Bending and folding can often be undertaken with the panel in position on the frame structure itself, or with the panel held between two pieces of wood or angle iron. Pad the clamps so that they do not mark the sheet. A hammer blow will also mark the sheeting, so a piece of wood should always be interposed between hammer and sheet. It is preferable to use a boxwood mallet rather than a hammer.

When folding a long stretch of metal, use a short length of wood to spread the force of the impact of hammer or mallet, and fold gradually, by hand at first if you can, rather than trying to finish one section first and then moving on to the rest.

Before clamping a panel in place ready for riveting, spread a layer of silicone sealant over the framework. This will prevent corrosion by electrolytic action, and will help to make the joint between frame and panel watertight. Using sealant will also stop any creaks and groans if the structure flexes.

Mark the panels out ready for the rivets, making sure that you follow the contours of the edge of the panel carefully, using a pair of compasses or dividers to ensure neat, regular spacing at 2in (50mm) intervals, and centre-punch each position to stop the drill wandering when you make the holes. The holes should be ⅛in (3.2mm) diameter, and aluminium pop rivets should be used, long enough

Fig. 15.9. Quite small holes can be cut accurately with a pair of straight snips.

to grip comfortably the various thicknesses of metal.

Curved sections such as the bonnet top, scuttle and rear panel need different treatment. A long length of wide diameter pipe is very useful for forming the bonnet top. I use a length of 6in (150mm) diameter stove pipe, and exert gentle pressure by hand. This is a slightly awkward job because of the size of the panel, and a second pair of hands is useful.

Covering the scuttle either with mild steel or aluminium calls for the making of an accurate template, from which the metal can be marked out and cut. Mark the centre of the sheet and the scuttle, and clamp securely at each side, before 'spreading' the sheet downwards at either side with a piece of wood. Clamp the sheet at intervals to retain the shape before turning in any edges when you are satisfied with the panel shape.

Tight curves that require panels folded over them can be tricky. If the fold will be hidden, then you can cut V-shaped notches in the edge, which will make it easy. If the fold is not hidden, it is a question of patience, gradually forming the fold with the panel fixed or clamped on each side of the length you are working on.

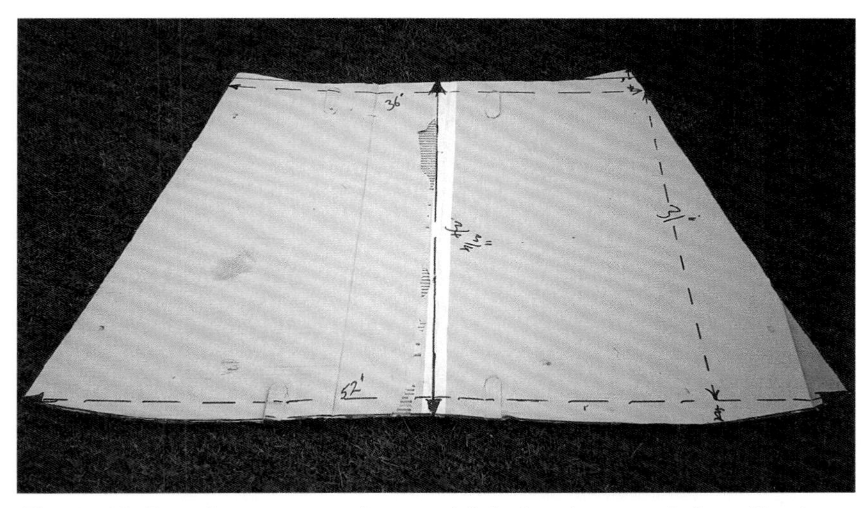

Fig. 15.10. Templates are used to establish the shape and size of body panels. This is for the bonnet.

Unfortunately, the more you beat metal, the harder it becomes, through a process called 'work hardening'. The cure for this is heat. With mild steel you need to heat the area concerned with a blow lamp until it is red hot. After the metal has cooled it will work much more easily. If you are using aluminium, either rub ordinary soap on the surface and heat gently until this blackens, or heat the surface and keep stroking a piece of wood lightly across it; when the wood leaves a mark on the surface, remove the heat.

This process is known as 'annealing', and you may care to practise it on some scrap metal before you start in earnest. If the metal needs a lot of beating, it will gradually harden again but you can continue to anneal it as necessary.

If you finish up with a few wrinkles, these should be hammered as flat as possible and can then be filed flat.

When you have finished panelling the flat and curved areas, you are left with the difficult, compound areas such as the mudguards, and the nose cone or radiator surround. If you are building a fairly standard version of the 'Seven', you will be able to buy GRP items that will fit well and look like the originals. You can also buy aluminium versions of these parts from specialists, but these are very expensive. Alternatively,

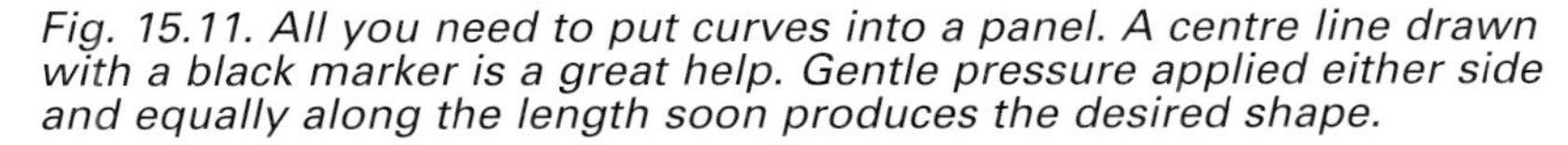

Fig. 15.11. All you need to put curves into a panel. A centre line drawn with a black marker is a great help. Gentle pressure applied either side and equally along the length soon produces the desired shape.

Fig. 15.12. Bending a light gauge tube to the desired radius. The template is cut out of a piece of blockboard and screwed to a bigger sheet of wood. A strip is screwed as shown to hold the tube and the free end of the tube is pulled up against the radius.

Fig. 15.13. Folding aluminium sheet around a tube.

Fig. 15.14. Securing aluminium sheet to a tube that will be part of the framework.

you can make your own compound sections from GRP.

SEPARATE CHASSIS

A space-frame is useful because it provides the framework for the body as well as forming the chassis, but if you are using a separate chassis, you will need to build a body that is either self-supporting or has a framework of wood or metal to support the panels. Wood framing has already been mentioned, but it is worth noting that the frame can also be made in metal as was done on many Italian cars, and also on Aston Martins and Bristols.

Light-gauge mild-steel tubing of about ⅝in (16mm) or ¾in (19mm) diameter is quite easily bent round formers made of wood, and sections can be welded or brazed together.

If your chassis is well designed, with a substantial bulkhead structure for the scuttle on which the dashboard is mounted, you can make the whole body quickly detachable by bolting it down to, say, eight points on the chassis.

Aluminium panelling can be used, as on the space-frame, with the edges wrapped around the tubing and riveted on the inside. This is an easy way of making a body but, again, it suffers from the fact that compound curves cannot be used unless you recruit a panel beater. However, there is no reason why you should not have a mix of aluminium and GRP. In any case, with a little ingenuity it is possible to build a body that looks good without compound curves.

Another easy way of building a body is to use plywood to make a 'tub', rather like boat building. Plywood is strong, and is easily worked with a jigsaw and ordinary woodworking tools. The only drawback is the soft surface, and the difficulty in obtaining a good paint finish. This problem can be overcome by sticking thin aluminium sheet to the outside of the plywood. Use outdoor-quality plywood, 9mm thick for the floor and bulkheads and 6mm thick for the sides and any top panels.

If, as suggested earlier, you make a model of the car first, you could do this in card or sheet balsa and, when you are satisfied with the shape, scale up the dimensions to full size, using your ingenuity to ensure minimum waste from the plywood sheets. The sheets can then be cut out, and the edges can be finished smooth. Sheets can be joined using resin and glassfibre tape or mat cut into strips 4in (100mm) wide. The structure is built up from the floor one piece at a time, making sure that each panel is square (or at the angle you want) before fitting the next piece.

Glassfibre resin is painted on to about 2½in (63mm) each side of the joint, and a strip of tape is then stippled or rolled on each surface so that the tape is thoroughly wet before a second strip is applied. Where one side of the join will be seen, as on the outside of the bottom of the body, masking tape should be used to prevent the resin from leaking through, and four strips of tape should be used on the inside, instead of two, the third and fourth being twice the width of the first two. Metal plates, brackets or tubular structures can be used for localised strengthening and bonded into the resin.

A trial assembly of all fittings should take place before the aluminium cladding is fitted and the body is stripped to the bare tub again. This will ensure that any surface damage or unwanted holes and any other mistakes that took place in construction will be covered by nice, shiny aluminium. It is wise to make templates of any tricky areas to ensure that the cladding will cover accurately when folded over the edges.

Although the cladding will remain in place because of the folds over the edges, and because various attachments such as mudguard stays and the windscreen are bolted through both layers, you may feel safer, particularly on the larger panels, if the sheets of aluminium cladding and the wooden panels are glued together, if only to stop any possibility of vibration and resonance. To do this, first roughen the inside of the metal panels with coarse emery cloth, then spread on a contact adhesive. Do not wait for the adhesive to dry, but put the panels in place immediately. Any final forming required can be done after the adhesive has dried.

This method of construction is perhaps the ideal one for utility-type vehicles, like the Jeep or Hustler, where compound curves are not essential. Ordinary curves can be made with the plywood. If necessary, two or three layers of thinner plywood can be laminated together to give the required section. If you want more exotic shapes, you will have to use GRP.

The body must be insulated from the chassis. Sit the body on closed-cell foam rubber strip or the sort of plastic strip that builders use for damp courses in brickwork.

Fig. 15.15. An AK Cobra body in GRP, straight from the mould.

GLASS-REINFORCED PLASTIC

GRP (or glassfibre) is a material much used in the building of specials, kit cars and many industrial fabrications. Its great merits are that it is strong, light in weight and can be moulded into almost any shape.

GRP consists of a liquid resin that is solidified by the addition of a hardener. On its own this makes a very good adhesive, but to make sections or panels, it is used in conjunction with a cloth ('mat') made of strands of glass, obtainable in various thicknesses or weights. The resin is worked into the mat and, when set, becomes hard and glossy, but can be easily worked with metal-working tools. GRP is waterproof and a good electrical insulator, but it is flammable (although many people seem unaware of the fact).

Fig. 15.15 shows a completed Cobra body-shell made in GRP. You too can make a body like this, or nose cones, or wings, or almost anything else. First, you must make a pattern and a mould, and this is where the good news becomes less good. Pattern-making is time consuming, especially if you only want to produce a one-off component from it, but it is worthwhile if you are setting up a production line. However, there is often no alternative and it is not difficult to make a pattern.

The pattern can be made in almost any hard material, including chicken wire impregnated with plaster of Paris, and of course, GRP itself. The finished component will be the *exact* shape and size of the pattern, so it follows that the pattern itself must be correct in every detail, and highly finished on the side(s) that will show. A component produced from a mould cannot be better than the mould itself. It can be as good – but it may be worse!

The mould must be so shaped that you can remove the finished part without cutting. If the part is complex you will have to make several part-moulds and bond the finished parts together afterwards.

Professionals make patterns mainly from wood; this can require a high degree of woodworking skill, especially on curved sections, but amateurs have used hardboard, cardboard and, as mentioned above, chicken wire and plaster of Paris. Chicken wire can be folded or moulded into shapes, using several layers and bunching it up to provide some strength, and then filled with the plaster, moulding it to the appropriate shape. When the plaster has set, it can be finished with sandpaper to ensure a good smooth surface and the right shape. Although somewhat messy, it is often a quick, cheap and effective way of producing intricate shapes. Instead of the plaster you can perhaps use polythene sheet laid over an armature of wire, depending on the shape to be produced. Either way you are likely to spend a long time producing a good finish, but it is worth the effort.

The next step is to make the mould using GRP. The pattern is first covered with a 'release agent' so that the resin will not stick to the pattern and can easily be parted from it. Ordinary wax-based car polish will do, but several coats (perhaps as many as six or seven) will be needed, well rubbed in and polished smooth.

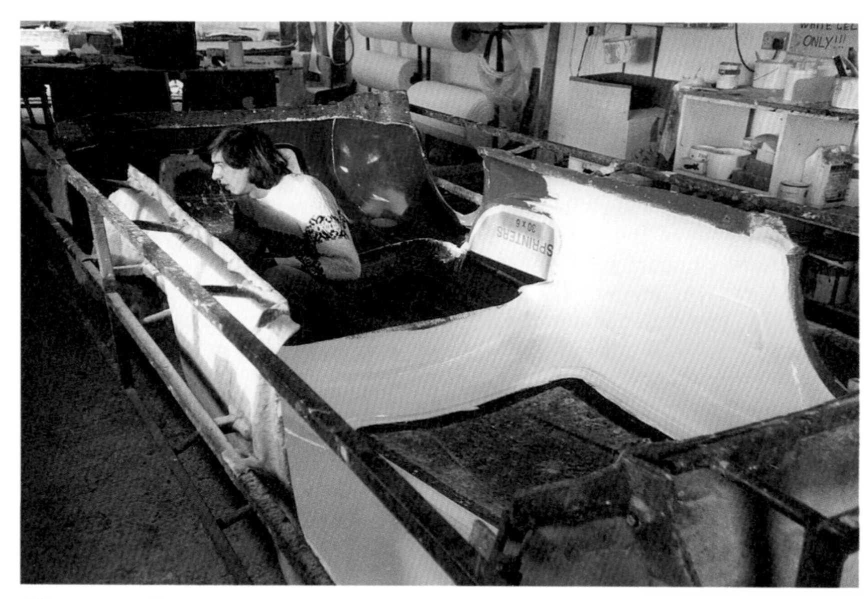

Fig. 15.16. Beginning laying-up the GRP for the body. The white gel coat is being 'painted' on the blue, waxed mould.

Once the release agent has been applied, this should be followed by a 'gel' coat, which is simply a coat of resin. Glass mat and resin dust are irritants, especially when drilled or sanded, and a mask and protective goggles are essential when working it, or even when sweeping up after using it. Latex gloves must be worn when dealing with resin, and a well-ventilated work area is necessary to allow the fumes given off to escape. No naked lights should be allowed when working with resin. As you will need much more material than is available in the kits sold in accessory shops, you will have to buy from the specialist suppliers who have standard printed information on safety – which you should read and follow.

After it has been mixed with

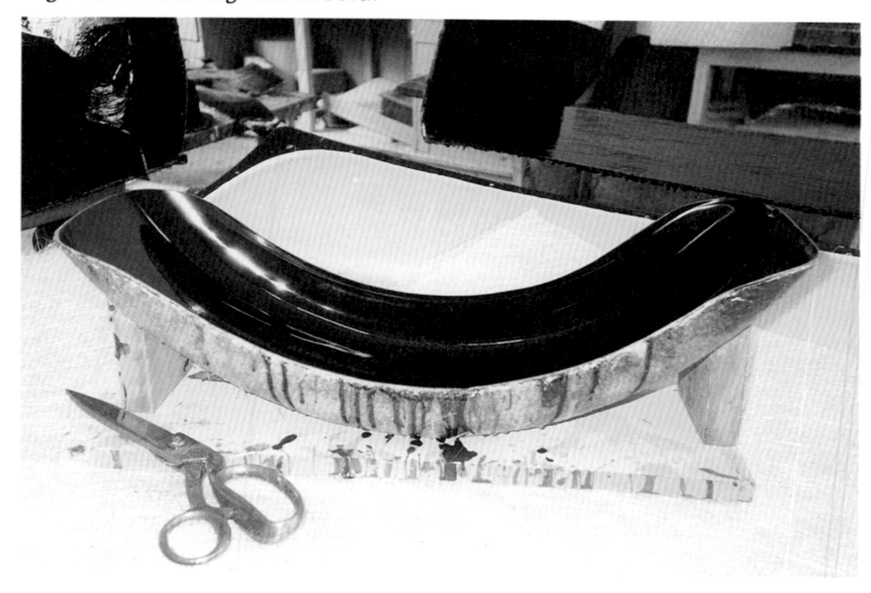

Fig. 15.17. A mudguard mould.

hardener the resin is painted on with a brush. When the resin has set, the first layer of glass mat should be applied. The first layer should be cut with scissors to an approximate fit, piecing up as necessary so that there is complete coverage, and then stippling and rolling with resin until the mat is completely saturated and clings to the shape of the pattern. The first layer is immediately followed by the second layer, which should again be stippled and then rolled to exclude all air and to ensure that it lies flat against the pattern.

The mould now needs time, and preferably a warm atmosphere, to 'cure', and is best left overnight before being parted gently from the pattern. You should now have the exact opposite of what the finished component will be like; any minor imperfections such as pitting can be filled with Plasticine or 'Bluetack', and carefully smoothed, or alternatively the imperfections can be filled with resin, smoothing it with wet-or-dry paper used wet, and polishing when set. If the mould is a large one, it should be braced and supported to prevent it sagging or twisting.

You can now mould the finished part. Polish the inside of the mould with the wax polish several times, and paint on the gel coat, which can be coloured with special pigment if you wish, as this will be the outside, shiny coat. Follow by 'laying-up' with the first layer of mat. There are various weights, but for bodies and wings, two layers, one of 2oz (56g) and one of 1½oz (42g), will be adequate – suitably reinforced locally, if required. A final gel coat on what will be the inside of the moulding will ensure that the colour is 'solid' and will finish it off neatly. After curing, the moulding should be detached from the mould and any surplus mat trimmed off. You now have a finished moulding, self-coloured or ready for painting.

Fig. 15.18. An orange mudguard out of the mould and ready for trimming.

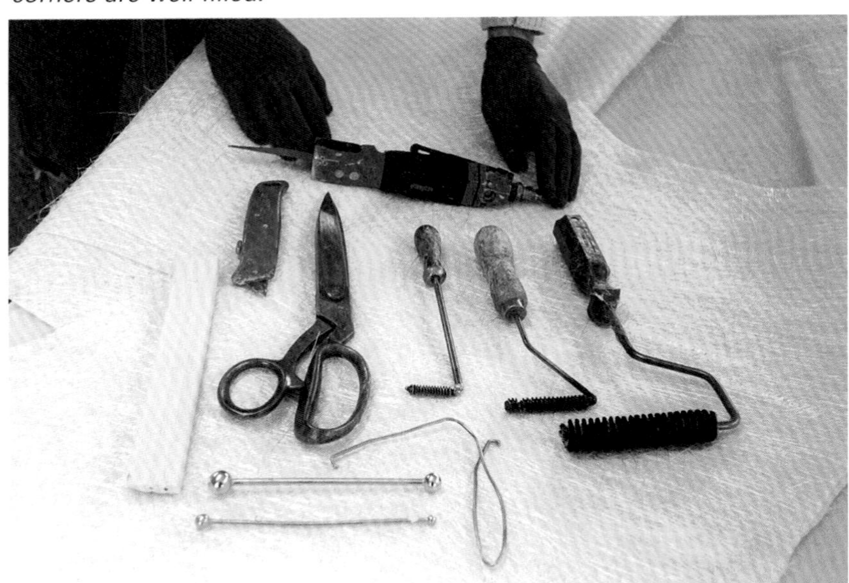

Fig. 15.19. The tools you need for working in GRP. The ball-ended tools are for smoothing fillets, and the piece of wire is for ensuring that corners are well filled.

Chapter 16

Painting

THE EVOLUTION OF VEHICLE PAINTING

Until the introduction of pressed-steel panels, cars were hand-painted. This was a laborious and slow process made necessary by the amount of preparation required on bodies constructed in the traditional manner. These bodies needed heavy and slow-drying fillers to hide the imperfections of the bodywork, and the paint used for the final coats was also slow drying. (It was because black-pigmented paint dried more quickly than any other colour that at one period Henry Ford used it almost exclusively on his Model T production line, famously pronouncing that customers 'could have any colour they liked, provided it was black.')

The painting process got a lot quicker with the dawn of pressed-steel panels in the 1920s, because far less preparation was required and cellulose spray-painting took over from hand-painting. Indeed, it was not long before body preparation – consisting of cleansing, rinsing, rust-proofing and priming – was done by dipping the whole body shell into various preparations, leaving only the finishing coats to be sprayed on, a process which is now done automatically.

A wide range of products is available to the industry today, in addition to the cellulose-based paint products, but all except cellulose-based products need special equipment, either to hasten the drying time or to protect the user from the toxic fumes (cyanide, in the case of one popular finish) given off by the paint. The amateur, therefore, is well advised to stick to cellulose products and should be prepared for a certain amount of hard work during the rubbing-down processes, confident in the knowledge that a good result can be achieved.

The first thing to consider is where you are going to carry out the work. If the car is not too large, and you can work round it in the garage space available, you may be able to manage, but there is always a lot of overspray, so move or protect anything that you do not want painted. If you can keep the car mobile, so that it can be wheeled outside, it is very helpful, as quantities of water are required during the 'flatting-off' processes. Flatting leaves a fine white dust which you can do without when you are trying to get a good paint finish, and with the car outside you can hose it down easily. If you are spraying in fine warm weather (and ideally this is what you want) you can also undertake some of the preliminary coats outside, but whether working inside or outside, a dry warm atmosphere is important during the finishing stages. Much of the process is the same whether you are painting steel, aluminium or GRP, but the initial stages of preparation are different. We will start with the ordinary steel body.

STEEL

Preparation and finishing

If you are restoring or repairing a car that is already painted and you have merely put new panels on it, you should be able to limit the

Fig. 16.1. There is only one cure for paintwork like this – strip it to bare metal and respray completely.

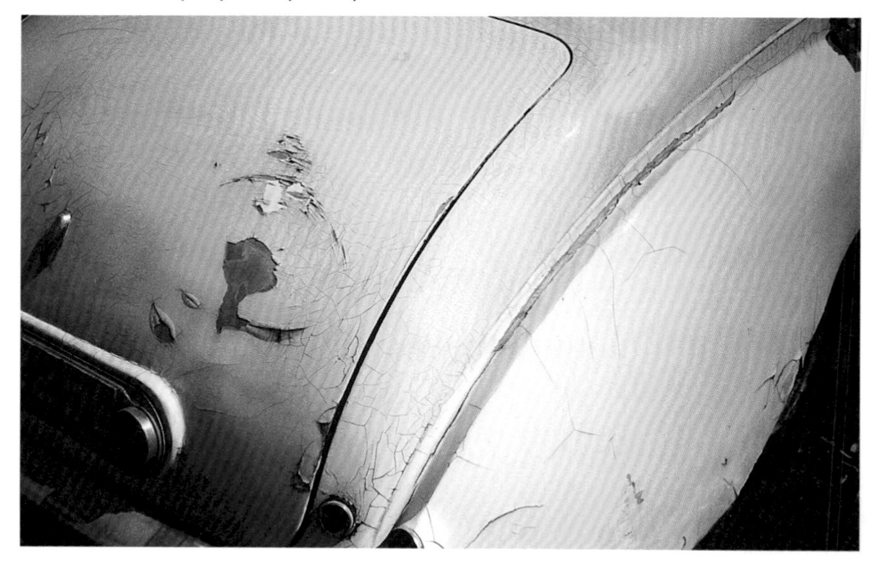

Fig. 16.2. All you need to strip paint – plus a lot of hard work.

painting to the new panels, provided you can match the colour. For many years most cars have had a code number on a plate under the bonnet or in the boot, which identifies the colour and shade of paint used on the car originally. If you can find this code, you can order the correct paint using the code. Whether it will match exactly is another matter, since when paint ages it can change colour slightly, especially by fading: reds are particularly prone to fading. If you need a precise match, the paint supplier will require a sample of the existing paint to which the new paint can be compared, and this could be achieved by removing a small panel, such as the flap over the petrol filler cap, where applicable.

For a really first class job, you need to strip all the old paint off the area to be re-sprayed, as you will be doing if you are re-spraying the whole car, especially if you are changing its colour. This is a very laborious job, normally undertaken by using a chemical stripper such as 'Nitromors' and a scraper, but there are mobile shot blasting units that will visit you and blast the paint off the car, leaving behind a heap of grit and paint (often to the annoyance of neighbours if the wind is blowing in the wrong direction) which will need careful cleaning up. If you use chemicals, be sure to neutralise the surface afterwards, especially in crevices, according to the maker's instructions.

All removable fittings should be taken off, and anything that you do not want painted but cannot detach must be masked-up by covering with several layers of paper and masking tape. Newspaper used to be used for this purpose, as it was cheap and available. However the newspaper printing process now contains a silicone-based preparation, and silicones are one of the painter's worst enemies as they can cause minute bubbles in the paint finish (often some time after the paint has been applied) and can ruin an otherwise perfect finish. Painters now use a special type of brown paper, often taken from a roll that automatically feeds masking tape onto one edge, ready for application.

This paper is also more durable than some newsprint, and therefore stands up better to the repeated soaking during the rubbing-down process.

Masking must be done thoroughly, bearing in mind that it will be wetted with water several times during the rubbing down process. Be especially careful with the rubber window surrounds – the professionals take them out, together with the window glass. Wheels should be covered with plastic sheeting as this is easily removed when you want to move the car.

When the paint has been removed, surface preparation can begin. This consists of first inspecting the whole body carefully, especially those areas that have been welded or where rust is likely, such as the wheel arches and sills. Look at the panels in a strong light to see whether

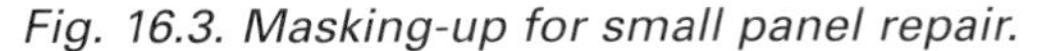

Fig. 16.3. Masking-up for small panel repair.

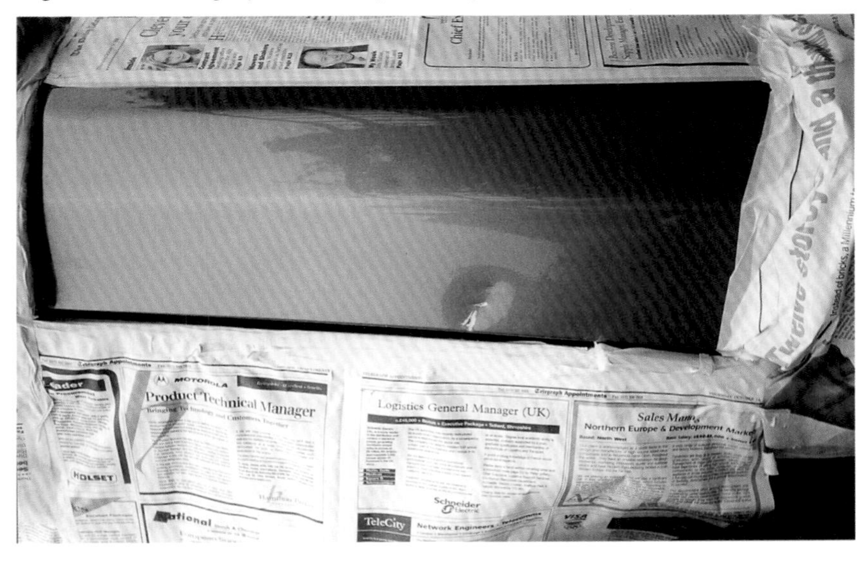

there are deep scratches or other damage.

'Wet-or-dry' abrasive paper is used to prepare the bodywork. This comes in various grades, the lowest number being the coarsest. A shaped rubber block is essential – never carry out rubbing down with using paper held directly by hand. The abrasive paper should be cut to size, then folded and inserted into the block. Most purpose-made blocks have some means of securing the paper.

Wet the paper thoroughly in a bucket of water and rub it with a piece of hard soap – this provides 'lubrication', and helps to stop clogging of the abrasive. Start rubbing, keeping everything wet, and frequently wash off the residue with a leather or sponge to get rid of the fine dust. Where an unpainted area adjoins a painted one (if you are not stripping the whole car) the existing paint edge must be 'feathered' to lead gradually into the unpainted area, otherwise the join will be very noticeable. Surface rust must be rubbed down until bare metal is reached, or in severe cases, the corroded section must be cut out and repaired.

When the body, or the section to be sprayed, is in bare metal, and has been thoroughly washed and dried, it can be primed. Priming is done by spraying if the area is a large one, or by brush on small areas and edges. (Some professionals would start with an 'etch primer' on bare steel, as this bites into the metal and gives maximum adhesion. It is normally a two-pack system but can be obtained as an aerosol.) Check the manufacturer's instructions on the drying time of the primer – indeed on all preparations, and if in doubt allow more time rather than less. Primer comes in different colours, and some are matt while others have a slight sheen which can be helpful in showing up minor imperfections.

When the primer has dried, attention can be paid to very minor imperfections. Paste filler with a resin base is used to fill larger indentations, but 'stopper', a sort of putty, is used for minor imperfections in the paintwork. Stopper tends to shrink and should be applied in thin layers. Stopper can be left standing proud of the surface of the panel, as successive flatting-off and coats of paint will deal with this. Body filler should be finished flush with the surrounding surface.

A 'primer surfacer' is applied next. Heavy coats of this material are usual, two or three on top of existing paint and from three to five over bare metal. When thoroughly dry, the primer surfacer is rubbed down with 280 or 320 grade paper, but before doing so it is as well to spray a thin coat of colour as a 'reference' or 'guide' coat. (This is a good opportunity to get rid of part tins of cellulose paint or aerosols.) The purpose of the

Fig. 16.4. These items will be needed for flatting-off and preparation.

Fig. 16.5. This body has been primed with polyester paint.

guide coat is to colour the surface so that when rubbing down takes place the colour will be removed from all but the 'low' areas. More flatting will need to be carried out locally to remove the guide coat, or more filling or stopping may be required to fill any low areas if warranted.

Work on a small area at a time using plenty of water, wiping off the panel thoroughly as you proceed. A pair of rubber gloves is an asset, particularly where you need to use the abrasive paper, folded, by hand in the places where the block will not go.

When buying the paint for the finishing coats you must establish whether an undercoat is required. Generally, sufficient coats of cellulose top coat are applied for the finish to become opaque, but it is worth asking. If an undercoat is used, the undercoat should be flatted before applying the finishing colour coats.

The first colour coat should be a thin, light 'mist' coat to seal the filler, then two full coats should be applied, with about 30 minutes in between each coat. Once the second full coat has dried, the finish should be closely inspected, and any minor imperfections should be 'stopped-up', rubbed down with 320-grade paper after hardening, and sprayed over. Two more colour coats should then be sprayed and left to dry thoroughly.

Flatting-off then takes place with 400-grade paper, with soap and plenty of water. Assuming that you have produced a 'solid' colour finish you can progress to the final spray coat. If you are still not happy that the finish is 'solid', two more coats and more flatting-off should be enough to give a satisfactory finish.

The last colour coat is made up of 75 per cent thinners and 25 per cent paint. Before applying this final coat, make sure that there are

Fig. 16.7. A reference coat is flatted off, the painter preferring to do it dry in this case.

Fig. 16.6. Refinishing a damaged wing. The repair has been filled and rubbed down. The panel is being wiped with a cloth saturated with 'panel wipe' to ensure that it is clean before the final, colour, coats are applied.

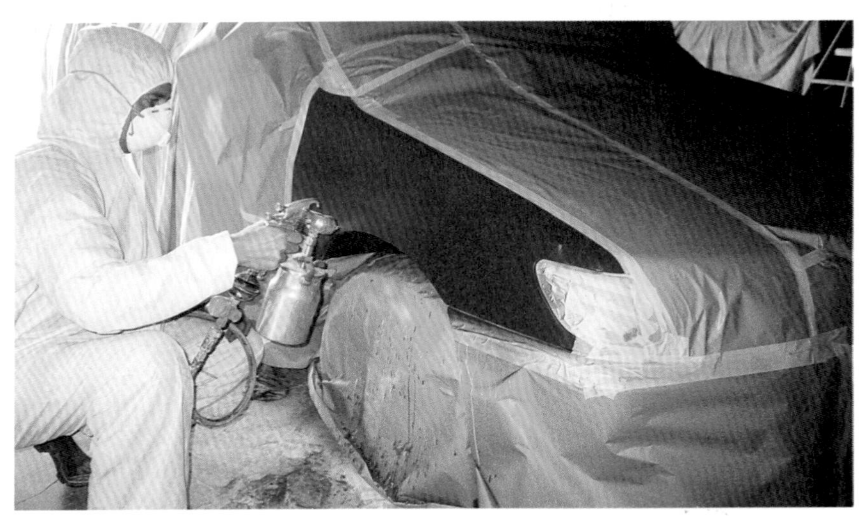

Fig. 16.8. Spraying the colour coats. Note the painter's mask and protective clothing.

no foreign bodies or dust on the paint surface by wiping it down with a 'tack cloth', which will remove all unwanted contamination. Once the final coat of paint has dried thoroughly, remove all the masking.

Burnishing is the next step. The best thing that you can now do is to go on holiday for a fortnight, to give the paint time to harden. In that way you will not be tempted to touch the paint surface to see how it is getting on. If you decide to stay at home, do have patience and leave it an absolute minimum of 24 hours, and ideally longer, before burnishing.

The burnishing operation (also known as 'compounding' or 'cutting in') consists of rubbing the surface with a very fine abrasive compound. The compound is a liquid, or a paste, and is applied with a clean, damp cloth and a lot of elbow grease. A small quantity of paste is put on the cloth and is rubbed backwards and forwards over a small area until a smooth, high-gloss finish is produced. Turn the cloth frequently and wash it out periodically, as it quickly becomes impregnated and discoloured with paint. Be careful not to be too enthusiastic when working on edges, as you will quickly work through the paint. After burnishing, a polish with a liquid polish should give you the finish you set out to achieve in the first place (avoid the use of silicon-based polish if possible, as it can cause problems later if you need to carry out any further painting or touching up).

If you are not happy with the final finish, do not despair, because you can correct it.

Rectification

If you apply paint that is too thin, you may get runs in the finish. If you are too slow in moving the spray gun, or if you concentrate too much on one area, you will get a build-up of paint that will 'sag'. If the paint is not properly thinned, or if the spray gun is held too far from the surface, the finish will be 'dry' and may resemble orange peel in texture. A whitish, cloudy effect ('blooming') is the result of spraying in damp or humid conditions.

Runs and sags should be rectified as they occur before moving on to the next operation, flatting the imperfections down and respraying locally. It should be possible to rectify the blooming effect when compounding, but if not, local re-spraying will be necessary. Orange peel, or other signs of a 'dry' finish can be corrected by flatting with progressively finer papers, if necessary progressing to 1,000 or even 1,200 grade. Indeed, if disappointed with the final finish of the car, the whole surface should be flatted with 1,200 grade paper before final compounding.

ALUMINIUM

Because most aluminium car bodies will have been hand-made, it is likely that there will be more surface imperfections than is the case with pressed steel bodies, and different preparation is required at the start of the painting process.

A coat of etch primer is essential on aluminium to 'key' paint to its surface, and the etch primer should be followed by a coat of zinc chromate primer. As explained earlier, etch primer aerosols are available, and for repairs this will prove more economical than spraying etch primer with a spray gun.

A heavy-bodied filler is then applied. The number of coats required will depend on the surface of the panels. A minimum of three coats will be required, more if imperfections are still apparent.

A professional would use either a different spray gun, or a gun nozzle with a larger orifice, to apply heavy-bodied filler, in order to achieve the required coverage with as few 'passes' of the gun as possible. An amateur's air-compressor may not be powerful enough to enable the spraying of heavy-bodied filler, but it is possible to brush on this type of filler, as long as plenty of time is left for each coat to dry before the next is applied. A polyester-based filler is now available and is easier to apply – the body shown in *Fig. 16.5* was sprayed with this type of paint.

When adequate coverage has been achieved, a guide coat should be sprayed lightly over the filler, which is then flatted-off with 180-grade paper. Once flatting has been completed, any stopping or filling can then be done. If all is well, the normal procedure (as described previously for steel panels) can then start at the primer-surfacer stage. The primer-surfacer acts as a seal, and only two or three coats should be necessary.

GLASS-REINFORCED PLASTIC (GRP)

GRP may already have a perfectly satisfactory coloured finish, and may not need painting. If you are painting metal panels surrounding GRP components, it may be worth considering painting the GRP as well, especially if the surface of the GRP is not too smooth, since any subsequent changes in colour brought about by fading or retouching may vary across the different panels because of the different base material.

It is important to ensure that no trace of the release agent (the wax polish used to ensure that the GRP component separated from its mould) remains on the surface to be painted, and a thorough wipe down with white spirit will ensure this. If you used a non-wax-based release agent, especially with a silicone base, rubbing down with fine abrasive paper, followed by a good wash, will prepare the surface for painting.

Some ordinary primers work well on GRP, but it is worth consulting the supplier for recommendations, especially if you are painting the complete body.

After the preparation procedure has been completed, the remainder of the finishing procedure is as described previously for steel panels.

SPRAY PAINTING

Safety

It is essential to use a mask while spraying, even out-of-doors and, as solvents are flammable, no naked lights should be allowed during the spraying process.

Equipment and techniques

Spray painting is a job that requires skill and the right equipment. When watching professionals at work, or a new car being painted automatically, it is marvellous to see how quickly a body in primer suddenly becomes a bright, gleaming object. The amateur, with normal equipment, will soon find that to obtain a similar finish (which is entirely possible) will take a lot longer and demands much hard work and patience.

As there now seem to be no paints available for brush finishing coachwork, spraying is the only way. To spray paint successfully, an air-compressor and a spray gun will be required.

It is possible to hire professional spraying equipment, but make sure that you hire a compressor which you can run from your mains supply.

If you are buying spraying equipment, get the most powerful compressor with the biggest air receiver that you can afford (and can run on your electricity supply), and a spray gun matched to the compressor's output. Spray guns are of two basic types, suction feed, with the paint container attached underneath, and gravity feed, with the paint container on top. The suction feed is preferred, as it holds more paint and is less likely to drip paint, so is especially suited to amateur use.

Paint is too thick to be used straight from the can, and has to be

Fig. 16.9. Spray guns – the one at the rear is for cleaning fluids.

Fig. 16.10. Doors and removable panels are taken off and prepared separately so that the edges can be painted.

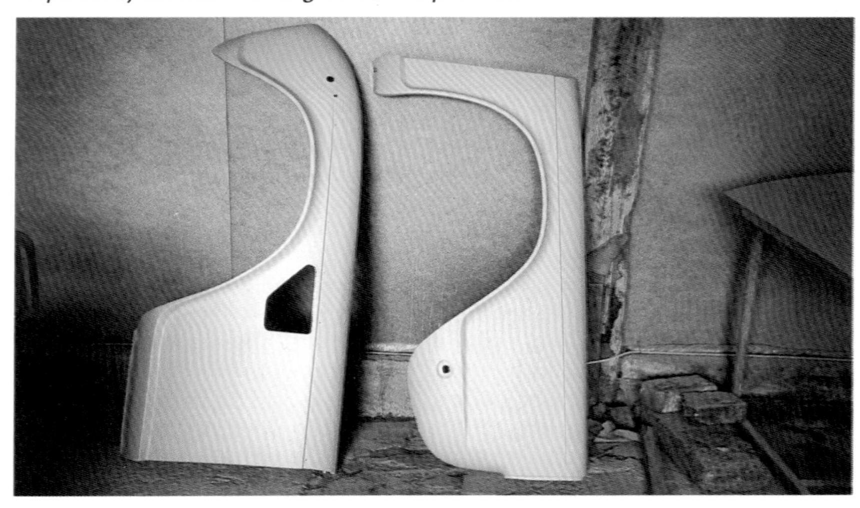

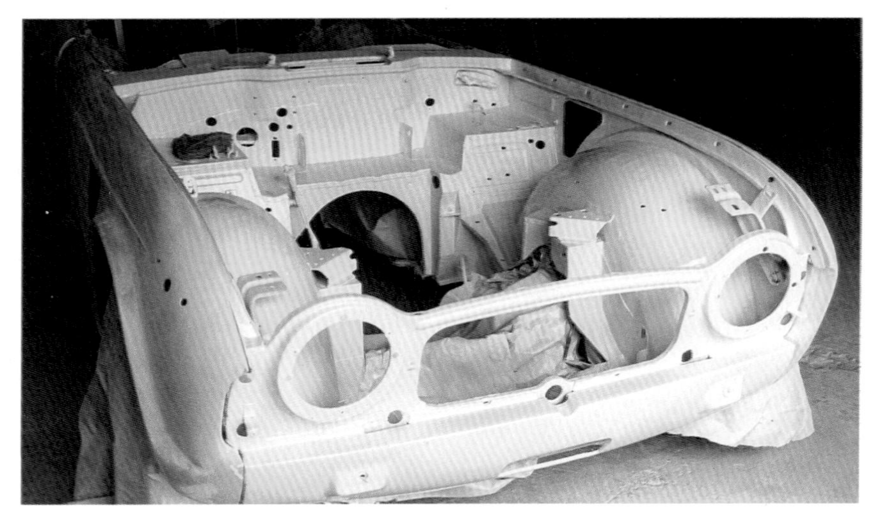

Fig. 16.11. The interior is finished first.

Fig. 16.12. The finished bodyshell awaiting 'fitting-up'.

thinned with the appropriate type of thinners. You will need quite a lot of thinners, which is not cheap, but you can buy a cheap grade which, while not suitable for mixing with paint, will do for cleaning the spray gun. The greater the volume of air produced by the compressor, the thicker the paint that can be applied in any one 'pass' of the gun. It is, therefore, necessary to match the size of the gun nozzle to the performance of the compressor, and the thickness of the paint to both.

The level of thinning required for use with professional equipment will be recommended by the paint manufacturer. The less powerful your equipment the more thinning you will need, and you will have to experiment with each type of paint – primer, filler and top coat – before using it on the car.

In theory, the operation of the spray gun is simple – you merely connect the gun to the compressor, switch on and, when air is available, press the trigger and point the gun at the prepared surface. The gun should be held from four to nine inches away from the surface, and moved from left to right, parallel to the surface. Press the trigger to start spraying just before the edge of the panel, and release the trigger to stop spraying just after the edge of the panel to prevent a build-up of paint at the edges. The nozzle should be set to give a vertical 'fan' shape. Each pass of the gun should overlap the previous pass, and the gun should be moved at a speed which allows adequate paint coverage without becoming so 'wet' that the paint runs or sags. Do not attempt to achieve a finish in a single coat; subsequent coats will blend in to earlier ones and give the required 'thickness' or opacity of finish.

Before starting work on the actual job, you obviously need to practise your technique, and experiment with the settings of the gun and the air pressure. If in doubt about the air pressure, set it to 55psi (3.8 bar). An old oil drum or some scrap sheet metal, finished to the same state as the car, is very useful for practising and, of course, spraying the various coats of primer and filler gives you the opportunity to practise on the car itself before spraying the final colour coats.

After use, clean the gun by washing out the paint container in thinners, then spray neat thinners to clean the nozzle. Wipe the outside of the gun and paint container with a cloth soaked in thinners, and check that the air hole in the paint container cap is clear. Do not immerse the gun itself in thinners, as this will cause deterioration of the seals.

Chapter 17

Upholstery and trim

GENERAL

Unless you are going racing, when all you will want in the way of trim and upholstery will be a piece of foam in a bucket seat, you will need to do something about the comfort and appearance of the inside of your car.

Trim panels cover the interior 'walls' of the car, hiding the structure and providing an attractive finish and sound insulation. Seats are, of course, a necessity and need to be adequately comfortable and supportive to make travel in your car a pleasure. You may also want the protection of a hood and tonneau cover if you have an open car, but such items are likely to require the use of an industrial sewing machine and a lot of experience, so are best left to the specialists.

For those who want, and can afford to pay for, modern seats for their kit cars and specials, there is a wide range available from specialist suppliers. If you cannot afford 'off the shelf' seats, or you want something traditional, like the seat shown in *Fig. 17.2*, it is not too difficult to make your own. Alternatively, pay another visit to a breaker's yard where you may be able to find something suitable, perhaps in leather.

Fig. 17.1. Basic racing seat in GRP, which can be upholstered.

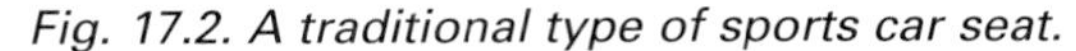

Fig. 17.2. A traditional type of sports car seat.

SEATS

Methods of seat construction differ considerably. Modern seats of complicated shape are moulded from polystyrene-type foam on a metal frame; others have the seat formed from a rubber diaphragm stretched on a metal frame with a moulded and upholstered back.

Fig. 17.3. A partially stripped oak-framed seat from a luxury car.

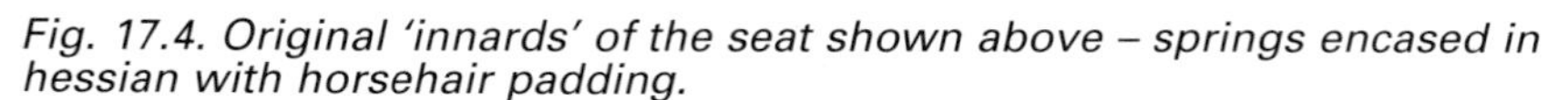

Fig. 17.4. Original 'innards' of the seat shown above – springs encased in hessian with horsehair padding.

Some seats are of a more traditional construction, with padding over a sprung frame, which are not too difficult to repair but would be tricky to make. The most basic seats, which are easy to make and quite comfortable, have a wooden base, with thick foam cushioning and a covering of vinyl.

If you decide to visit a breaker's in search of seats, go armed with the measurements of the car interior – especially the width – and buy the runners as well as the seats.

Some cars had leather seats, either as an option or as standard on the more expensive models, and it is worthwhile looking for these, as they are very comfortable and can often be repaired, rejuvenated and dyed.

Vinyl-covered seats come in all shapes and sizes, and their appearance is nearly always improved by a good scrub with soap and water. You can buy various preparations for cleaning vinyl seats and changing their colour, but they are difficult to repair satisfactorily. Whilst it may be possible to get hold of some patching material and adhesive to deal with small cuts, more major damage will have to be repaired by renewing the complete panel.

Cloth-covered seats are often very attractive, but tend to soil easily and can fade, although they can often be cleaned and freshened-up with the appropriate upholstery cleaner. Their use should be restricted to closed cars, as cloth soaks up water, which is not only unpleasant to sit in, but will also leave watermark discoloration.

To make the type of seat shown in *Fig. 17.2*, typical of many traditional sports cars, a base board of ⅜in (9mm) or ½in (13mm) thickness is cut from plywood or chipboard to the shape required for the seat cushions and the back (see *Figs. 17.5 and 17.6*). Measurements will, of course, vary from car to car. The measurements shown are those used for my Locost. Foam of about 1in (25mm thickness) is then cut to the same dimensions, and

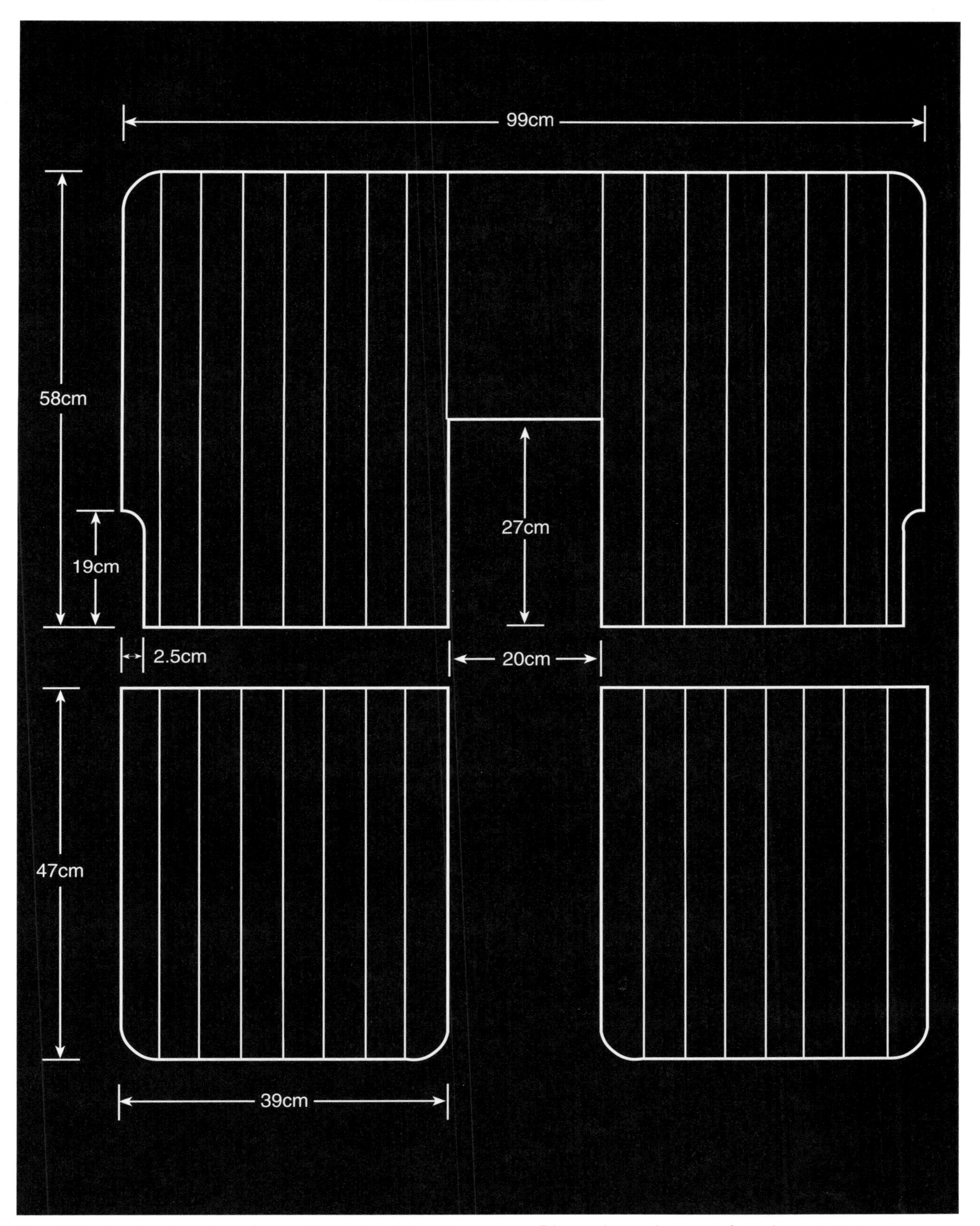

Fig. 17.5. A cut-out pattern for making a traditional type seat. Dimensions given are for a Locost seat.

additional foam shaped (using a sharp knife or hacksaw blade) and stuck on to create the overall profile (see *Fig. 17.7*).

Paper patterns are made to use as templates when cutting out the vinyl covering. Once the covering has been cut out, it is then lined with ½in (13mm) soft foam. The pleats are made by sewing the vinyl to a backing piece of calico, and filling the 'pockets' so made with ½in (13mm) foam strip, pushed down with a ruler or something similar. Alternatively, the vinyl can be sewn through, as shown in *Fig. 17.9*. The piping is

Fig. 17.6. A back-board, like this one for a Locost, can be cut out from ⅜in (9mm) or ½in (13mm) chipboard or plywood.

Fig. 17.8. Marking out the seat cover for the pleats.

Fig. 17.7. Adding shape to the back of the seat.

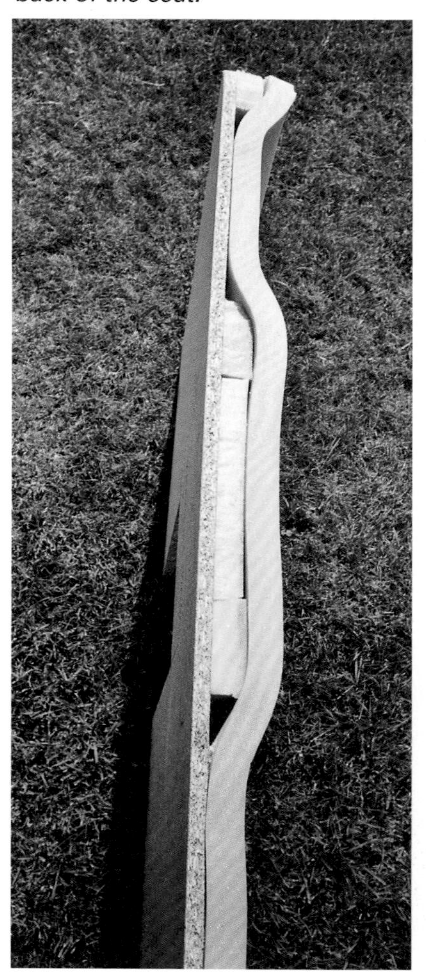

Fig. 17.9. The pleats being machine-sewn into the 'sandwich' made up from the vinyl cover material, foam and calico backing.

Fig. 17.10. Making up the piping.

Fig. 17.11. Piping sewn to the edge of the panel for the seat bottom.

optional, but it sets the finished seats off nicely and, like the vinyl, is available in different colours. A domestic sewing machine should be just about adequate for this work, but it might protest a bit when there are several thicknesses of vinyl and the piping to be sewn together.

When the covering is completed, it is pulled over the foam-lined base and stapled to the back (see *Figs. 17.13 and 17.14*).

If you do not fancy the sewing required for the pleats, you can still make very effective seats in the same way, merely by stretching the vinyl covering over the foam and stapling it to the back of the wooden bases, being careful to get the corners to fold over neatly. As an alternative to vinyl, leather could be used, but a domestic sewing machine would be working quite hard to cope with it.

The law requires that seats are positively located. You can use runners if you want the seats to be adjustable, but if no adjustment is required then can simply be fixed to the floor direct. To secure the seats, captive bolts are made by

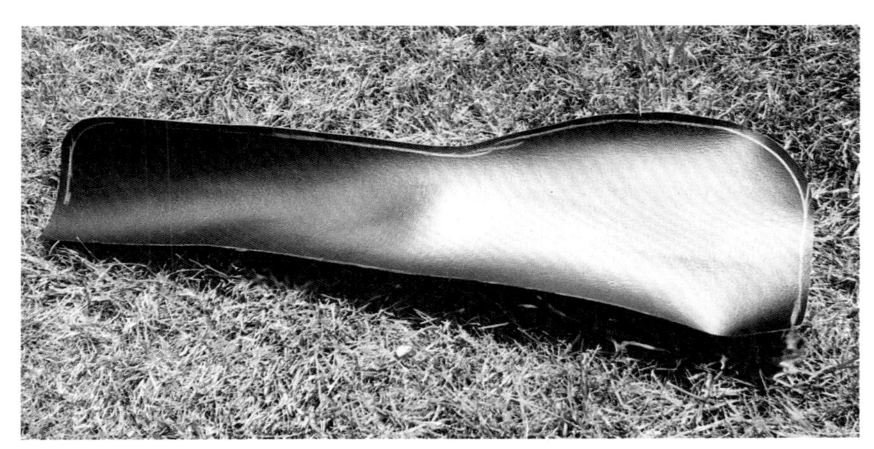

Fig. 17.12. Material cut out to form a panel for the seat bottom side.

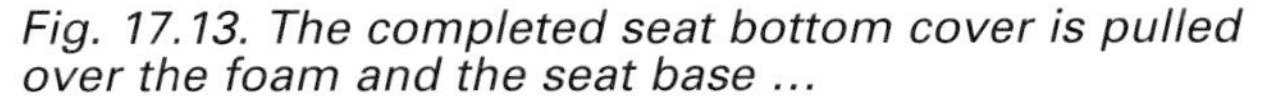

Fig. 17.13. The completed seat bottom cover is pulled over the foam and the seat base ...

Fig. 17.14. ... and stapled to the wooden base.

Fig. 17.15. Metal plates with captive bolts are screwed to the seat base and bolted through the floor of the car.

brazing the bolt head (thinned on the lathe if you have one) to a small plate screwed into the wooden base, as shown in *Fig. 17.15.*

TRIM PANELS

These can be made in hardboard (or thin ply if you are making a quality car), using the thinnest outdoor grade obtainable, cut to paper patterns carefully drawn to fit the sides and doors.

The panels can be lined with thin foam, stuck on with a spray adhesive, then covered with vinyl. Allow about 1in (25mm) overlap, which can be folded neatly over the back of the panel, cutting out V-shaped notches at corners or tight curves so that there is only one thickness of material to be glued to the hardboard or ply.

Unless you use very thin backing, the backing will need chamfering along those edges which will be visible when fitted, to ensure that you get a smooth finish rather than a square edge. A strip of piping stuck to the back of the panel gives a professional finish, especially if a contrasting colour is chosen.

The panels are attached to the framework by means of self-tapping screws. These should be of the 'raised-head countersunk' variety for preference, and should be used in conjunction with screw cups. Chromium-plated screws never seem to last very long before discolouring, and one solution is to use stainless steel screws from a yacht chandler, especially if you are building a car open to the elements.

When working on door trim panels, you will, of course, need to cut out the necessary openings for the door furniture (window winders, interior door handles, etc.) If there is room in the thickness of the door you will find a map pocket handy. This is no more than a shallow box, rather like a letterbox, and needs covering inside before fitting to the back of the panel.

Areas that suffer a lot of wear, especially from the shoes, such as the lower area of the side trim panels near the pedals, and the bottom of the door trim panels, can be covered in carpet instead of vinyl. The transmission tunnel also looks good finished with carpet.

CARPETING

The floor itself needs carpeting. Having spent so long over the build or rebuild of your car, do not spoil it by using the spare piece of carpet left over from when you re-carpeted the spare bedroom, but go for purpose-made car carpeting, available from a specialist supplier – patterned carpet does not look good in a car!

Felt or rubber underlay helps to prevent wear and gives good sound insulation against noise of the engine and running gear. The carpet under the seats and on any vertical surfaces should be glued in place with spray or contact adhesive, but that under the feet should be made removable for easy cleaning. Carpets must not be left loose, otherwise they bunch up and, on the driver's side, tend to get caught under the pedals.

Special carpet fasteners are available, which have a stud that screws into the floor, and a thin metal ring that pushes into the carpet and is secured underneath by a socket which clips on to the stud. These fasteners are virtually invisible and very effective, but care should be taken when fitting the rings, as the three prongs are viciously sharp.

Removable carpets should have their edges bound to stop them from fraying, and to present a professionally finished appearance. A strip of the vinyl used for the seat or panel trim will do for binding, and can be sewn or stuck to the carpet edge, allowing about 3/4in (19mm) overlap and carefully mitreing the corners.

The top edges of open bodywork sometimes create a problem, depending on how the metal body panels are finished. If the panels cover the top of the door or aperture completely and fold down over the inside, the unfinished edge of the panel will be covered by the trim panel, but if the panel finishes at the top, it will need covering. This can be done with trim material and padding, with a broad strip of extruded aluminium, or with 'Hidden Banding' which is fixed with tacks or small screws which are hidden when finished. Hidden Banding has a leathercloth finish and is offered in a small range of colours.

A padded armrest makes driving more comfortable, and is easily made with a roll of foam covered in vinyl trim material mounted on a piece of shaped aluminium.

Chapter 18

Putting it on the road

After many hours of work, and much expenditure, your gleaming new (or newly restored) car now sits in the garage, ready for the road. So how do you go about preparing for your first drive?

TAX AND INSURANCE

In the UK a car needs to be taxed and insured, but before you can do either the car must have an identity and must be registered. If your project is a restoration, it will already have an identity, and you can insure it.

MOT TEST

If the car is more than three-years-old, it will have to pass an MoT test before you can tax it. To obtain a test certificate, make an appointment with your local MoT Test Centre (you can drive your car there for its test, but nowhere else). As you have no opportunity for road testing beforehand, all you can do to prepare for the test is to ensure that all the systems work – lights, windscreen washers and wipers, flashers, etc.

As you will probably not have had access to the equipment required to carry out some of the checks and adjustments required for the MoT test, if you explain the position to the Centre when you make the appointment, you may be able to arrange for them to adjust your headlights and check the brakes for you before the Test, as they will have the proper equipment to carry out this work.

REGISTERING A CAR

Before a newly-built car can be put on the road, it must first be given its own exclusive identity and then have this registered, but before registration it has to be examined

Registration of vehicles comes under the aegis of the Driver and Vehicle Licensing Authority (DVLA), which publishes helpful pamphlets on the subject. The relevant publication for our purpose is INF 26, which is available from the DVLA, Swansea or from one of its Vehicle Registration Offices (VROs). There are 40 VROs throughout England, Scotland and Wales and their addresses can be obtained from the DVLA, Swansea.

The type of registration issued will depend on the originality of the vehicle and its various components.

If you wish to retain the donor car's original registration number, enough of the donor's major components must be used to score more than eight points on a scale which includes chassis (or bodyshell), steering, suspension and so on, as detailed in the relevant pamphlet. If the score falls below eight points on the scale, then currently a 'Q' registration prefix letter is issued.

In the case of kit cars, if all the parts are supplied new by the manufacturer, the DVLA will treat the car as a new vehicle, and will issue a current registration mark. If not all the components are new, and one or more reconditioned component has been used, provided that the 'reconditioning' is certified as being to 'as new' standard, a current registration can be issued.

'Reconstructed Classics' (vehicles built from genuine period components of the original specification, and all over 25 years old) will be given an age-related registration, provided that the appropriate vehicle enthusiast's club confirms the authenticity of the components.

As with all production cars, self-built/restored vehicles must carry a Vehicle Identification Number (VIN), and this number forms an important part of the description of the vehicle on the Vehicle Registration Document (V5) which is issued to the owner of the vehicle.

This VIN is allocated by the local VRO. The car cannot be registered without this number, and the VRO will need to inspect the vehicle to ensure that it has in fact been marked 'on the offside of the vehicle, in a clearly visible and accessible position, and by a method such as hammering or stamping, in such a way that it cannot be obliterated or deteriorate.' If this requirement sounds like red tape, it must be remembered that it forms part of a system designed to limit theft and fraud. You will find that you get a real sense of achievement when you have put the VIN number on your car and attached the registration plates. This is official recognition that you have created a real car!

After the VIN number has been allocated, but before you can register the car, you have to prove that the car is safe and roadworthy.

Since 1998 all amateur-built vehicles have had to pass the Single Vehicle Approval inspection and must be granted a Minister's Approval Certificate (MAC) before the VRO will give you a registration number. The SVA is similar to the production car Type Approval test (to British or European standards), the purpose of which is to ensure that '... vehicles have been designed and constructed to acceptable safety and environmental standards before they are used on public roads.' Information about the scheme is given in the Department of the Environment, Transport and the Regions (DETR) pamphlet SVA 2. SVA inspections are carried out at the existing Heavy Goods Vehicle test stations, of which there are 16, and again their addresses can be obtained from the DVLA, Swansea.

The Vehicle Inspectorate produces a manual for use by its inspectors, which details the requirements of the legislation, the standards applicable and the procedures to be followed for checking the relevant components or systems. This manual may be purchased from The Vehicle Inspectorate (see Appendix 2), and is invaluable when designing and constructing your special.

THE FIRST DRIVE

I always think that the time you really learn to drive is immediately after you have passed the driving test, when for the first time you are allowed out in the car on your own, when you have to make your own decisions with no help available to you. This is when, if you have any sense, you proceed cautiously and gradually build up your skill with experience. Putting a newly-built, or completely restored, car on the road for the first time is a bit like this and if, as soon as your car is road legal, you go screaming off down the nearest main road or try out its cornering ability at speed on twisty country roads, you are asking for trouble. Even such firms as Mercedes Benz, after all their testing and development, occasionally (very occasionally!) get it wrong, as the much publicised 'elk test' with the 'A' class cars showed when they were first introduced.

As your car is not allowed on the road before it passes its MoT, testing and development will have to be done afterwards. Drive gently and get a feel for the car's handling, ride and steering characteristics, and its braking performance on different road surfaces and in different weather conditions. After a while, you will be able to build up a picture of the car's behaviour. This way you can make informed decisions about spring rates, tyre pressures, shock absorber settings and all the other variables. Often, quite minor adjustments can transform the feel of a car.

Now is the time to check on items such as the oil pressure when the engine is hot, the efficiency of the cooling system, and whether there are any unusual vibrations. If there are any shortcomings, you can sort these out by modifying the offending parts. In short, you can now do what the manufacturers are able to do on their test tracks before production, and perfect your creation!

Chapter 19
Buying and maintaining

BUYING SECOND-HAND

If, now that you have read about building your own car, you have decided that you do not have the time, facilities or skill to build your own car, but you would nevertheless like to own and run something that is different from the mass-produced car, you may want to look for a ready-made special or kit car. In this case, how do you go about it?

Kit cars are not hard to find. Dedicated magazines have pages of advertisements for completed cars, and uncompleted projects, and some of the kit car manufacturers also sell completed cars themselves. With well-known makes, you should be assured that the chassis and specialised mechanical parts have been well designed and have stood the test of time. If the manufacturers supplied the original parts, the workmanship should be of professional standard, and the only question should be how well the car was put together.

As always when buying second-hand, it helps if the car has some history. If you are buying the car from the original constructor, you can interrogate him or her and find out how complete the kit was before construction started. If all the parts were supplied by the kit manufacturer, and the constructor simply assembled the various components, a check of the security of the fastenings should give you some confidence that the job has been done properly.

The bodywork should be examined. If it has been correctly fitted to the chassis, there should be no distortion, with equal gaps and shut lines from side-to-side. The bodywork should be viewed carefully from each side, and from the front and rear, before getting underneath it to check the security of the mounting arrangements.

Bodies made of GRP can suffer from crazing, especially at stress points, and any signs of this should be carefully investigated to establish whether it is merely cosmetic damage, or of more sinister origin. As on any second-hand car, you need to establish whether it has suffered accident damage and, if so, how well it was repaired.

The security of items like the steering column, the seats and, of course, the seat belts needs checking, and you will need to ascertain whether the wheels and tyres are in good condition. Nearly all kit cars and specials will have wheels that were not original equipment on the donor car. Apart from examining the condition of the wheels themselves, especially if alloy (to establish that they are not cracked or damaged), you need to know that they have the correct type of wheel nuts (or bolts) that go with the wheels, as some alloys rely on having steel inserts, and others sleeved nuts, in the fixing holes.

Do the tyres match the wheel rims or are they oversize, and is wear equal across the tread? Tread wear, if irregular, will tell you a lot about the steering geometry and suspension set up – and, by inference, about the owner who allows it to go uncorrected.

If the vendor is not the constructor, but also bought the car second-hand, you will not be able to get answers to all of your questions, and you will need to be even more thorough in your checking. Find out how long the car has been on the road and how many owners it has had. If the car has had a large number of owners, then there must be some reason for numerous people wanting to get rid of it; do you want to join them?

A test drive will indicate how well the car goes, the performance of the steering, suspension and brakes, and how pleasant the car is to drive. If you have any doubts at all, ask a knowledgeable friend or a well-respected local garage to vet the car for you and reinforce your own observations.

Specials are much more rarely advertised than kit cars, and it is unclear whether this is because there are fewer of them, or because owners, having designed and built them from scratch, tend to cherish them more and continue to develop them.

Those specials built for a particular purpose, such as racing or hillclimbing, tend to become well known within their club or with the followers of their particular sport, and probably change hands privately without being advertised, or are advertised only in the relevant club magazine.

If you are tempted by an 'unknown' special, you have to be doubly careful, as not only do you need to assess the quality of the build, but you also need to assess how well-conceived the design is.

If you have read through the various sections of this book, you will be able to form some idea about the power/weight ratio and the suitability of the chassis design for its intended purpose.

Examine the chassis joint by joint, and check each weld. Check whether the suspension units have been home-made or taken from a donor car. If the latter, was the complete unit, sub-frame or other mounting arrangement used, or only a part of the system? If the whole unit from the donor was used, at least some degree of engineering integrity is implied, but if everything is to the builder's design, you need to be sure that the design is sound.

The car may, of course, be superb in design and construction, and it may exist because there is no commercially available equivalent to touch it, or because the builder had an overwhelming desire to express himself – both of which are good reasons for building a special – but you will need to be sure.

In addition to driving the car yourself, watch the car while it is being driven slowly past you, and especially while it is travelling away from you, and note whether the rear wheels follow the track of the front ones. If they do not, then there is something seriously amiss with the chassis or suspension layout, and it is likely that the components are not correctly aligned or have been damaged.

Unfinished projects are worth considering if only as a source of parts for your own project. The owner may have done much of the work in collecting the various parts, cleaning and restoring them, and may have bought expensive accessories such as seats, wheels or instruments that he or she is anxious to convert into cash, much to your advantage.

The potential dangers of buying a second-hand home-built vehicle made before SVA legislation are greater than buying a mass-produced vehicle. Caution and the help of a 'knowledgeable friend' are essential. A current MoT certificate is an asset, but only tells you that the various items checked are working or in serviceable condition. The MoT does not comment on the design or construction of a vehicle.

If the vendor has faith in his or her vehicle and has nothing to hide, then a professional examination of it will not be objected to. If you have any doubts, leave it alone. There are other cars available, and the experience you gain in examining them will help you to choose the right one in the end.

MAINTENANCE

The maintenance of specials is fundamentally similar to that of production cars as far as engine adjustments, oil changes, brakes, etc are concerned, but other factors need consideration.

The main cause of vehicle breakdowns is electrical faults, sometimes in components and sometimes in the wiring. It is a good idea to check periodically that all connections are correctly made and secure and that all terminals are clean. An occasional squirt of water repellent (such as WD40) on to terminals will prevent corrosion. Also check that the wiring harness is well supported, and that its weight is not tending to pull the connectors off the terminals.

A 'Seven' look-alike will probably have rubber bushes in the suspension, as indeed will many cars. These are fine when they are precisely aligned, but it is easy to weld their housings a few degrees out of line and still get them to fit. This means that the bushes will wear more quickly, and an eye should be kept on them. This is particularly true of rear radius rods, which are very short – they should really have their front pivots in line with the forward end of the propeller shaft for perfect geometry – and tend to wear quite quickly, especially if you use the full performance of the car. These bushes are, however, easily and cheaply replaced.

GRP bodywork has already been mentioned, but aluminium panels over steel can lead to problems of corrosion through electrolytic action – salt and wet roads are the cause of this. The two types of metal should be separated by silicone or plastic strip whenever possible during building. Also note that aluminium rivets fixed into the steel frame have metal-to-metal contact, so should occasionally be inspected, and any necessary remedial action taken immediately.

Chapter 20

The author's current project

CHASSIS, SUSPENSION AND STEERING

As mentioned in a previous Chapter, a while ago I visited a breaker's yard which I had never visited before, and I was able to pick up a chassis, complete with suspension, from a 1936 Fiat 'Topolino' (or 'Little Mouse'). The Topolino was a two-seater saloon of only 500cc, but with a 'proper' front-mounted, water-cooled four-cylinder engine, and with independent front suspension which consisted of a transverse leaf spring at the top and wishbones at the bottom. The chassis was much used by builders of specials, particularly builders of hillclimb specials and 500cc racers, because of the lightness of the chassis frame and especially because of the independent front suspension, which was very unusual in the 1930s, particularly on a cheap mass-produced car. At least one such special used parts of two chassis, providing all-round independent suspension.

I decided to build a lightweight special, based on the Fiat chassis. The chassis frame was complete in itself, and liberally drilled, as much of the car's strength lay in the body. (In reality the 'Topolino' chassis formed a mounting for the suspension components and engine.) The cross-bracing that originally existed had been removed before I saw the chassis, and it was obvious that the frame would not be strong enough in its current condition, so I 'boxed' it. Normally, a channel-section chassis member is boxed merely by welding a plate on the open side of the channel section, but I thought that even more strengthening was required, so I welded in another channel section inside the existing channel to complete the box, and drilled this to match the original.

As I intended to use a Ford Escort rear axle, I pulled the rear ends of the chassis side members slightly apart so that the Fiat spring ends would mate with the original

Fig. 20.1. Showing the additional channel section welded on to the original to strengthen the chassis frame.

Fig. 20.2. Fabricating a cross-member, the clamps hold the three pieces together for welding to each other and to the end plates.

Fig. 20.3. The cross-member welded.

spring seats on the axle. This meant that the original rear cross-member was too short, but fortunately, with minor modifications, the original cross-member fits under the gearbox and will form the gearbox mounting. A new rear cross-member was made out of 40x60mm section steel, as shown in *Figs. 20.2* to 20.5. This new cross-member was clamped in position to achieve the right length, welded and drilled, and finally bolted into position on the chassis plates originally provided for the shock absorbers.

The chassis layout is very simple, and if you want to build a similar one, you do not have to find an old Fiat 500, as a chassis can be made quite easily, using 100mm diameter tubing for the side members, or alternatively box section mild steel of 40x60mm with a wall thickness of 3mm. The dimensions of my chassis are shown in *Fig. 20.6*, and you can lighten it or not depending on the type of suspension and running gear you have and what engine you propose to use. To cut the large lightening holes you need a circular cutter, run at very slow speed. I use my lathe to power the cutter whenever possible, because this has a slower speed than any of my power tools. The framework for the front suspension – a pressed and welded structure on the original – is easily built up from box-section material and welded into place. If you do not want to use a transverse leaf spring, wishbones can be fabricated and used in conjunction with coil-over-shock absorber units.

I have deliberately used non-independent rear suspension, as I am merely adapting the chassis from the original rather than building it from scratch. If you want to use independent rear suspension (IRS) you will have to build a structure capable of

Fig. 20.4. The finished cross-member, complete with drilled lightening holes, bolted in position.

Fig. 20.5. The new chassis cross-member in place, with the original moved forward to act as a mounting for the gearbox.

Fig. 20.6. Chassis frame dimensions.

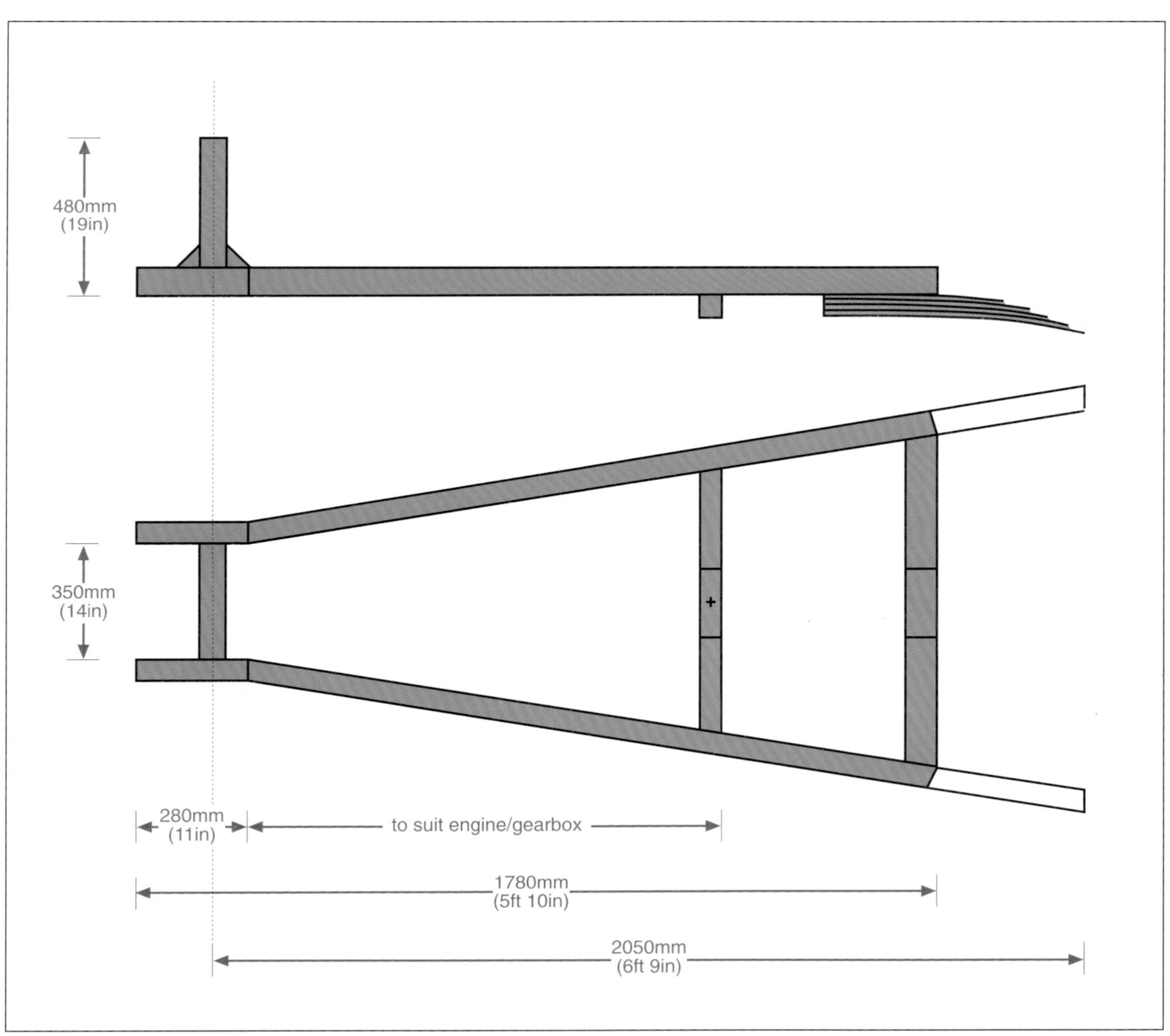

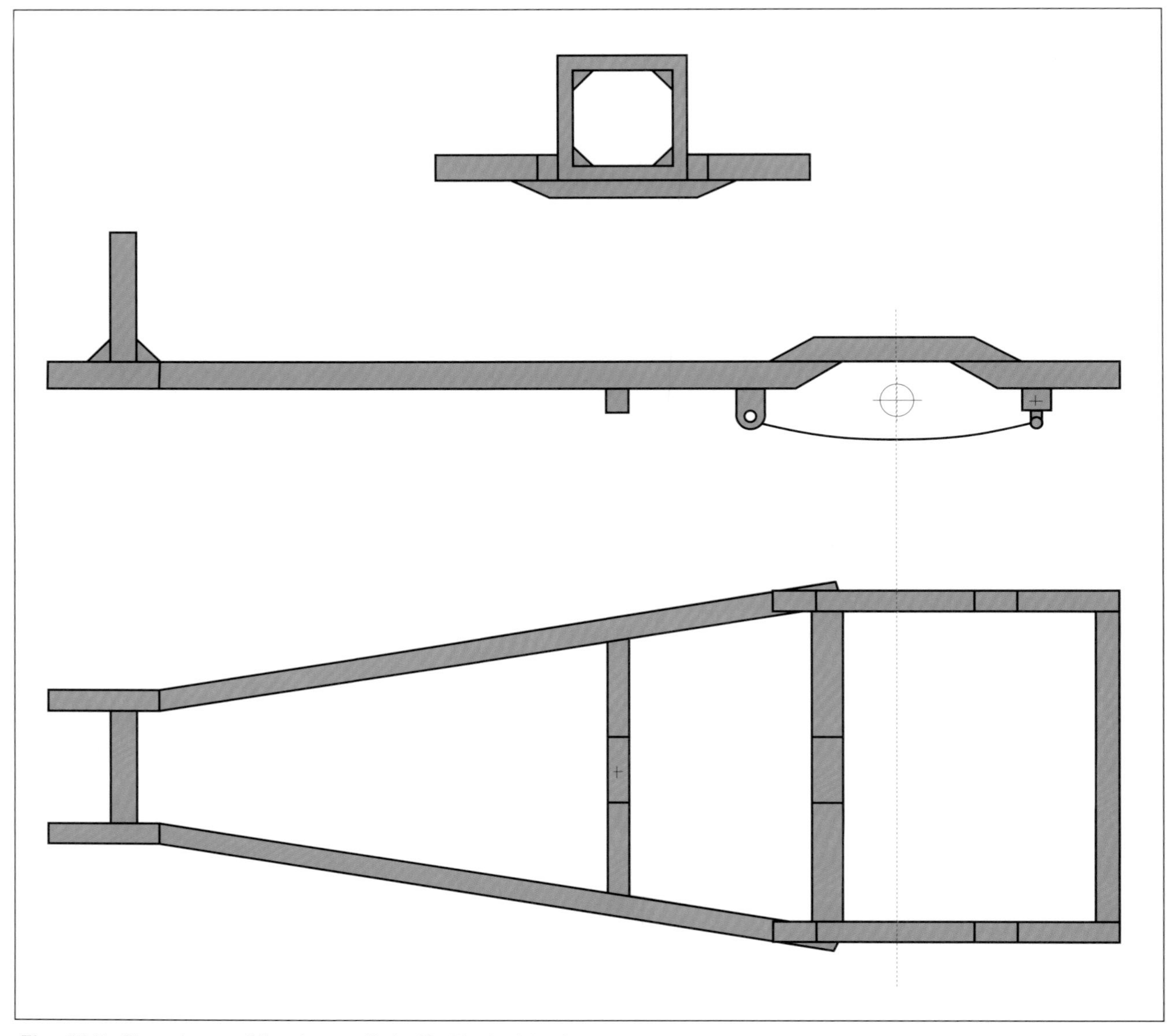

Fig. 20.7. Chassis modification to fit half-elliptical leaf springs.

carrying it, similar to that used for the front suspension. If independent rear suspension is used, it will also be necessary either to fabricate hub carriers for the rear wheels or, preferably, to use some from the breaker's, from a rear-wheel-drive car with independent rear suspension such as a Sierra, Jaguar, Triumph or similar.

The early Fiat chassis were fitted with quarter-elliptical springs at the rear, as shown, but were later altered to accept the more normal half-elliptical leaf springs. If you decide that you want to use these later springs, then you will have to modify the chassis as shown in *Fig. 20.7*. With a 'full' chassis it is easier to fit the bodywork, as the chassis to the rear of the axle will carry some weight, whereas if the short chassis is used, the weight of the body at the back will have to be carried by the body frame itself. Moreover, the radius arms originally used to locate the rear axle when using quarter-elliptical springs become unnecessary, as the later half-elliptical springs will locate the axle.

In fact, the radius arms are a bit of a nuisance as they are anchored at the chassis end on plates that will intrude into the seat area, making a high seating position necessary. In order to prevent the axle twisting, and the nose of the differential dipping every time the gear is changed and the clutch is let in, the radius arms need to form a parallelogram with the spring, and therefore need to be the same distance from the spring anchorage points as the spring eye is below the centreline of the axle. I used two existing spring platforms on the axle, which are rather low, and by cutting these off and making new brackets it will be possible to obtain about 1in (25mm) or a bit more, so that the radius arm anchorage can be moved accordingly. When my friend Ron Champion (author of Haynes's *Build Your Own Sports Car For As Little As £250 – And Race It!*) saw my design, he was delighted and said 'This is in the real spirit of special building.' We went on to discuss numerous points, particularly engine height and the radius arms. He asked what I intended to do about the sideways location of the rear axle, pointing out that though originally the springs would be adequate for the modest power of the 'Topolino', and the skinny cross-ply tyres it used would in any case 'give' a little under side loads, using the wider radials fitted to my special which would be transmitting a lot more power would alter the situation. Ron suggested that using wishbone type links from the back axle to the chassis cross-member would locate the axle laterally and, if suitably positioned, could also take the place of the existing radius rods. Ron's advice is always welcome, so it is back to the drawing board to design a revised system similar to that shown in *Fig. 20.9*.

Like most builders, I have a collection of parts, including a set of the classic alloy Dunlop wheels, that I wanted to use. These wheels had a stud pattern for a Ford, which did not fit the stud pattern of the Fiat hubs. Although I could have used adaptor plates to make the wheels fit the hubs, I did not like the look of the original Fiat brakes which, although hydraulic in keeping with the modern design of the rest of the car, were only 6in (15cm) in diameter, which I thought

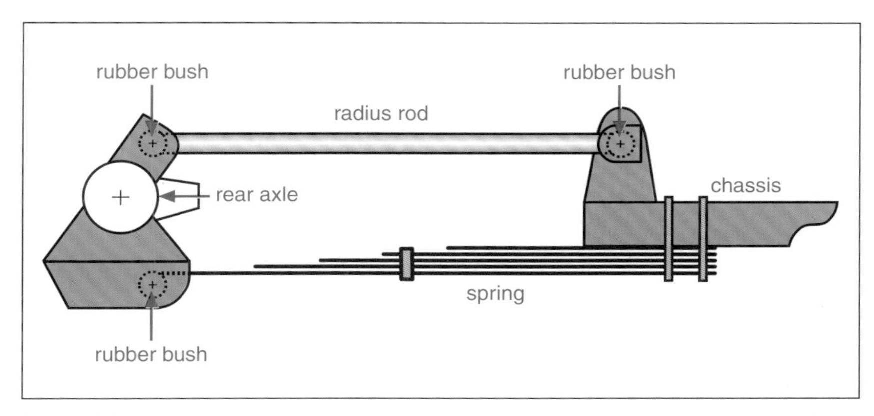

Fig. 20.8. Parallelogram arrangement necessary with quarter-elliptical springs to prevent axle twisting under load/braking.

Fig. 20.9. By making the radius rods into wishbones the rear axle is controlled laterally as well as vertically.

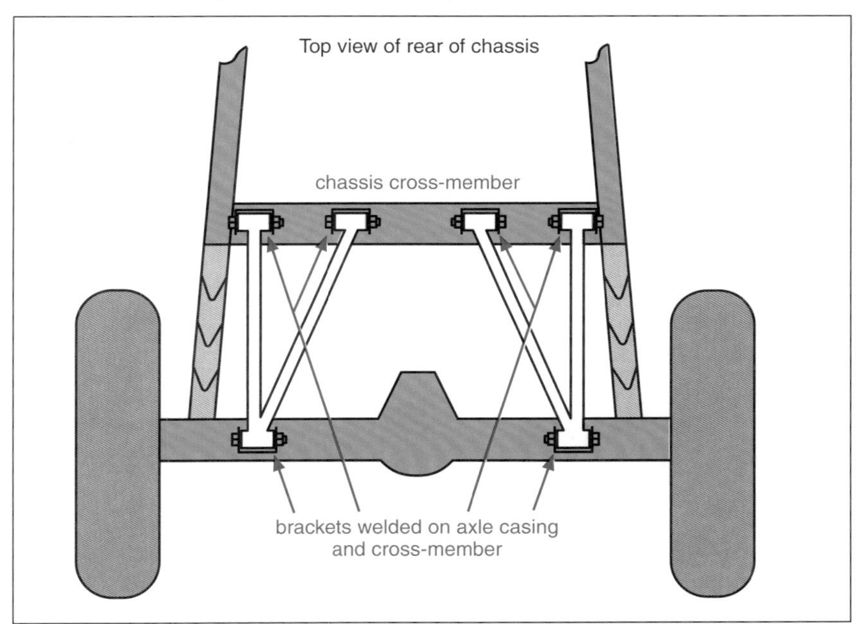

Fig. 20.10. The nearside front Ford stub axle and drum brake modified to fit the Fiat suspension.

Fig. 20.11. With the front suspension rebuilt with new bushes and some new pins turned up on the lathe, the result looks serviceable.

would be inadequate for modern road conditions and the power output of the engine I planned to install. The sensible thing was to use Ford stub axles complete with brakes, but some surgery was necessary to mate the Ford stub axle and brake assemblies with the Fiat uprights. The steel sections necessary to make the modification were welded professionally, and I drilled and reamed them out on the lathe to accept the Fiat king pins. With the front suspension rebuilt using new bushes, and some new pins turned up on the lathe, the result looks satisfactory. It will be seen that I used drum brakes from an early Escort MkI rather than the later disc brakes which might have been too powerful for the set up, and in any case drum brakes are more in keeping with the type of car I have in mind.

The front shock absorbers are the original hydraulic units that are still in excellent working order. They are directly coupled to the cross-shaft that connects the arms of the wishbones, and should be adequate for the weight of the new car. However, I note from photographs of specials using this chassis and suspension that many of them have telescopic shock absorbers, so it may be that the originals will not be up to the job and will have to be augmented or replaced with something more modern. The original rear shock absorbers were missing, but were a hydraulic lever type, and will be replaced by more modern units, probably from a Morris 1000.

The steering is by rack and pinion, also ex-Ford. I might have used the original steering, but the steering box was missing. As the rack is slightly too long, I modified it by cutting a small piece out of each of the two track rods, and made collars to fit over them which were then welded on (see *Fig. 20.11*). Steering rack mounts were made and welded to a cross-member to suit the rack and its clamps. The steering column will be left until I have made the bulkhead and can get an accurate idea of its length and position.

The bulkhead and scuttle structure is of great importance, as it can add substantially to the strength of the chassis as well as the body. I shall make mine with a framework of 1in (25mm) square tubing or angle iron, sheeted in with riveted aluminium sheet which, when welded or bolted to the chassis frame, will provide a quite rigid 'box', and will give the chassis torsional rigidity. This is important, since I want my bodywork to be easily removable, and it will not add much strength to the total structure. The scuttle part of the structure can either be made to be visible, as part of the bodywork, or can be hidden by the bodywork if you are building an all-enveloping body. In either case, the structure can be made complete to take the dashboard and instruments so that the car is driveable without the body.

ENGINE

I also had in stock an engine from a Sunbeam Talbot that I wanted to use. This 930cc, all-aluminium engine is very light and, having an overhead camshaft, produces a

Fig. 20.12. The chassis frame with trial assembly of the main components of the running gear.

Fig. 20.13. Another view of the rolling chassis with trial fitted main components.

respectable amount of power (the engine is derived from the Coventry Climax FPF engine by way of the Hillman Imp). However, the Imp engine has two drawbacks, one being that it is rather tall as many OHC engines are, and the other that having been designed originally to be mounted transversely in the back of the Imp, the water cooling arrangements are slightly odd if the engine is used fore-and-aft at the front. If I had not already obtained this particular engine, I should probably have used a Reliant OHV unit, which is smaller than the Imp engine and also very light, but less powerful.

The radiator just happens to be from a Triumph Spitfire for no other reason than it happened to be another item that I already had in stock. This radiator was designed to cool a 1200cc engine and should therefore be more than adequate for the 930cc unit that I am using.

BODYWORK

Figs. 20.12 and 20.13 show the chassis frame and a trial assembly of the main components of the running gear. Most of the welding is tack-welding, as I may need to alter the position of some of the components later if I have second thoughts, and I may need to strengthen various parts including the engine mounts. I would like to be able to lower the engine in the chassis frame, but the water pump sticks out on the offside and the frame is not wide enough at this point to allow the engine to go much lower. I might manage to lower the engine by an inch or so, or more if I can re-position the water pump or if I can afford to replace the existing pump with an electric one.

Before starting on the bodywork the car will be completed as far as possible while there is good access for the installation of brake lines, fuel lines and wiring.

Fig. 20.14 shows a simple balsa-wood model of what the bodywork may look like. The intention was to give the car a 'retro' look, since the component parts of it are very dated and the high bonnet line is dictated by the height of the engine. The original intention was to build a single-seater, but I have compromised by making it into a two-seater with the driver as the main consideration.

The body will be built using aluminium panels on a frame of light tubing, with the compound-curve sections made from GRP. Mudguards will be either bought-in aluminium ones or commercially available GRP, perhaps modified slightly to give them a more individual appearance.

Light-gauge steel tubing of about ⅝in (16mm) diameter will be used, as this can easily be formed into gentle curves over wooden formers, bent cold as shown in Chapter 15, and then brazed or welded together and secured to the chassis with welded-on brackets. The aluminium panels can be wrapped around the tubes for neatness and secured with pop-rivets on the inside.

Fig. 20.14. A simple balsa wood model of the bodywork for the author's current project

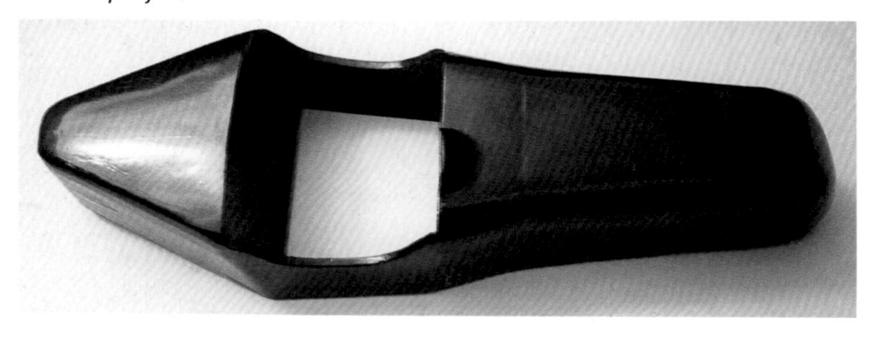

The design of the rear of the bodywork is capable of further development or complete redesign. A flat slab-tank in typical MG style is a possibility, or a barrel back with a spare wheel housed in the end is another possibility. A completely rounded back would also be possible, but I intend to keep the number of curved panels to a minimum. The rear structure will require some thought, as there will be no support for it from the chassis. The structure will therefore have to be kept very light and, with no provision for carrying anything very heavy, the petrol tank will be bolted to the back of the seat, and the spare wheel may be carried on the side of the car, in classic 'retro' fashion. An alternative would be to make the rear of the seat into a substantial bulkhead, and to use this to anchor the rear end, but I am rather hoping to make the whole of the body easily removable with perhaps only six or eight fixing points to the chassis.

Of course, if your chassis is full length then the problem of support for the rear of the body does not arise.

Appendix 1

Useful information

MAGAZINES

There are many magazines dealing with different aspects of motoring. The restorer and builder will find the following of interest. The order is alphabetical.

Car Mechanics
(Kelsey Publishing Ltd)
Cars and Car Conversions
(Link House Magazines Ltd)
**Classic and Sports Car*
(Haymarket Publications Ltd)
Classic Car Mart
(Trinity Publications Ltd)
**Thoroughbred and Classic Cars*
(EMAP Active Ltd)
Classics
(SPL)
Kit Car
(Kit Cars International Ltd)
Kit Cars International
(Flame Ltd)
Practical Classics and Car Restorer
(EMAP Active Ltd)

Those asterisked are of more general interest, but often contain articles on completed restorations.

Apart from helpful articles and practical instruction in the restoration or building of cars and their components, these magazines contain advertisements from suppliers of goods and services that are very useful. Many advertisers offer catalogues, and you can soon build up a very useful collection for reference.

Classic and Sports Car gives away with one of its issues a directory, updated annually, called 'The Owner's Bible' which lists dealers, restorers, specialist services and much other useful information.

REFERENCE BOOKS AND MANUALS

The Motor Vehicles (Approval) Regulations 2001 (The Stationery Office)
This publication covers the Single Vehicle Approval regulations in detail.

SVA Inspection Manual (The Vehicle Inspectorate)
Automotive Electrical Manual (Haynes Publishing)
Build Your Own Sports Car For As Little as £250 – And Race It!, Ron Champion (Haynes Publishing)
Fault Diagnosis (Lucas Technical Series)
How to Restore Wooden Body Framing, A. Alderwick (Osprey)
SU Workshop Manual (Burlen Fuel Systems)
Automotive Carburettor Manual (Haynes Publishing)
Zenith and CD Catalogue (Burlen Fuel Systems)

Haynes Publishing have in print many specialist books and manuals on different aspects of building, restoring and modifying cars, in addition to their well-known car service and repair manual series which covers a wide variety of models. Every builder or restorer ought to have a copy of the relevant manual for his or her car or donor vehicle.

SPECIALIST SUPPLIERS

There are a number of specialist suppliers of accessories, components and services who advertise in the magazines listed above and in appropriate club publications. Many specialise in a narrow range of parts or services, but amongst those who offer a wider range of parts and accessories, and who produce catalogues, are the following. The addresses and telephone numbers were believed to be correct at the time of going to press. However, as they are subject to change, particularly telephone area codes, no guarantee can be given for their continued accuracy.

Demon Tweeks
75 Ash Road South
Wrexham Industrial Estate
Wrexham
N Wales LL13 9UG
Tel. 01978 664466
Fax. 01978 664462
Two motorsport parts and accessories catalogues with thousands of items. A really fantastic treasure trove.

Europa Specialist Spares
Fauld Industrial Estate
Tutbury
Burton-upon-Trent
Staffs DE13 9HR
Tel. 01283 815609
Fax. 01283 814976
Parts and accessories catalogue with a wide range of goods.

Merlin Motorsport
Castle Combe Circuit
Chippenham
Wilts SN14 7EX
Tel. 01249 782101
Fax. 01249 782161
Parts and accessories catalogue with the emphasis on motorsport, as you would expect from the address.

Grand Prix Racewear
Mail Order Dept.
Power Road
Chiswick
London W4 5PY
Tel. 0181 9875500
Fax. 0181 74289999
Catalogue contains chiefly helmets and race wear but some hardware also.

Racer's Hardware
8 South Street
Crowland
Peterborough PE 6 0AJ
Tel. 01733 211311
Fax. 01733 211258
Price list of race parts for suspension, steering, transmission and other components.

Holden Vintage Classics
Linton Trading Estate
Bromyard
Herefordshire HR7 4QT
Tel. 01885 488000
Fax. 01885 211258
Catalogue specialising largely in replacement electrical equipment but many other items of interest also.

Appendix 2
Synopsis of *Single Vehicle Approval Inspection Manual*

The following is a guide only, and is not intended to be a comprehensive list of requirements for SVA. It is strongly recommended that the *Single Vehicle Approval Inspection Manual* be consulted before and during construction to ensure that your car complies with the necessary requirements.

Full details of what is tested and how is described in the Vehicle Inspectorate's *SVA Inspection Manual*. It should be possible to obtain a copy of this publication from a library or possibly one of the car clubs, or a copy can be purchased from:

The Vehicle Inspectorate,
PO Box 12,
Swansea,
SA1 1BP.

APPLICABILITY

- SVA is applicable to:

Passenger vehicles with four or more wheels and not more than 8 seats.
Passenger vehicles with three wheels and a maximum gross weight of more than 1,000kg and 410kg unladen.
Passenger vehicles with three wheels and a maximum gross weight of not more than 1,000kg and 410kg unladen and either having a design speed of more than 31mph (50kph) or an engine capacity of more than 50cc.
Goods vehicles with three or more wheels and a maximum gross weight not more than 3500kg.

- The inspection relates to construction and not condition.
- Vehicle must be 'inspectable' – clean, easy of access, and have a VIN (vehicle identification number). Driver must be present to operate controls as required.
- Inspection limited to parts that can be seen without dismantling (except carpet/trim).
- 'Amateur built' means build (or substantial part) carried out by individual for personal use, and individual did not have business constructing motor vehicles.

SECTION 1

Anti-theft device

- Must be fitted in addition to ignition switch.
- Must not operate on brakes.
- If an anti-theft device is, or incorporates, any mechanical device that acts on a system that affects control of the car (eg, steering), it must not be possible to start the engine in the normal way until every such mechanical device has been deactivated. If must no be possible to activate any such mechanical device when the engine is running, and the action of any such device must be distinct and separate from that of stopping the engine.

SECTION 2

Defrosting/demisting

- Required except if vehicle not equipped with windscreen (so aero screens OK) or has opening windscreen, or one that has its top edge below a horizontal plane defined in *SVA Inspection Manual* (eg, racing deflector).
- Must clear area for driver to have adequate view of road in front and forward, and forward of sides of vehicle.

SECTION 3

Windscreen wiper(s) and washer(s)

- Wiper required if there is a windscreen (except if it opens fully below the specified horizontal plane).
- Must automatically clear area sufficient for driver's view.
- Operational frequency a minimum of 45 sweeps per minute.
- Wiper blade must automatically park out of driver's normal vision, at or beyond the outer edge of the area swept by the wiper.
- Must be capable of being lifted from screen for cleaning.
- Washers must provide sufficient liquid for wiper(s) to be effective.

- Reservoir must hold a minimum of 1 litre.
- With jets blocked, must be able to withstand stated pressures.

SECTION 4

Seats and anchorages

- Must be firmly attached to load bearing part of vehicle structure.
- Movable seat backs and displacement systems must have automatic locking systems for all normal positions.
- 'Displacement' seat/back must have control accessible from open door and rear seat immediately behind, if suitable for adult.

SECTION 5

Seat belts

The Regulations are very detailed but include:

- Each seating position must have anchorage points sufficient for type of belt fitted (3 front, 2 rear).
- Anchorage, fixing and surround must be strong enough.
- Must be permanently marked with acceptable approval marking.
- Locking mechanism must work.
- Retracting mechanism must take up all slack when seat unoccupied.
- Anchorage location of lap belts must allow belt to rest on pelvic area of body.
- Shoulder belt must be positioned so that it does not slip off shoulder.
- Drawings and measurements of upper belt anchorages are given.

SECTION 6

Interior fittings

The Regulations are very detailed but include:

- No surface, other than the surface of a window which can be contacted by a sphere of 165mm diameter and is within the specified zone (see appropriate EEC Directive) shall include any fittings or design features which have any 'dangerous roughness' or sharp edges likely to be contacted by the occupants.
- The rearward and upward facing parts of front seat frames must be covered in non-rigid material with a radius of 5mm or more.
- The gear lever in any forward gear and the handbrake in the fully released position (unless under dash) must have a radius of curvature of more than 3.2mm.
- There are specific regulations referring to projections from roofs.

SECTION 7

Radio suppression

- Effective suppression must be fitted.

SECTION 8

Glazing

- Driver must have full view of the road forward.
- Windscreen/sidescreens/ windows must be securely fitted.
- Windows/windscreens must be of safety glass of approved standard (BS 857/BS5282/BSAU178 at the time of writing).
- Opacity must not be greater than 30 per cent.

SECTION 9

Lighting

SVA reinforces the existing Road Traffic Lighting Regulations.

- All lamps/reflectors visible from the front must be white (except amber indicators).
- All lamps/reflectors visible from rear must be red (except amber indicators).
- All obligatory lights must be correctly positioned and working.
- Rear fog lamp must have a 'tell-tale' light that can be seen by driver.
- There must be a visible or audible 'tell-tale' warning for the indicators that may be shared with the hazard warning lights.

The *Manual* defines the required angles of visibility, both horizontal and vertical, for the indicators and rear lamps.

SECTION 10

Mirrors

The *Manual* gives a diagram showing the areas of required visibility for each mirror.

- An interior rear view mirror and off-side exterior mirror are required.
- If an interior mirror could not be effective, a near-side mirror is obligatory.
- Mirrors must have a European Approval Mark and be securely mounted and vibration free.
- External mirrors must be capable of hinging inwards under impact and must be adjustable from the driver's seat.

SECTION 11

Tyres

- Must be of the correct nominal size for the wheel and have a speed rating appropriate for the maximum design speed of the vehicle.
- Tyres of the same construction (radial/crossply/bias belted) and aspect ratio must be fitted to the same axle.
- If radial tyres are fitted to the front axle, they must also be fitted to the rear, and if crossply tyre are fitted to the front axle, radial or crossply tyres must be fitted to the rear.
- Tyres must have an approval

mark ('E' or 'e') and have permanently moulded the following information:

Nominal size
Construction type
Load capacity
Speed capability.

The *Manual* contains tables for speed categories and tyre capacities.

SECTION 12

Doors, latches and hinges

- Doors must be capable of being securely latched when closed. They must show that they can be used easily and that the edges are not sharp. Handles, locks, etc. must be easily accessible from the adjacent seat.
- Any 'aperture covers' – boots, bonnets, etc. – must be capable of being secured when closed.
- Door locks must have both intermediate and fully-latched mechanisms that will withstand a force of about 30kgf (66lbf) in both positions.
- Where hinges are used, the hinges must be fitted to the front edge of the door. Hinges may be fitted to the rear or top edge of the door if a device is fitted which automatically closes the door if it is unlatched when the vehicle is moving forward, or a safety bolt is fitted to prevent unlatching, along with an audible warning device which activates if the vehicle is driven without the bolt in place.

SECTION 13

Exterior projections

This is a particularly important section affecting the basic design of the car, and the regulations should be read fully (the regulations are too detailed to cover comprehensively here). It seeks to eliminate features likely to 'catch on or increase the risk of seriousness of injury' to anyone who could come into contact with the car.

- The regulations are concerned with an area between the 'floor line' and a height of 2 metres. It excludes jacking points, exhaust tail pipes emerging from under the body, wheels, and assumes that wheel arches are filled in.
- The 'floor line' is determined by means of a cone segment with a 30-degree angle. The 'floor line' is where the cone touches the vehicle at any point.
- Mascots and other decorative objects projecting more than 10mm from the mounting surface must retract or detach under a load not exceeding 10kgf (22lbf), the base or mount must then not project more than 10mm.
- All hard features projecting more than 10mm from the floor line must terminate in a radius of not less than 2.5mm.
- Note that wheel nuts of the eared, knock-on, variety may not be used, but side-mounted exhausts are permitted provided that they conform to the 'floor-line' conditions.
- The ends of the bumpers shall be turned inwards or recessed or integrated within the bodywork.

SECTION 14

Steering

- The steering wheel must not have spokes with holes or slots in them and should have edges with a radius of not less than 2.5mm.
- The wheel and column assembly should be designed to offer protection to the driver in a collision. It is, therefore, essential that the column consists of two or more parts so that displacement to the upper part is minimized. (The *Manual* contains helpful diagrams and information showing six examples of the normal type of collapsible steering columns. The builder of a special can select any of these types from a suitable donor car, modifying them in length if necessary but retaining the mechanism that enables them to collapse under impact.)
- The upper bearing and mounting must be strong enough to 'resist' upper column movement under impact to allow the collapsible mechanism incorporated in the system to operate properly.

The *Manual* points out that a 'well-designed car will minimize injury' and that the structure in front of the steering box or rack is important as it can absorb energy in a collision before it affects the steering column. A steering rack or similar mechanism that lies behind the centre line of the front wheels is therefore preferred.

SECTION 15

Vehicle design and construction, general

- Inspectors will check 'all aspects and construction of the vehicle' to ensure that no 'danger is likely to be caused to any person in the vehicle or other road users.'
- Structure/chassis/suspension/steering; these will be checked for adequacy of components, when vehicle driven, especially when fully laden.
- Mounting of components, sub-frames to be checked, and welds and fastenings.
- Steering to be checked under normal load to ensure that it does not cause fouling of wheels/steering/transmission/brake drums or discs.
- The fuel system to be checked for security/leakage/positioning/ in respect of vibration and the environment.
- Tank caps must seal and lock positively.
- Electrical equipment/wiring

checked for security/ positioning/ insulation/capacity.

SECTION 16

Brakes

- Must operate on all wheels and 'slow down' vehicle by means of a single operation from the driver's seat without removing hands from steering wheel.
- Four-wheel vehicles must have split circuit capable of operating a minimum of two wheels, one on either side of the car. Three-wheel vehicles can have split circuit or adequate handbrake.
- Parking brake must be capable of being applied from driving seat, on all wheels of at least one axle, independently of the service brake, and be mechanically restrained in the 'on' position.
- Visual check of master cylinder/operating linkage/mounting, and of disc/drum brake assemblies. All brakes must be capable of individual adjustment; front must be automatic.
- Assessment of overall adequacy of vehicle braking system in relation to vehicle weight/performance.
- Hydraulic fluid reservoir must have low-level warning lamp, or transparent container with minimum level marked.
- A roller brake test to be carried out to check braking efficiency, on each wheel and axle.
- Four-wheel-drive vehicles to be road tested instead, with decelerometer.

SECTION 17

Noise

- Must have complete exhaust system, including silencer.
- Noise level not to exceed 101db(A) measured at 0.5m from the exhaust outlet at 45° to the axis of the outlet pipe, in a horizontal plane.

SECTION 18

Emissions (spark ignition engines)

A table is given showing the maximum values allowed.

SECTION 19

Speedometer

- Must be fitted and working, and read in mph, up to a maximum of the design speed of vehicle, and be capable of being read at night (illuminated).
- Speedometer and drive must be from same donor car and be accurate within the limits detailed.

SECTION 20

Design weights

The calculations are given for the Maximum Permitted Axle Weight and Maximum Gross Weight.

Index

Other books from Haynes Publishing

Build Your Own Sports Car
for as little as £250 – and race it! (2nd edition)
by Ron Champion
ISBN 1 85960 636 9

Competition Car Suspension (3rd edition)
Design, construction, tuning
by Allan Staniforth
ISBN 1 85960 644 X

Competition Car Composites
A practical handbook
by Simon McBeath
ISBN 1 85960 624 5

Competition Car Downforce
A practical handbook
by Simon McBeath
ISBN 1 85960 662 8

Competition Car Preparation
A practical handbook
by Simon McBeath
ISBN 1 85960 609 1

Two-Stroke Performance Tuning (2nd edition)
by A. Graham Bell
ISBN 1 85960 619 9

Four-Stroke Performance Tuning (2nd edition)
by A. Graham Bell
ISBN 1 85960 435 8

Modern Engine Tuning
by A. Graham Bell
ISBN 1 85960 866 3

Tuning the A-Series Engine (3rd edition)
The definitive manual on tuning for performance and economy
by David Vizard
ISBN 1 85960 620 2

Tuning Rover V8 Engines
How to get the best performance for road and competition use
by David Hardcastle
ISBN 0 85429 933 5

Rebuilding and Tuning Ford's Kent Crossflow Engine
by Peter & Valerie Wallage
ISBN 1 85010 938 9

Rebuilding and Tuning Ford's CVH Engine
by Peter Wallage
ISBN 1 85960 006 9

Building, Preparing and Racing Your Mini
by Bill Sollis with Dave Pollard
ISBN 1 85960 621 0

For more information please contact:
Customer Services Department, Haynes Publishing, Sparkford, Yeovil, Somerset BA22 7JJ, UK

Tel: 01963 442030 Fax: 01963 440001
Int. tel: +44 1963 442030 Fax: +44 1963 440001

E-mail: sales@haynes-manuals.co.uk
Web site: www.haynes.co.uk